What Color Is
Your Parachute?

Other Books
by Richard N. Bolles

Where Do I Go From Here With My Life?
(co-authored with John C. Crystal)

*The Three Boxes of Life, and How To
Get Out of Them*
(Publication: Summer, 1978)

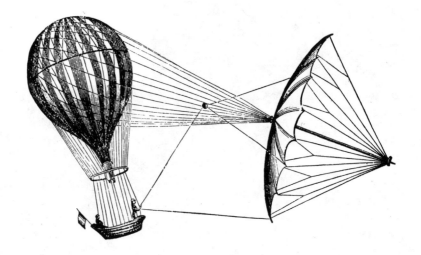

REVISED 1978

What Color Is Your Parachute?

A Practical Manual
for
Job-Hunters
& Career Changers

RICHARD NELSON BOLLES

TEN SPEED PRESS 1☉

What Color Is Your Parachute?
is published by
TEN SPEED PRESS
Box 7123
Berkeley, California 94707

You may order single copies prepaid
direct from the publisher for $9.95 + $.75 per copy
for postage and handling (clothbound), or
$5.95 + $.50 per copy postage and handling (paperbound).

Library of Congress Catalog Card Number 72-92348
ISBN paper 0-913668-91-5
ISBN cloth 0-913668-92-3
21st printing January 1978
Beverly Anderson Graphic Design
Printed in United States of America
by Consolidated Printers, Berkeley, California

Why This Book Was Written
COMMONLY CALLED THE INTRODUCTION OR PREFACE

"Give me a fish, and I will eat for today; teach me to fish, and I will eat for the rest of my life." (*Ancient Proverb*)

This book is an attempt to teach you how to fish, with respect to the most difficult task any of us faces in life: the job-hunt (whether it be a hunt for a career, or for a way to 'do your own thing,' or just for bread, to make ends meet).

This book is an attempt to, in other words, empower the job-hunter, so that no matter how many times you have to go about the job-hunt during your life, you will know how to do it.

And how many times will you have to go about the job-hunt? Who can say, in your particular case? But you may be interested to know that according to experts, the average worker under thirty-five years of age goes about the job-hunt once every one-and-a-half years! And the average worker over thirty-five, once every three years!

And in this process, experts estimate, the average worker will change careers, now, three to five times in his or her lifetime—i.e., go into a new field for which (upon first examination) his previous experience would not seem to qualify him or her. Sometimes, you and I may go into these new careers because we want to; other times, because we have to (i.e., our old one is being phased out of our society; cf. aerospace engineers, the energy crisis, etc.).

Our society has taken pity on the job-hunter and career-changer, and invented all kinds of helps for him or her, in their plight: federal-state employment agencies, private employment agencies, classified ads, job counselors, computerized job banks, and so forth. None of these works very well; in fact, the number of people who turn to any one of them, without getting a job as a result, is simply mind-blowing. But even when they do work, they only—at best—give you a fish. They rescue you from your present predicament (maybe), but often in jobs which are vastly below your abilities, and which bore you out of your mind. And always, they do this without giving you even a clue as to how you should go about the job-hunt the next time (like, maybe one-and-a-half to three years from now). Some fish!

It is time, in our society, when we thought it worthwhile to try a noble experiment: to stop giving the job-hunter a fish, half a fish, or no fish at all; and instead, teach him how to fish.

Hence this book, which you hold in your hands. Hopefully, you will find it a very practical manual, and one you can use again and again—whether you are a high school student, or someone facing the question of what to do in retirement, or somewhere in between those two experiences.

In order that this book could be written in the first place, endless travel and research was conducted around the country. I want to thank all those who kept pointing out to me what was wrong with this country's whole job-hunt process—countless, conscientious, creative souls who have often been given the feeling that they are voices crying in the wilderness. They are too numerous to name, but I want to single one out in particular—a genius named John Crystal, who emptied his file drawers onto my desk (via the mails) so that I might have documentary evidence for the principles in this book. God Bless, John.

I want also to thank those countless victims of our country's outdated, outmoded and Neanderthal job-hunting apparatus, who shared with me their woes, their difficulties, and—ultimately—their victories, as they tested the principles in this book and found that they work, beyond their wildest dreams. Women, minorities, students, the aging—everyone.

Okay, so here it is. A book with practical step-by-step instructions for you, based on the most creative, practical method of job-hunting known in the world today (if we find a better one tomorrow in our continuing ongoing research, we'll say so, in the next annual revision of this book).

If you are good at following instructions, by yourself, this should be sufficient. If you need help, there are the appendices.

My concluding plea: if you are a worker today, you will be a job-hunter tomorrow. If you are a job-hunter more than once, you will also be a career-changer —odds are.

Learn how to do the job-hunt the most effectively, so that your talents really get used. Learn how to change careers, without going back to college for arduous retraining.

Learn how to fish.

You are setting out on an exciting (if somewhat difficult) journey, whether you be 16 or 60. The light-hearted tone of this book is not intended to deny the seriousness of all this for your life and being; but it is intended, hopefully, to make the journey a little lighter and more enjoyable. Why should job manuals be dull?

Peace and shalom.

R.N.B.

Contents

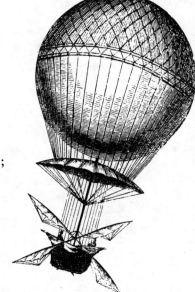

YOU'RE GOING TO GET YOUR *BREAD* OUT IN THE WORLD

START ↓

MOTIVATION CITY

You determine to give this transition your very *best*.

10

INVENTORY AVENUE

You know you must know *what you want to do,* so you inventory your achievements.

11

SKILLSVILLE

You pick out your strongest skills: done best and enjoyed the most by you.

12

HAPHAZARDS-VILLE

You figure this is as easy as rolling off a log; oh, right on!

1

operation

CLASSIFIED SQUARE

You read the ads in your daily paper looking for $15,000 jobs.

2

> A NEW GAME FOR JOB-HUNTERS TO PLAY AND ONE ON WHICH NO

AGENCY AVENUE

You visit agency after agency, getting no help at all.

3

DIRECTIONS
for 379 players

you need:
   yourself, and
   5 private employment agency counselors
   50 executive search firm executives*
   2 United States employment service counselors
   300 employers to whom you send your resume
   15 advertisers whose ads you respond to
   5 friends who give you well-meaning advice
   1 professional job counselor whom <u>you</u>
         pay handsomely.

* *these may not know they are players*

FRIENDSFIELD

You go to all the appointments and lunches your friends set up for you; but it leads nowhere.

4

FUNK CITY

Deep depression. The old job looks more and more like a nice safe womb...

5 PAYMENT PLACE

You decide you're going to pay someone to do the job of job-hunting for you.

6 SUSPICION STREET

Tests, some hand-holding; you begin to wonder if you're being taken.

¿JOB!?

You get a job — sort of.
Anyone can drive a taxi; go back to *START*.

CONSTELLATION COURT

You research different fields to identify what career uses your strongest skills the best.

13

PICKA COUNTY

You must determine where you would most enjoy working, and begin to research.

14

VISIT PLACE

You must, after researching, *go there* and get to know the economy.

15

16

COUNTDOWN CITY

You visit organizations that, at a distance, looked interesting, to see if they really are.

parachute

RESEARCH LAND

17

You now research each organization on the (manageable) list you now have of places that interest *you*.

> WHEN SEEKING CAREER TRANSITION
> OCCUPATION HAS A MONOPOLY

FOCUS STREET

18

You focus on organizations *you* like that have problems you can solve and you identify the top man responsible for solving that problem.

DIRECTIONS
for 50 players*

you need:
    yourself, and
    1 competent coach (or book)
    40 interviewers, whom <u>you</u> choose
        and <u>you</u> interview in order
        to get the information
        <u>you</u> need at various steps
        along the way
    8 men with The Power to hire you
        for the position <u>you</u> want
        in the organizations
        <u>you</u> choose.

* number may vary at your discretion

APPOINTMENT WAY

19

In each organization, you go to that man and explain how *you* can help *him* with his problems.

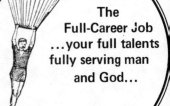

RESUME ALLEY

7

You send out 300 resumes but no offer comes.

⟵ Go back to *Funk City.*

RESUME RALLY

8

200 more resumes; one passable offer. You take it.

⟵ Go back to *"Job!?"*

DESPERATION GULCH

9

Repeat steps 1 through 6 —or try some other arrows— beginning with number 10.

The Full-Career Job ...your full talents fully serving man and God...

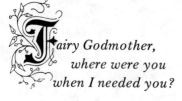 *airy Godmother,*
where were you
when I needed you?

Cinderella

CHAPTER ONE

A Job-Hunting
We Will Go

Okay, this is it.
You've been idly thinking about it, off and on, for
some time now, wondering what it would be like.
To be earning your bread in the marketplace.
Or maybe you're already out there,
And the problem is choosing another career.
Anyhow, the moment of truth has arrived.
For one reason or another, you've got to get at it —
Go out, and look for a job, for the first time or the twentieth.
You've heard of course, all the horror stories.
Of ex-executives working as doormen.
Of former college profs with two masters degrees
working as countermen in a delicatessen.
Of women who can only get a job as a secretary.
And you wonder what lies in store for you.

Of course, it may be that the problem is all solved.
Maybe you're going to "drop out" and just go
"do your own thing." The subsistence-survival game.
Or, if not, maybe some friend has button-holed you
and said, "Why not come and work for me?"
So, your job-hunt ends before it begins.
Or, it may be that you came into your present
career after a full life doing something else, and
You know you're welcome back there, anytime;
Anytime, they said.
And, assuming they meant it,
no problem, right?
So long as that's what you still want to do.
But for the vast majority of us,
that isn't how it goes.
Not for us the Horatio Alger role;
ah no! In retrospect it seems
We play a kind of Don Quixote; and
the job-hunt is our windmill.

2

Those who have gone the route before,
   all say the very same thing.
      This is how we go about it, when our time has come:
         We procrastinate,
            That's what we do.
               Busy winding things up, we say.
                  Actually, if the truth were known,
                     we're hoping for that miracle;
                        you know the one:
                           that if we just sit tight a little longer,
                           we won't have to go job-hunting, no
                           the job will come hunting for us.
                        Right in the front door, it will come.
                     To show us we are destiny's favorites,
                  And that God loves us.
               But, it doesn't come. And of course,
            eventually, we realize that time
         and money
      are beginning to run out.

   Time to begin in earnest.
   And all of our familiar friends immediately
   are at our elbow, giving advice —
   solicited or unsolicited, as to what we should do.
   "Jean or Joe, I've always thought you would make a great teacher."
   So we ask who they know
   in the academic world,
   and, armed with that name,
   we go a-calling. Calling, and
      sitting, cooling our heels
         in the ante-room of the Dean's office,
            until he asks, at last,
               "And what can I do for you, Mr. or Ms. ?"
                  We tell him, of course, that we're job-hunting.
                     "And one of my friends thought that you ..."
                        Oops. We watch the face change,

And we (who *do* know something about body language),
  Wait to hear his words catch up with his body.
    "You feel I'm 'over-qualified'? I see.
     "Two thousand applications, you say, already in hand
      For one hundred vacancies? I see.
      No, of course I understand."
       Strike-out. Back to the drawingboard. More advice.
       "Jean or Joe, have you tried the employment agencies?"
       "Good thinking. No, which ones should I try?
      The ones which deal with professionals? Which ones are they?
     Okay. Good. Down I'll go."
     And down we do go.
    Down, down, down.
   The ante-room again.
  And those other hopeful, haunted faces.
 A new twist too: our first bout
with the Application Form.
  "Previous jobs held.
 List in reverse chronological order."
Filling all the questions out. Followed by
That interminable wait.
And then, at last, the interviewer,
She of the over-cheerful countenance, and mien—
She talks to us. "Now, let's see, Mr. or Ms.,
What kind of a job are you looking for?"
"Well," we say,
"What do you think I could do?"
 She studies, again, the application form;
  "It seems to me," she says, "that with your background
   —it is a *bit* unusual—
    You might do very well in sales."
   "Oh, sales," we say. "Why yes," says she, "in fact
    I think that I could place you almost immediately.
     We'll be in touch with you. Is this your phone?"
    We nod, and shake her hand, and that is the
     Last time
      We ever hear from her.
       Strike out, number two.

Now, our ballooning hopes that we would quickly land a job
    are running into some frigid air,
      So we decide to confess at last
        Our need of help—to some of our more prosperous friends
        in the business world (if we have such)
        Who *surely* know what we should do
      At this point. The windmill is tiring us. What would they suggest
      we do?
    "What kind of a job are you looking for?"
  Ah, *that*, again! "Well, you know me well, what do you think
  I can do? I'll do almost anything,"
we say, now that the hour of desperation is snapping at our heels.
  "You know, with all the *kinds* of things I've done—"
we say; "I mean, I've done this and that, and here and there,
It all adds up to a kind of kaleidoscope;
Well, anyway, there must be *something* I can do?"

"Have you tried the want-ads?" asks our friend.
"Have you gone to see Bill, and Ed, and John, and Frances and Marty?
Ah, no? Well tell them I sent you."
So, off we go—now newly armed.
We study the want-ads. Gad, what misery is hidden in
Those little boxes. Misery in miserable jobs which are built
As little boxes.
We dutifully send our resume, such as it is,
To every box that looks as though
It might not be a box.
And wait for the avalanche of replies, from bright-eyed men
Who, seeing our resume, will surely know
Our worth; even if, at this point, our worth seems
In question in our own eyes.
Avalanche? Not even a rolling stone.

Time to go see those friends that our friend said we
ought to see.
You know: Bill, and Ed, and John, and Frances and Marty.
They seem slightly perplexed, as to why we've come,
And in the dark about exactly
Just exactly what they can do for us.
We try to take them off the hook; "I thought, Mr. President,
Your company might need—of course, my experience *has*
been limited, but I am willing, and I thought perhaps
that you..."

The interview drags on; downhill, now, all the way
As our host finishes out his courtesy debt,
A debt not to us but to the friend that sent us; and we go.
Boy, do we go! over hill and valley and dale,
Talking to everyone who will listen,
Listening to everyone who will talk
With us; and thinking that surely there must be
Someone who knows how to crack the job-market;

This job-hunt seems the loneliest task in the world.
Is it this difficult for other people?
The answer is *YES*.

Are other people *this* discouraged, and desperate
And frustrated, and so low in self-esteem after
A spell of job-hunting?
The answer is *YES*.

*Well, yes, you do have
great big teeth; but, never mind
that. You were great to at
least grant me this interview.*

Little Red Riding Hood

CHAPTER TWO

Rejection
Shock

OUR NEANDERTHAL
JOB-HUNTING PROCESS

Sure, the preceding account of the job-hunt is rather bleak.

But it has happened, is happening, and will continue to happen to countless millions of job-hunters in just the fashion described (or even worse).

Why?

Is it because they are different from other people? No. This happens to about 95% of all the people in this country who get involved in the job-hunt at one time or other in their lives. Let us put the matter simply and candidly:

The whole process of the job-hunt in this country is Neanderthal.

In spite of the fact that nearly every adult American man and, presently, some 45 million women have been or will be involved in the job-hunt at some time in their lives, we are condemned to go about the job-hunt as though we were the first person in this country to have to do it.

Year after year, our 'system' condemns man after man and woman after woman to go down the same path, face the same problems, make the same mistakes, endure the same frustrations, go through the same loneliness, and end up either still unemployed after an inordinately long period of time, or—*what is much more likely*—underemployed, in the wrong field, at the wrong job, or well below the peak of our abilities. Neanderthal, indeed!

And when we turn to the "experts" in this field to say, "Show me a better way," we are chagrined to discover that the genuine experts (who *do* exist) are few and far between, and awfully difficult to find; while most of those whom the world accounts as experts (so-called "personnel people" or "human resource developers") are—in their quiet, meditative moments, and in their heart of hearts—*just as baffled by this job-hunt, and just as aware that they haven't yet come up with the answer to it, as we are.*

This is never more clear than when *they themselves* are out of a job, and have to join the multitude in "pounding the pavements." You would think that they would absolutely be in their element, and know just precisely what to do. Yet the average executive (even the personnel executive) who yesterday was screening, interviewing, hiring any number of people, is just as much at a loss as anyone else *to know how to go about the job-hunt systematically, methodically, and successfully.*

Very often, the best plan they can suggest to themselves is the best plan they could suggest, in the past, to others: "The numbers game." That's right, the numbers game. It sometimes has a somewhat more sophisticated title (like, say, *systematic job search*), but in most cases this is what it comes down to, and this is what a number of experts are honest enough to call it.

THE NUMBERS GAME

In its original evolution, someone must have worked it all out, *backwards*. It wasn't all that hard. The logic would have gone like this:

For the job-hunter to get a job he or she really likes, he or she needs to have two or three job offers to choose from, from different employers.

In order to get two or three offers, the job-hunter probably ought to have *at least* six interviews at different companies.

In order to get six interviews he or she must mount a direct mail campaign, sending out x resumes to prospective employers, with covering letters, or whatever other kind of mail will titillate a prospective employer and his or her screening committees (personnel department, executive secretaries, et al); like: telegrams, special delivery letters, or whatever. So, how many is "x"? Well surveys have indicated that each 100 resumes sent out will get 1-2[1], or 2-3[2] or 3-4[3] invitations for the job-hunter to come in for an interview, —the figure varying, depending on which expert you are talking to, listening to, or reading.

Consequently, the conclusion of this game is that you should send out at least 500 resumes, with some experts saying 1000 or 1200, and others saying that there is no limit: send out 10-15 each day, they say, keeping a card-file on them, recording the outcome—responses, interviews, and so forth.

In a nutshell, that is The Numbers Game—the best that the personnel system in this country has been able to come up with (except for a creative minority — more about them, later).

You like?

Most of the books you can pick up at your local bookstore for a fiver, or so, will sell you this game.

Most of the job counselors you can go to (paying fees up to $3000 and higher) will sell you little more than this game—with maybe a little psychological testing and interview-role-playing thrown in.

Most of the personnel people in whose offices you may sit, will counsel you for nothing, ...but *in this game.*

There may be a few variations here and there: and sometimes the old game is hidden under an exquisitely clever new vocabulary, so it sounds like a very different invention. But you will suddenly awake to realize it is, in the end, The Little Ol' Game We've All Come To Love and Know So Well: Numbers.

HOW WELL DOES IT WORK?

Now, let's face facts: no matter how much of a gamble it sounds, for some people this numbers game works exceedingly well. They luck in. They end up with just the job they wanted, and they are ecstatically happy about the whole thing ... especially if they were engaged in only aimless job-hunting behavior prior to stumbling upon this plan. This works just beautifully, by contrast—*for some people.*

For other people, this numbers game works passably. They end up with a job of sorts, and a salary, even though in retrospect it is not really the kind of work they had been hoping for, and the salary is quite a bit below what they really needed or wanted. But ... a job is a job is a job. Parenthetically, the one thing that the job-hunt system in this country does, and does exceedingly well, is scaring people to the point where they are more than willing to lower their self-esteem and hence their expectations as to what they will settle for. So, the numbers game works passably, so far as some people are concerned.

But for the vast majority of people who use this 'system' (some 80-95% of them, we would guess) it just doesn't work at all—and most especially for those who are essentially aiming at a new career. Despite vigorous exceptions, as a group second-careerists have the most difficulty with this system.

Some job-hunters have sent out 400, 500, 600, 700, 800 resumes or more, without getting a single invitation to come in for an interview. Only the polite acknowledgment ("thank you for yours of the sixteenth. We regret ...") or the polite turn-down ("we will however keep your resume on file (in the wastebasket!) and should anything..."), or—no answer whatsoever.

PEOPLE-IN-THE-FORM-OF-PAPER

Nor, from the *company's* point of view, is it difficult to see why. Some companies receive as many as 250,000 resumes in a year. And even small companies may receive as many as ten to fifteen a week. The employment world floats on a sea of resumes, as some experts have observed.[4]

Hence, in dealing with resumes at employers' headquarters, the key word for the personnel department (and executive secretaries) is not selection, but *elimination*. (Of course, if you're agriculturally minded—or Biblically minded—you may prefer: winnowing the crop.) Here, to a particular organization, flows in this endless stack of People-in-the-Form-of Paper, day after day. If you're working there, what do you do with the stack? Well, of course. You go through it, to see if you can get the stack down to more manageable size. You look to see who you can eliminate.

Who gets nominated for this dubious honor? Well, $75 a week file-clerks who are applying for the President's job. And $75,000 a year Presidents who are willing to settle for file-clerks' jobs. And, resumes so poorly written you can't tell anything about the men or women behind them. And resumes so slickly written (usually by a hired professional) that you can't tell anything about the men or women behind them.

And . . . people applying for a job for which they look as though they have not had the necessary qualifying experience or credentials. Those resumes which have the greatest difficulty in getting through this Screening Process are those belonging to Zig-Zag people, Second Careerists who've accumulated a lot of experience in their old Zig profession, and now are trying to Zag. Their resumes (unless they are done extremely cleverly—about which, more in a later chapter) find that this Screening Process is their Dunkirk.

Well, all in all, how likely is your resume to survive the Process? A recent study of a number of different companies revealed that those companies sent out one invitation to an interview for every 245 resumes that they received *on an average*. But, this average represented a range between companies which consented to one interview for every 36 resumes they received, and companies which only sent out one invitation to an interview for every 1188 resumes they received.[5] In terms of the first process that resumes are subjected to, therefore, the Screening Out Process searches for reasons to eliminate 35 out of every 36 resumes if we are lucky; or for reasons to eliminate on up to 1187 out of every 1188 resumes received if we're dealing with a tough company market.

You are free, of course, to doubt these statistics and find them simply unbelievable. Or you may want to redouble your efforts to make your resume *the one that gets through.* Or, you may want to know a better system than the Numbers Game. We will try to point out aids for all three groups of people: the Doubters, the System-beaters, and the Alternatives-seekers.

REJECTION SHOCK

But, first of all, every job-hunter owes it to him- or herself to *understand* the system. What it is. How it works. What its limitations are. What its out-and-out defects are.

Why? Well, first of all, to save him- or herself from Rejection Shock. Rejection Shock occurs when you set out to look for a job, confidently follow all the instructions that you are given about the Numbers Game (via books, articles, friends and paid professionals) only to discover that none of this works *for you,* and after a lengthy period of time you are still unemployed. You then go into Shock, characterized by a slow or rapid erosion of your self-esteem, a conviction that there is something wrong *with you,* leading to lower expectations, depression, desperation and/or apathy. This assumes, consequently, all the proportions of a major crisis in your life, your

14

personal relations and your family, leading to loneliness, irritability, withdrawal, where divorce is often a consequence and even suicide is not unthinkable.[6] *(One major executive career counselor did a survey of 15,000 clients, and discovered that 75% of them were either facing, in the midst of, or just out of, a marital divorce.)*[7]

Rejection Shock also occurs when you set out to look for a job, confidently follow all the instructions you are given about the Numbers Game, only to discover that this only *partially* works for you, and after a lengthy period of time (often) you have gotten a job in which you are *under-employed.* You are in the wrong field, or at the wrong job, or well below the peak of your abilities. You go into Shock, consequently, because you feel under-valued, ill-at-ease, underpaid and poorly-used, and you think you must be content with this under-employment *because something is fundamentally wrong with you.* In the midst of Shock, as you are, it never occurs to you that perhaps something is fundamentally wrong with *the whole job-hunting system in this country.*

A NATIONAL TRAGEDY

It should be every job-hunter's high purpose to avoid not only the obvious devil of Un-employment, but also the less-obvious devil of Under-employment, with every resource that is at your command. And, more than that, that you should determine to help others to understand the system, so that they, too, may be spared the blight of these two devils.

Insiders estimate that, currently, 80% of our working people are Under-employed.[8] Or more.[9] This is a national tragedy. But people submit to it because they regard Under-employment as preferable to Un-employment. They prefer pounding a typewriter to pounding the pavements.

And in this instinctive fear, they are quite right. Insiders again and again bring forth statistics which reveal that those who regard the job-hunt as an occasion for leaping to a better job are taking a big gamble, and especially so if they are either on in years (polite euphemism) or unemployed, or both. Witness these statistics with regard to men in particular:

Of the several thousand middle-aged men who lose their

jobs this month, one year from now 80% will be unemployed, under-employed (at lesser salary than before), or eking out a private income, estimates one insider.[10]

Three million people are trying to get better jobs (at over $12,000 a year), and of these, 75% will not succeed in finding them — estimates another insider.[11]

A year from now, 20% of those middle-aged men who lose their jobs will still be unemployed.[12]

The cause: *in large measure,* failure to understand the job-hunting system in this country.

The result: Rejection Shock.

Tragedy.

HOW TO USE THE NUMBERS GAME, INSTEAD OF BEING USED BY IT

A second reason why every job-hunter ought to understand the numbers game, in all its parts, is you may want to use *some* parts of it to *supplement* your main program as outlined later on.

A study of *The Job Hunt* by Harold L. Sheppard and A. Harvey Belitsky[13] revealed that the greater the number of auxiliary avenues used by the job-hunter, the greater the job-finding success. It makes sense, therefore, to know of *all* the avenues, how they work, and what their limitations are, so that you can choose *which* avenue or avenues you want to use, and *how* you want to use them. You are in the driver's seat about these matters, as you should be.

The parts of this game most commonly spoken of are: mailing resumes; contacting executive search firms; answering newspaper ads; placing newspaper ads; going to private employment (or placement) agencies; going to the government employment agency; contacting college placement firms; using executive registers or other forms of clearinghouses; and making personal contacts, through friends, personal referrals, and so forth.

Let us look at the virtues, and defects, of each of these, in rapid succession; to see why they usually don't work—and how you might get around their defects.

HEADHUNTERS, OTHERWISE KNOWN AS EXECUTIVE SEARCH FIRMS

If you play the numbers game, and especially if you pay someone to guide you in it, you will be told to send your resume to Executive Search firms. And what, pray tell, are *they*? Well, they are recruiting firms that are retained by employers. The employers want these firms to hire away from other firms or employers, executives who are employed, and rising. From this, you will realize they know of, and are dealing with, vacancies known to exist. That's why, in any decent scatter-gun, Numbers Game sending out of your resume, you are advised—by any number of experts—to be sure and include Executive Search firms. Not surprisingly, there are a number of places which make a thriving business of selling lists of such firms.

EXECUTIVE RECRUITERS

<u>Name</u>: Executive recruitment consultants, executive recruiters, executive search firms, executive development specialists, management consultants.

<u>Nicknames</u>: head-hunters, flesh peddlers, body snatchers, talent scouts.

<u>Number</u>: variously estimated between 500-800 on up to 1500-2000 because some firms doing other things also do this.

<u>Volume of business</u>: in 1963, these firms took in an estimated $15 million in fees [14], in 1967, $30 million.[15] In 1978, who knows?

continued

Percentage of market: some insiders say they handle 25% of all openings above $15,000 annual salary; some say they fill 50% of *all* top jobs, and one insider says 80%.[16]

Number of vacancies handled by a firm: each staff member can only handle 6-8 searches at a time (as a rule)[17]; so multiply number of staff that a firm has (if known) times six. Majority of firms are one-two staff (hence, are handling 5-10 current openings); a few are four to five staff (20-25 openings being searched for); and the largest have staffs handling 80-100 openings.

You can get lists of such firms from:

1. The Association of Executive Recruitment Consultants, 347 Madison Avenue, New York, N.Y., in a booklet entitled *A Company's Most Valuable Asset.* Free.

2. The American Management Association, Inc., 135 West 50th Street, New York, N.Y. 10020, in a list entitled *Executive Recruitment Organizations and Executive Job Counselling Organizations.* $2.00.

3. Performance Dynamics, Inc., Publishing Division, 17 Grove Avenue, Verona, New Jersey 07044 has a list entitled *The Performance Dynamics Worldwide Directory of Job-Hunting Contacts: A Guide to 2400 Employment Recruiters.* $9.95; $12.50 for the executive list. Prices subject to change.

4. Manford F. Ettinger, P.O. Box 495, Springfield, Missouri 65801, has a *Directory of Executive Recruiters* of 1,024 firms. Only Regional lists are available: NYC $7.00; East (not including NYC) $6.50; Chicago $4.00; Midwest (not including Chicago) $4.00; South and Southwest $3.00; Pacific $3.00; Foreign based $2.00.

The question is: do you *want* these lists (even the free ones), i.e., are they going to do you any good?

Well, let's say you regard yourself as a professional, and so you decide to send them your resume (unsolicited—they didn't ask you to send it, you just sent it). The average Executive Recruitment Firm or Executive Search Firm may get as many as 100 to 300 unsolicited resumes a week. Or letters. And, as we saw on our filing card (previous page) the majority may be handling five to ten *current openings,* for which they are looking for executives who are presently employed and rising.

Well okay, that Executive Recruiter is sitting there with 100 to 300 resumes in his or her hands, at the end of that week — yours (and mine) among them. You know what's about to happen to that stack of People-in-the-Form-of-Paper. That old Elimination, Winnowing, or Screening Process again. *Our* chances of surviving? Well, the first to get eliminated will be those who a) are not presently executives, or b) employed as such, or c) rising in their firm; i.e., you and me.

That's why, even in a good business year, many experts say: *Forget it!*[18]

Of course, you may be one who likes to cover all bets. In that case, get a free list, and check out Antell, Wright & Nagel; Boyden Associates; Canny Bowen Howard Peck; William H. Clark Associates; George Haley; Heidrick & Struggles; Spencer Stuart Associates; and Ward Howell Associates.[19]

ANSWERING NEWSPAPER ADS

Experts will advise you, for the sake of thoroughness, to study the newspaper advertisements *daily* and to study *all of them, from A to Z* — because ads are alphabetized, in some sections, according to job title; and there are some very strange and unpredictable job titles floating around. Then if you see an ad for which you qualify, even three-quarters, you are advised to send off:

      a) Your resume OR

      b) Your resume and a covering letter OR

      c) Just a covering letter.

In short, you're still playing the Numbers Game, when you answer ads. And the odds are stacked against you just about as badly as when you send out your resume scatter-gun fashion. How badly? (Better sit down before reading further.) A study conducted in two sample cities recently revealed (and I quote) "that 85 per cent of the employers in San

NEWSPAPER ADS

Where Found:
1. In business section of the Sunday New York Times (Section 3) and education section (Section 4); also in Sunday editions of Chicago Tribune and Los Angeles Times.
2. In business section (often found with Sports section) of your daily paper; also daily Wall Street Journal (especially Tuesday and Wednesday's editions).
3. In classified section of your daily paper (and Sunday's, too).

Jobs Advertised: usually those which have a clear-cut title, well-defined specifications, and a job for which either many qualify, or very few.

Number of Resumes received by Employer as Result of the Ad: 20-1000, commonly.

Time It Takes Resumes to Come In: 48-96 hours. Third day is usually the peak day, after ad is placed.[20]

No. of Resumes NOT Screened Out: Only 2-5 out of every 100 (normally) survive. 95-98 out of every 100 answers are screened out.

NEWSPAPER ADS continued

Beware of:

● Blind ads (no company name, just a box number). These, according to some insiders, are particularly unrewarding to the job-hunter's time. ● Fake ads (positions advertised which don't exist)—usually run by placement firms or others, in order to garner resumes for future use.[22] ● Phone numbers in ads: don't use them except to set up an appointment. Period. ("I can't talk right now. I'm calling from the office.") Beware of saying more. Avoid getting screened out over the telephone. ● Phrases like "make an investment in your future" which means *you have to put money down* (often quite a lot of thousands) to buy in, on the job.

Francisco, and 75 per cent in Salt Lake City, did not hire any employees through want ads" in a typical year. Yes, that said *any* employees, *during the whole year.*

Of course, you may be one who still likes to cover all bets, and if so, you want to know how *your* resume can be the one that gets through the Screening Process. (Let's be honest: answering ads *has* paid off, for some job-hunters.)

Most of the experts say, *if* you're going to play this game:

1. All you're trying to do, in answering the ad, is to get invited in for an interview (rather than getting screened out). So, quote the ad's specifications, and tailor your resume or case history letter (if you prefer *that* to a resume)—so that *you* fit their specifications as closely as possible.

2. Omit all else from your response (so there is no further excuse for Screening you out).

3. *If* the ad requested salary requirements, some experts say ignore the request; others say, state a salary range (of as much as 3 - 10 thousand dollars variation) adding the words "depending on the nature and scope of duties and responsibilities," or words to that effect. If the ad does not mention salary requirements, *don't you either.* Why give an excuse for getting your response Screened Out?

21

PLACING ADS YOURSELF
IN THE NEWSPAPER

PLACING ADS

Name of Ads (Commonly): Positions wanted (by the job-hunter, that is).

Found in: Wall Street Journal, professional journals and trade association publications.

Cost: Varies. Wall Street Journal, for example, varies from $20.72 to $68.32, per column inch, for one time—depending on the regional edition that you want the ad to appear in.

Effectiveness: Very effective in getting responses from employment agencies, peddlers, salesmen, and so forth. Practically worthless in getting responses from prospective employers, who rarely read these ads.

Recommendation: Forget it. Unless, just to cover all bets, you want to place some in professional journals appropriate to your field. Study other people's attempts first, though.

ASKING PRIVATE EMPLOYMENT
AGENCIES FOR HELP

PRIVATE EMPLOYMENT AGENCIES

Number: Nobody Knows. There are at least 8000 private employment or placement agencies in the U.S. with 2000 dropping out, to be (in effect) replaced with 2000 new ones each year. [23]

Standards: Maintained by National Employment Association, 2000 K Street N.W., Suite 353, Washington, D.C. 20006. It is alleged that there are 1700 in good standing, who subscribe to those standards. [24]

Specialization: Many specialize in executives (about 600 agencies[25]), financial, data processing, or other specialties.

Fees: Employer or job-hunter may pay *but only when and if hired.* Fees vary from state to state. Tax deductible. In New York, for example, fee cannot exceed 60% of one month's salary, i.e. a $15,000 a year job will cost you $750. The fee may be paid in weekly installments of 10% (e.g. $75 on a $750 total). In 80% of executives' cases, employer pays the fee. [26]

Contract: The application form filled out by the job-hunter at an agency *is* the contract.

Exclusive handling: Don't give it, even if they ask for it.

continued

23

Nature of business: Primarily a volume business, requiring rapid turnover of clientele, dealing with most-marketable job-hunters in what one insider has called "a short-term matching game."[27]

Volume: Places only 4% of those entering job-market, and only 15% of all Americans who change jobs.[28]

Effectiveness: In 1968, spokesman for Federal Trade Commission announced average placement rate for employment agencies was only 5% of their clients. (That means a 95% failure rate, right?)

Loyalty: Agency's loyalty in the very nature of things must tend to lie with those who pay the bills (which in most cases is the employer), and those who represent repeat business (again, employers).

Evaluation: An agency, with its dependency on rapid-turnover volume business, usually has not time to deal with *any* problems (like, career-transitions). *Possible exception for you to investigate:* a new, or suddenly expanding agency, which needs job-hunters badly if it is to get employers' business.

ASKING THE
FEDERAL-STATE
EMPLOYMENT SERVICE
FOR HELP

UNITED STATES
EMPLOYMENT SERVICE

Old Name: Was called USTES—United States Training
and Employment Service, 2400 offices in
the country, used by 10.9 million yearly, in
1965, or 14% of the work force at that time;
used by 9.9 million in 1970, or 11.5% of the
work force. [29]

Services: Most state offices of USES not only serve
entry level workers, but also have services for
professionals. Washington, D.C. had most
innovative one. Middle management (and up)
job-hunters still tend to avoid it.

Nationwide network: In any city (as a rule) you can
inquire about job opportunities in other
states or cities, for a particular field. Also
see Job Bank (page 28).

Openings: 8.3 million job vacancies listed with USES
in 1965; 6.7 million vacancies listed with them
in 1970. [29]

Placements: Of the 10.9 million who used USES in 1965,
allegedly less than 6.3 million (or 59%) found placement. Of the 9.9 million who used it in 1970, allegedly
less than 4.6 million (or 46%) found placement. [29]

A survey in one area raised some question about the
quality of placement, moreover, when it was discovered
that 57% of those placed in that geographical area by
USES were not working at their jobs anymore, just 30
days later. [30] (That would reduce the placement rate to
20%, *at best*; an 80% failure rate. It's probably closer
to 13.7% placement rate; 86.3% failure rate.)

COLLEGE PLACEMENT BUREAUS

Where Located: There are alleged to be 1100 university placement offices in this country.[31] Actually, most of the 2686 institutions of higher education in this country (970 two-year community colleges, 765 four-year institutions, and 951 others) have some kind of placement function, however informal.

Helpfulness: Some are very very good. Others have become "locked in" to the old era of recruiters, when students had to be taught only how to respond; and do not know how to help students nowadays, when latter must take the initiative in job-hunting. [32]

Evaluation: Visit, to see whether they teach skills in "management by initiative," or only in "management by invitation." Not likely to be terribly helpful with alumni, though some, like UCLA's, are.

SUBSCRIBING TO REGISTERS OR CLEARINGHOUSES OF VACANCIES

REGISTERS OR CLEARINGHOUSE OPERATIONS

These are attempts to set up "job exchanges" or a kind of bulletin board, where employer and job-hunter can meet. The private clearinghouses commonly handle both employer and job-hunter listings, charging each.

Types: federal and private; general and specialized fields; listing either future projected openings, or present ones; listing employers' vacancies, or job-hunters' resumes (in brief), or both.

Cost to Job-Hunter: ranges from free, to $75 or more.

Effectiveness: A register may have as many as 13,000 clients registered with it (if it is a private operation), and (let us say) 500 openings at one time, from employer clients. Some registers will let employer know of every client who is eligible; others will pick out the few best ones. You must figure out what the odds are. A newer register *may* do more for you than an older one.

Loyalty: For most private registers, company pays the fee (like, 20% of first year's gross salary) if they hire a register client. As in case of private placement agencies, loyalty probably goes to those who pay bills, and offer repeat business. **continued**

This is a very popular idea, and new entrants in the field are appearing constantly. On the following cards, we list some examples:

REGISTERS ETC.
continued

General Clearinghouse Listing Present Vacancies:
> The State Employment Offices in over 43 states, comprising over three-quarters of the Nation's population, have allegedly set up a computerized (in most cities) *job bank* to provide daily listings of job openings in that city. If every employer cooperated and listed every opening he or she had, each day, it would be a great concept. Unhappily, employers prefer to fill many jobs above $10,000 in more personal, informal ways. So the job bank remains a rather limited resource for such jobs. *Can be a helpful research instrument*, however.

A Clearinghouse for College-Educated Women.
> Catalyst (National Headquarters: 14 East 60th Street, New York, New York 10022) used to maintain a National Roster, a national computerized listing, for women age 24 and over, who have had at least one year of college and were seeking part-time or full-time professional positions. This has now been discontinued however.

Private Clearinghouse for Executive Field: Executive Register, 72 Park St., New Canaan, Conn. 06840. Fee: $75 for six-month period of registry for the job-hunter, *if* you make $15,000+ per year (many people do, when they stop to add up everything), and *if* E.R. accepts you (they reject 15-20% who apply—they say).

Private Clearinghouses for Educational Field:
Educational Career Service (Paul Barringer, Managing Trustee), P.O. Box 672, Princeton, N.J. 08540. There is a membership fee of $36 for the first year.

Clearinghouses for Junior and Community College Vacancies: The American Association of Junior Colleges is now sponsoring a job placement program for two-year college teachers, which is essentially a register. It costs $20, for individuals interested in teaching in a junior or community college to register. Address: AACJC Career Staffing Center, P.O. Box 298, 621 Duke Street, Alexander, Virginia 22314. Phone 703-549-4134. Your name gets sent to 900 colleges, in December and April.
• Community College Job Listing Service: Registrants are sent a list of

vacancies in their field, each June. Their
condensed resume is sent to community
colleges in all the states they designated.
P.O. Box M-1007, Ann Arbor, Michigan
48106. $25.

REGISTERS ETC.
continued

A Clearinghouse for the Social-Economic-Ecology
Development Fields:
There have been registers in this field,
such as Sociocom, but they have suspended
publication because of "the continuing
curtailment of programs at all levels in the
Social-Economic field." Which is to say,
such registers had the 'Achilles heel' of
being able to find enough job-hunters, all
right, but not enough employers' listings.

Registers in the Church: A clearinghouse for clergy
has been set up in the American Baptist
Convention, the Lutheran Church in
America, the Episcopal Church, and the
National Council of Churches; under the
direction of Roddey Reid, Jr., 815 Second Avenue, New York, N.Y. 10017.

Evaluation: the very terms "clearinghouse" or "register"
can be misleading. The vision: one central place where you
can go, and find listed every vacancy in a particular field of
endeavor. But, sorry, Virginia; there ain't no such animal. All

you'll find by going to any of these places is *A Selected List* of some of the vacancies. But only some.

So far as finding *jobs for people* are concerned, these clearinghouses and agencies (like employment agencies) really end up finding *people for jobs*. (Think about it!) Heart of gold though they *may* have, these agencies serve employers better than they serve the job-hunter.

And yet there are *ways* of using such registers to gain valuable information for the job-hunter. So at the very least, the Federal job bank (if there is one in your city), and perhaps a relatively inexpensive Register, if there is one in your particular field, can serve as *auxiliaries* to your researching particular geographical areas — about which, more in a later chapter.

OTHER IDEAS

Your Resume in a Book: Some organizations circulate small booklets which are essentially mass distribution of people's resumes, in precise form. Forty Plus Clubs do this, through their *Executive Manpower Directory.* So do some of the executive registry places. Some other places used to put out such directories, but went out of business. Evaluation: It's a gamble, just like everything else in this Numbers Game system. A real gamble, if you are trying to start a second career. You have to boil your resume down to a very few words, normally. And then decide if you stand out. If not, forget it. If yes, well.... maybe.

List of Companies with Mailing Addresses: Auren Uris' book *Turn Your Job into A Successful Career* (1967, Simon and Schuster, p.71) lists these. Evaluation: most often, terribly outdated, and of dubious value, to say the least.

Off-beat Methods: Mailing strange boxes to company presidents, with strange messages (or your resume) inside; using sandwich board signs and parading up and down in front of a company; sit-ins at a president's office, when you are simply determined to work for *that* company, association, or whatever. You name it—and if it's kooky, *it's been tried.* Kookiness is generally ill-advised, however. $64,000 question every employer must weigh: if you're like this *before* you're hired, what will he or she have to live with *afterward*?

To summarize the effectiveness of all the preceding methods in some sort of table (you do like tables, don't you?), we may look at the results of a survey the Bureau of the Census made. The survey, made in the year 1972 and published in the *Occupational Outlook Quarterly* in the Winter of 1976, was of ten million jobseekers. The results were published in two tables, which are self-explanatory:

Table 1: Use and Effectiveness of Job Search Methods

Method	Usage[1]	Effectiveness Rate[2]
Applied directly to employer	66.0	47.7
Asked friends:		
About jobs where they work	50.8	22.1
About jobs elsewhere	41.8	11.9
Asked relatives:		
About jobs where they work	28.4	19.3
About jobs elsewhere	27.3	7.4
Answered newspaper ads:		
Local	45.9	23.9
Nonlocal	11.7	10.0
Private employment agency	21.0	24.2
State employment service	33.5	13.7
School placement office	12.5	21.4
Civil Service test	15.3	12.5
Asked teacher or professor	10.4	12.1
Went to place where employers come to pick up people	1.4	8.2
Placed newspaper ads:		
Local	1.6	12.9
Nonlocal	.5	[3]
Answered ads in professional or trade journals	4.9	7.3
Union hiring hall	6.0	22.2
Contacted local organization	5.6	12.7
Placed ads in professional or trade journals	.6	[3]
Other	11.8	39.7

1   Percent of total jobseekers using the method.
2   A percentage obtained by dividing the number of jobseekers who found work using the method by the total number of jobseekers who used the method, whether successfully or not.
3   Base less than 75,000.

Table 2: Effective Methods of Finding a Job, by Occupation *

Method	Professional and technical workers	Managers	Sales workers	Clerical workers	Craft workers	Operatives, except transport	Transport equipment operatives	Laborers, except farm	Service workers, except private household
Applied directly to employer	xx	xx	xx	xx	xx	xx	xx	xx	xx
Answered local newspaper ads	x	xx	xx	x	x	x	xx	x	xx
Asked friends about jobs where they work			x	x	xx	x	x	x	xx
Asked relatives about jobs where they work					x	x		x	x
Union hiring hall					xx	x		x	
School placement office	xx			x					x
Private employment agency		xx		xx					
Asked friends about jobs elsewhere		x							
State employment service						x			
Contacted local organization									x

* One "x" indicates that the method was successful for 20 to 24 percent of the people using it.
  A double "x" indicates that it was successful for 25 percent or more.

34

You will note that in Table 2 a so-called "Effective Method", deserving at least one "x" for a particular occupation, is by definition a Method which failed for 76 to 80% of the job-seekers who used it. And that, in Table 1, even *the* most effective method listed there failed to work for 52.3% of those jobseekers who used it. (Yes, I know, picky, picky, picky.)

Well, anyway, Mr. or Ms. Job-hunter, this just about covers the favorite job-hunting system of this country *at its best.* (Except personal contacts, which we give special treatment—Chapter Six.)

If it works for you, right off, *great!* But if it doesn't, you may be interested in *the other plan*—you know, the one they had saved up for you, in case all of this didn't work? Small problem: with most of the experts in our country, *there is no other plan.* And that is that.

---

1 *Executive Register*, 72 Park Street, New Canaan, Conn. 06840, cites this figure.
2 Albee, p. 137 cites this figure (see Appendix B).
3 Uris, p. 149 cites this figure in *Action Guide* (Appendix B).
4 Snelling, p. 129 (see Appendix B).
5 Deutsch, Shea & Evans, Inc., quoted on page 63 in *Electronic Design 16.*
6 Cf. Albee (Appendix B).
7 In a study conducted by J. Frederick Marcy and Associates.
8 Myron Clark, past president of Society for the Advancement of Management, quoted by Haldane, p. 186 (Appendix B). Also California State University at Fullerton, in its *CP & PC News*, reported a sixteen year study of 350,000 job applicants, which likewise concluded that 80% were in the wrong jobs.
9 Richard Lathrop, *Who's Hiring Who*, p. 19, 1977 Edition
10 Albee, *op. cit.*, p. 3.
11 Crystal Management Services, Inc. cited these statistics.
12 Albee, *op. cit.*, p. 3
13 See their book, described in Appendix B.
14 Uris, *Action Guide*, p. 58.
15 *Saturday Review*, December 30, 1967.

16 The first figure is cited by Executive Register; the second by Butler, p.97 (see Appendix B); and the third by M.L. Knight and Associates, of Los Angeles.

17 Butler, *op. cit.*, pp.160-1.

18 Uris, *op. cit.*, pp. 33, 69.
The job hunter must also beware of firms which have the word "search" or "recruiter" in their title, as this does not necessarily mean a) that they really are recruiters, or b) that they can or will use such facilities (even if they have them) to aid you ... glittering promises (mostly verbal) notwithstanding. *The Los Angeles Times* in November 1970 reported the indictment of an executive employment agency, for example, which ran ads saying "our clients are hungry for executives." In point of fact, however, records revealed that allegedly only one client out of a total of 361 was ever placed.

19 *Business Week*, July 25, 1970, p.89.

20 Uris, *op. cit.*, p.83.

21 Olympus Research Corporation, *A Study To Test the Feasibility of Determining Whether Classified Ads in Daily Newspapers are An Accurate Reflection of Local Labor Markets and of Significance to Employers and Job Seekers.* 1973. From: Olympus Research Corporation, 1290 24th Avenue, San Francisco, CA 94122.

22 *Washingtonian* Magazine, November, 1970, details how agencies list ads, allegedly, for positions which do not exist or for positions which are already filled. ("Hurry! Hurry! Hurry! Get Your Superjob Now," p.62).

23 Uris, *op. cit.*, p. 42.

24 Snelling, *op. cit.*, p.125.

25 Uris, *op. cit.*, p.43.

26 Ibid, p.40.

27 Albee, *op. cit.*, p.51.

28 Crystal Management Services, Inc. quoted the former figure; Snelling quotes the latter (p.124).
For an inside look at some of agencies' alleged practices, see the article in the *Washingtonian*, cited in footnote 22.

29 Quoted in the excellent study prepared by The Lawyers' Committee for Civil Rights Under Law, Sarah Carey, Assistant Director, and The National Urban Coalition: *Falling Down on the Job: The United States Employment Service and the Disadvantaged*, June, 1971.

30 The San Francisco Bay Area, for the period January 1966 thru April 1967, as reported in *Placement and Counseling In a Changing Labor Market: Public and Private Employment Agencies and Schools.* Report of the San Francisco Bay Area Placement and Counselling Survey, by Margaret Thal-Larsen. HR Institute of Industrial Relations, UC Berkeley, August, 1970.

31 *Careers Today* Magazine, March, 1969.

32 Wein, p.70 (see Appendix B).

Any new theory first is attacked as absurd; then it is admitted to be true, but obvious and insignificant; finally—it seems to be important, so important that its adversaries claim that they themselves discovered it!—"

William James

CHAPTER THREE

You Can
Do It!

YOU *CAN* DO IT.

If you decided to hop around in this book, rather than reading it from the very beginning, the odds are great that this is one of the first chapters you decided to look at—right?

So for those who have just joined us, we will summarize what has transpired thus far in our saga. Through all the preceding pages, two facts have stood out—like Mt. Everest—above all others:

(1) The whole job-hunting system in this country is a big fat gamble, in which the dice are loaded against *any* job-hunter who wants more than "just a job." *Any* job-hunter.

(2) The job-hunting system in this country poses especial difficulties for *all those who seek a second career*—And that is, according to statistical studies, four out of every five job-hunters, before their life is through.

Now, on with our story.

There are a few heroes in this country, who belong to what might be called "the creative minority" in this whole field. They are a very diverse group. Some of them live in the big city; some out in the country. Some teach and do research at universities; others are professional career counselors. But, despite these outward differences, these unsung heroes have at least two denominators in common, maybe three:

First of all, they have refused to accept the idea that the job-hunting system has to be as bad as it is, or as much of an out and out gamble as it is.

Secondly, instead of just criticizing the system, they have sat down and figured out how it could be done better. And, not too surprisingly, they have all come up with methods which are strikingly similar to one another.

Third, in spite of widely teaching their methods over a number of years and in a number of places, they have been rewarded by *being studiously ignored* by the "manpower/ human resources development / personnel / experts" in this country, from the Federal government on down (or up, depending on your point of view).

For *any* job-hunter, this creative minority and their insights are important.

And, when it comes time for you to seek another career, you will discover this creative minority and their insights are crucial.

THE CREATIVE MINORITY'S DIAGNOSIS

What, then, is it that makes the present job-hunting system in this country so disastrous? That was the question which the creative minority, wherever they were, first asked themselves. What are the fatal *assumptions* that are so casually made, taught, propagated, and reproduced, by some of our best business schools and job counselors, without ever being critically questioned? To the creative minority, the fatal assumptions seemed to be these:

Fatal Assumption No. 1: The job-hunter should remain somewhat loose (i.e., vague) about what he or she wants to do, so that he or she is free to take advantage of whatever vacancies may be available. Good grief, said the creative minority, this is why we have so great a percentage (80 or whatever) of Under-employment in this country. If you don't state just exactly what you want to do, first of all to yourself, and then to others, you are (in effect) handing over that decision to others. And others, vested with such awesome responsibility, are either going to dodge the decision or else make a very safe one, which is to define you as capable of doing only such and such a level of work (a safe, no risk diagnosis).

Fatal Assumption No. 2: The job-hunter should spend a good deal of time identifying the organizations that might be interested in him or her (no matter in what part of the country they may be), since employers have the initiative and upper hand in this whole process. Nonsense, said the creative minority. This isn't a high school prom, where the job-hunters are sitting around the edge of the dance-floor, like some shy wall-flower, while the employers are whirling around out in the center of the floor, and enjoying all the initiative. In many cases, those employers are stuck with partners (if we may pursue the metaphor) who are stepping on their toes, constantly. As a result, although the employer in theory has all the initiative as to whom he or she chooses to dance with, in actuality he or she is often praying *someone will pay no attention to this silly rule, and come to his or her rescue by cutting in.* And indeed, when someone takes the initiative with the employer, rather than just sitting on the sidelines with *I'll-be-very-lucky-if-you-choose-me* written all over their demeanor, the employer cannot help thinking *I-am-very-lucky-that-this-one-has-chosen-me.* People who cut in are usually pretty good dancers.

Fatal Assumption No. 3: Employers see only people who can write well. Pretty ridiculous, when it's put that way. But, say the creative minority, isn't that just exactly what our present job-hunting system is based on? To get hired, you must get an interview. To get an interview, you must let the personnel department see your resume first. Your resume will be screened out (and the interview never granted), if it doesn't make you sound good. But the resume is only as good as your writing ability (or someone else's) makes it. If you write poorly, your resume is (in effect) a Fun House mirror, which distorts you out of all proportion, so that it is impossible to tell what you really look like. *But no allowance is made for this possibility, by personnel departments, except maybe one out of a thousand.* Your resume is assumed to be an accurate mirror of you. You could be Einstein or Golda Meir, but if you don't write well (i.e., if you write a terrible resume) you will not get an interview. Employers only see people who can write well. Ridiculous? You bet it is. And, say the creative minority, this is an assumption which is long overdue for a rest. It just doesn't have to be this way.

THE CREATIVE MINORITY'S PRESCRIPTION

Once the fatal assumptions of the present system were delineated, it wasn't all that difficult to create a new system. Once you have said that the fatal assumptions are: that the job-hunter should stay vague, that employers have all the initiative as to where a job-hunter works, and that employers only see people who write well, the prescription almost writes itself, as to *the new assumptions that are the key to success:*

Key No. 1: You must decide just exactly what you want to do.

Key No. 2: You must decide just exactly where you want to do it, through your own research and personal survey.

Key No. 3: You must research the organizations that interest you at great length, and then approach the one individual in each organization who has the power to hire you for the job that you have decided you want to do.

[These steps, with minor variations, have equal applicability, whether you decide to work for industry, business, colleges, the government, associations, foundations, agencies, or whatever—though for the sake of simplicity, we will speak of "organization" as an all-inclusive term.]

For any job-hunter who wants more than "just-a-job," but a job which employs his or her abilities and interests at the highest level possible, the above prescription of the creative minority is crucial.

But for the job-hunter who is trying to strike out in some new directions, or who must of necessity do some different things than he or she has done heretofore, the prescription of the creative minority is (careerwise) *a matter of life and death.* It will be a rare new-careerist, indeed, who seeks employment without paying attention to these steps in the job-hunting process, and does not wind up Unemployed or, what is in some ways just as much a crime, Under-employed.

Since this book that you are presently ploughing your way through is intended, above all else, *to save you from making the mistakes that literally thousands before you have made,* the remainder of this book will be devoted to explaining *these three keys* to a truly successful job-search campaign.

AN EXERCISE WORTH
HALF A MILLION DOLLARS

As you review the three keys on the previous page, you will doubtless say to yourself something like, "my goodness, that looks like *an awful lot of work.*"

My friend, you are very very right!

It is a lot of hard, hard, work.

Some people say *the hardest work you will ever have to do*

is the job of getting a job. After all, it involves divining who you are, what you want, and where you are going with your life. So, think of it as a job in and of itself. Designate yourself Marketing Manager for the whole period of job-hunting. Marketing what?

You.

And if you need an incentive, say these insiders, look at it this way. Say you are forty years old, and a professional of one kind of another. And when you find a new career, you intend to work at it until you are sixty-five. That's twenty five more good years you have left as Man or Woman, the Worker. Maybe much more. And now, let's say you start at $14,000 a year and get a thousand dollars raise (on the average) each year for even ten years out of the twenty-five. That would leave you at an average earnings of between $18,000 and $20,000 per year. Multiply this by your twenty-five years and you get a total sum, for earnings, of something in the neighborhood of half a million dollars.

If you are much younger, just getting out of college say, the amount of bread you are talking about may be proportionately larger—unless you are going 'the subsistence route.' Even so, you may find yourself earning half a million before your life is over. Who knows?

Considering the above half a million dollars not crassly but stewardship-wise, as we think ultimately you should, how much time do you think a good steward should put in, to be sure that the half a million is brought to fruitfulness, rather than being—so to speak—buried?

Impatience, the desire to get it over with, fast, can cost you and your loved one (or ones) many thousands of dollars over the next decade or two, as well as condemn you to a fruitless occupation in which you continually feel undervalued, misused, and miserable. So, how much time to do it right?

Well, the job-of-getting-a-job at your highest level is going to cost you something like three months (at least) on up to nine, full-time, if the average experience of others who successfully sought a job *at their highest level,* is any guide.[1]

The higher the level of job you aim at, the more certain this time period is, since you will find decisions about hiring at higher levels—as a general rule—take longer to be made, particularly since they are so often done by a committee, rather than just by one individual.

But, you are aiming at a package which includes job satisfaction, full use of your talents, and the stewardship of perhaps half a million dollars over the next twenty-five years.

And the irony of all this is: considering the present chaotic mess that the national "job market" is, *it can take you just as long to get a poor job which pays much less and ignores the talents God gave you, as it can take you to get a good job.* The person who is unemployed stays without a job for an average (at this writing) of 115 days, regardless of the job-hunting method he or she uses.

As one member of the creative minority, John Crystal, says, the absolute first lesson to be learned in the job-hunting process is *there are no shortcuts.* And the frantic hurry to get the whole process over with can be deadly.

In charting your own job-search campaign, you are going to have ample opportunity to teach yourself the importance of Commitment—commitment, whole-heartedly, to this task that is in front of you. Time, thought and action. All are going to be required of you. And, lest such categories as these remain sounding terribly hazy, let us emphasize that they are spelled: h-a-r-d w-o-r-k.

In addition, if you are saddled with any of the special handicaps that are alleged to bog down a successful job-hunt: viz., being female, or member of a minority, or over-qualified, or under-qualified, or over forty, or under twenty-two, or a felon, ex-mental patient, or whatever, you will find the creative minority's process so much more effective than the "numbers game," that you will thank God for every hour you spent on it.

---

1 Some of the finest career transition counselors, for example, will not take clients unless they promise to spend this much time if necessary, on the whole process. Because of what has been discovered by experience.

"*Behold,
I send you forth
as lambs
among wolves . . .*"

Jesus Christ

46

CHAPTER FOUR

What About Getting Help?

WHAT ABOUT GETTING HELP?

"Okay," you say, "I'll buy the idea that a lot of hard work is involved in this process. But why do you keep saying that I have to do all this myself?

"I've heard—or read, or have been told—that there are a lot of professional agencies which will—for a fee—do a lot of this for the job-hunter.

"Maybe I don't have to do all this by myself, which would be a welcome relief."

True, true.

There *are* resources which can be of help to you—but only on two conditions:

1. If you know exactly what kind of help you need and want, because you've read and tried to use this book.

2. If you know exactly what these resources can do and what they can't do.

TYPES OF RESOURCES: LET US BEGIN BY OUTLINING THE KINDS OF HELP THAT YOU MIGHT NEED AND WANT.

- Help with particular parts of the job hunting process.
  - [1] Help with deciding just exactly what you want to do (Chapter Five).
    - A) In the way of vocation (what kind of exterior furniture do you want?)
    - B) In the way of personal growth (what to do with your interior furniture?)
  - [2] Help with the personal survey to help you decide just exactly where you want to do it (Chapter Six).
  - [3] Help with researching at length the organizations that interest you and how to approach the man who has the power to hire you for the job you want (Chapter Seven).

- Help with the whole process of the job-hunt (all of the above).

NOW, LET US LOOK AT WHAT RESOURCES THERE ARE, AND JUST WHAT THEY CAN AND CANNOT DO FOR YOU.

I. *Your own research.* This is to be preferred above all resources, for any number of reasons. First of all, knowledge which you gain for yourself is more meaningful than knowledge that is simply handed to you by others. Secondly, the job-hunt process rightly understood is itself a preparation for, and training in, skills you will need to exercise once you get the job; to deprive yourself of the opportunity to get valuable practice in these skills during the job-hunting process, is to make it just that much more difficult for yourself on the job. Thirdly, even if you pay money (and a whole lot of it) to one kind of professional agency or another, there is no guarantee that they will do the process any better than, or even as well as, you would do it yourself.

MORAL: *Every investment of your money is a gamble unless you have first tried to do it on your own, know what you did find out, what you did not find out, and therefore what kind of help you now need from others.*

II. *Books, pamphlets and other printed material.* If you need help this is the first resource to check out. (You already know that, or why are you reading this?) This kind of resource is inexpensive, and it may give you just the extra push you need, to get past whatever bottleneck is holding you up. If information, a clue, a glimmer—is all you need.

III. *Free professional help.* People rush off to press money into the hands of paid professionals when if they would just stop to analyze exactly what they need at that moment they might discover there is professional help available at no cost. Examples of such help: your local librarian, resources at the nearby university, the chamber of commerce, business friends, fellow alumni from your college who live in your area (write your college and ask for the alumni list), and others.

IV. *Professional Help for a Fee.* A. From the university. Example: vocational testing is given for a modest fee. Recommended if you have tried all the techniques in the next chapter of this book first, without getting any satisfactory answers. B. From your own professional group. For example, if you are a clergy person there are a number of church career development centers around the country. These are able to give help in certain specific areas. Check out Appendix B, for your profession. C. From the business-consultant world: (1) those which will accept all vocations as clients; (2) those which concentrate on serving specialized groups. If you are interested in these, the rest of this chapter is for you. (If not, skip to the next chapter now, before this puts you to sleep.)

BEWARE OF FALSE PROPHETS

Whether you are religious or not, you would do well to re-call the words of Jesus Christ, at this point in our survey of resources:

> Beware of false prophets, which come
> to you in sheep's clothing, but inwardly
> they are ravening wolves.
> *Matthew 7:15*

For when you come into the field of professional help for a fee, to aid you (allegedly) in the job-hunt, you are a lamb ripe for the shearing. And you can get sheared (some of your brothers and sisters already have) *to the tune of $3000.00 or more!!!* Nor should you scoff at the gullibility of your fellow sheep, at parting with so much wool, and think that it would never happen to you. The only thing that could make that certain is if you just don't have that much bread. (But neither did some of the others—until they decided to put themselves in hock.) Man, you haven't met some of those false prophets! They promise you the world. They promise you anything and everything, and they make it sound so plausible, so inexora-ble, that after a while you can't imagine why you are letting a piddling little $3000, or whatever amount they may name, hold you back from *Shangri-La.* You can easily become con-vinced by men masquerading as professional career counsel-ors, or whatever they call themselves, that these men have— alone— solved all mysteries to the job-hunt, that they hold keys to every executive washroom in your city, and that if you just put your fate (and your fee) in their hands, you will get that dazzling job you want, without your having to so much as lift a finger. Months later, after you have lost irre-placeable time, have gambled away on glittering, false prom-ises the money represented by their fee, you will know them for what they are, but it will be very late. And, still having no job or only a miserable excuse for one, you will have to begin all over again.

So, now, while you have not yet made such a devastating blunder, let us all recall together:

SOME BASIC TRUTHS ABOUT PROFESSIONAL HELP

In the whole, big field of The Job Hunt, all professional help divides up (one regrets to say) into the following inevitable categories:

1. Professionals who are sincere and skilled.
2. Professionals who are sincere but inept.
3. Professionals who are insincere and inept.

(One could list a fourth category, but charity must assert itself at some point—and, anyway, you have a good imagination.)

Now, the problem we all face when we are thinking of going to a particular professional is, of course, does he fall into category No.1, or into one of the other two (which of

the other two is really irrelevant, from the point of view of the individual job-seeker—ineptness is ineptness)?

The various clues which may at first occur to us are, upon more serious examination, not terribly fruitful. Let us tick off some of them, and see why:

✦ Clue No.1: Perhaps we can tell who is sincere and skilled, by the name of his vocation or agency. Difficulty: names vary greatly from one operation to another, even when the operations are similar. Among the names which some men or agencies bear, you will find: executive career counselors, executive career consultants, career management teams, executive consulting counselors, career guidance counselors, executive advisors, executive development specialists, executive job counselors, career advisors, executive recruitment consultants, professional career counselors, management consultants, professional placement specialists, executive search specialists, professional vocational counselors, etc. If, tomorrow, some legitimate counselor who is sincere and skilled takes on a new name, the day after that some counselor who is insincere and inept will copy the name directly. What it all comes down to, is this. Wolves need sheep's clothing. Names are sheep's clothing. Trouble is, hidden in there, are some genuinely helpful people. We need another clue.

✦ Clue No.2: Perhaps we can tell who is sincere and skilled by reading everything that the agency or counselor has written. Difficulty: both good and bad counselors know the areas where the job-hunter feels exceedingly vulnerable. Consequently, there are "turn on" words which occur in almost everybody's advertisements, brochures, and books: we will give you help, say they, with evaluating career, in-depth analysis of your background, establishment of your objective, in-depth analysis of your capabilities, your resume, names of companies, preparing the covering letter, background materials on companies, interview techniques, salary negotiations, filling out forms, tests, answering ads, aptitude tests, special problems—unemployment, age, too broad a background, too narrow a background, too many job changes, too few job changes, poor references, etc.—opening doors for you, and so forth. Both the counselors who are skilled and those who are inept will never get anyone in their doors if they don't mention the areas that have put the job-hunter in Desperation City. So this doesn't separate the sheep from the goats, unfortunately. One further warning: some founders of various agencies have written excellent books which it would appear some of their own employees haven't yet comprehended, sad to say. Next clue?

✦ Clue No.3: Perhaps we can tell who is sincere and skilled by the fee they charge; I mean, they wouldn't charge a high fee, would they, if they weren't skilled? Difficulty: as insiders say, low fees most frequently (with a few notable exceptions) mean shoddy, amateurish help. But the reverse of this is *not* true. As we have already mentioned, the vacuum created by the chaotic condition of our job-hunting process has attracted both competent people *and* people who are willing to prey upon the acute anxiety that job-hunters are often seized by. And when the latter say "Let us prey" they *really* prey. And they *thrive*. P. T. Barnum knew what he was talking about.* Next.

✦ Clue No. 4: Perhaps we can tell which professionals are both sincere and skilled, by talking to satisfied clients—or asking our friends who was helpful to them. Difficulty: what are they recommending?—the whole nationwide agency (assuming it is nationwide)? or the branch thereof that is in their city? or the particular counselor (or counselors) that they saw at that branch? If you stop to think about it, you will realize this most crucial truth: *all they can possibly speak to you about is the particular counselor or counselors that they worked with, at that agency, in that particular city.* Should you go to that same place, and get a different counselor, you might have a very different experience. One bad counselor in an agency that has say, six good ones, can cost you much money, time, and self-esteem, if *you* get that bad one as *your* counselor. The six good ones might as well be in Timbuktu, for all the good they'll do you. So, should any of your friends offer (or should you solicit from them) advice about a place they went to, be sure to find out the counselor

---

*A sucker is born every minute.

(or counselors) they worked with, there, *by name,* so you will know, who to ask for, if you decide to investigate or follow their lead.

Before we leave this clue, let us also observe that with most professional career counselors, though they will show you letters from satisfied customers, or even give you (in some cases) their names to check out, it is impossible to find out what percentage of their total clientele these satisfied persons represent: 100%? 10? 1? .1? a fluke? If you want a clue, you may make what you will out of the fact that the top officers of the largest executive counseling firm, which did over 50% of the business in the industry (allegedly) before it declared bankruptcy in the fall of 1974, (namely, Frederick Chusid & Co.) gave testimony in a New York Federal district court (during a civil suit) which indicated that only 3 or 4 out of every ten clients had been successful in getting a new job, during a previous six-month period.[1] Are these figures average for the industry? Better than average? Worse? Nobody knows. Outside courtrooms, executive counseling firms have been very reluctant to discuss their success rates, or else they have quoted success rates (uncorroborated or substantiated) that have caused *insiders* to raise their eyebrows. "Tell me another one!"

CAVEAT EMPTOR*, AND AGAIN I SAY

Now that we have seen which clues are not particularly helpful, we are ready to suggest some crucial guidelines for choosing a professional career counselor—*if* you decide you need one—now, or later on in your life:

Before you choose a professional career counselor (read these three times):

1. Try to do the three steps toward a successful job hunt (decide *what* you want to do, *where* you want to do it, and then research the organizations that interest you exhaustively before approaching *the one man* in each organization who has the power to hire you), by yourself or with the aid of family and friends. *If you bog down, make a list for yourself*

---

* Let the buyer beware

of exactly where you are bogging down. What steps in the process are eluding you?

2. Check out the recommended books (Appendix B) from your libraries, to see if you can get additional help with the particular steps that you made a list of (No.1 above). Also check out free professional help for those areas.

3. If you decide you need professional help with the whole process, consult the Directory (Appendix C), and choose *at least three places to check out personally.* How skilled they are is a judgment *you* must make for yourself and that is why you must do comparison shopping.

4. Before you visit or contact these places (or any others), we suggest you research a) this whole subject, and b) the specific agencies (if possible) that you are considering.

The whole subject is best researched through articles which have appeared about phony or questionable executive counseling services and firms; because, in making clear why these places are bad, guidelines appear regarding *all* career counseling. So run — do not walk — to your local library, and ask your librarian for help in finding the following articles. You could save $3000 and get an education, besides!

THE BEST ARTICLES:

"A Brief Case Against Executive Job Counselors: for up to $6,000 they sell mostly pep talks and promises to downhearted executives" by Caroline Donnelly, *Money* Magazine, November, 1973.

October 11, 1968: *The Wall Street Journal,* "Raising False Hopes? Firms Set Up To Counsel Executives Attacked As Promising Too Much; Mounting Complaints Spur Federal and Local Probes; Some Clients are Happy; Steep Fees and Rapid Talk," by Ronald Kessler.

January 15, 1970 *The Iron Age* Magazine, "Executive Job Counseling Woods Are Full of Confidence Men" "Unscrupulous Job Counselors Lure Many Executives" by S. H. Hockenberry.

September 1970 *The Retired Officer* Magazine "Unscrupulous Job Counselors Prove Expensive for Retired Officers."

OTHER ARTICLES:

"Executive Job Finding Rackets" by Sylvia Porter, May 2, 1965, *The Washington D.C. Sunday Star.* And "We Get You The Job You Deserve: Career Counselors Who *Can* Find You An Executive Position Are Leading The Fight To Get Rid of the Frauds Who, For A Fat Fee, Sell Nothing But False Hopes," by Thomas J. Fleming, in December 1968 *This Week* Magazine. And "Legislation to Regulate Executive-Counseling Concerns to be Sought" *The Wall Street Journal,* December 10, 1968. And January 4, 1969 *Business Week* Magazine column on criticism of job consulting. And July 25, 1970 *Business Week* Magazine column on paying a high fee for artful hand-holding. And October 3, 1970 *San Francisco Chronicle* article, "Jobless Executives and Agency Gyps." See also such books as *Move In & Move Up* by E. A. Butler (MacMillan).

You will also probably not find it a very wise investment of your time to visit your local Better Business Bureau, since neither their booklet on career counseling nor their evaluation of specific firms in your city is likely to be very enlightening, for your purposes.

5. Contact each of the three places you have chosen. These are exploratory visits only. Leave your wallet and your checkbook home, please! You are comparison shopping, not decision reaching!!

Make this unmistakably clear, when the interview begins. We also recommend *that you take careful, handwritten notes—to refresh your memory—and theirs.* Questions you will be seeking answers to, at each place—and please, write out these questions beforehand, and at each place ask *every* question (omitting none):

● *What is their program?* When all their gimmicks are set aside (and some have great ones, like rehearsing for interviews on closed circuit TV, or using video-tape or cassettes to record your resume, etc.) what are they offering: is it basically "the numbers game," *or* is it basically some variation of the creative minority's prescription (the Three Keys, on page 43)?

● *Who will be doing it?* Do you get the feeling that you must do most of it, with their basically assuming the role of coach? (if so, three cheers); or do you get the feeling that everything (including decision making about what you do, where you do it, etc.) will be done for you (if so, three warning bells should go off in your head)?

● *What guarantee is there that it will work?* If they make it clear that they have had a good success rate, but if you fail to work hard at the whole process, then there is no guarantee you are going to find a job, give them three stars. On the other hand, if they practically guarantee you a job, and say they have never had a client that failed to find a job, no matter what, *watch out.* Pulmotor job-counseling is very suspect; lifeless bodies make poor employees.

● *How many boxes are they building for you, as they talk?* A typical box in the *what-do-I-want-to-do?* area is: let's face it, you may have to settle for a job at a rather lower level than you might hope for. A typical box in the *where-do-I-want-to-do-it?* area is: let's face it, you may be unfair to yourself in trying to look for a job only in this particular geographical area—you may have to go where the work is. And so forth. *Press them about these kinds of limits.* The less boxes they build for you, the better; the more they build for you, the more demerits you should give them. The line between realism and pessimism is very thin in the head of an inept counselor; he or she will press you into a shape he or she can sell.

● *Are you face-to-face, and talking, with the actual persons who will be working with you, should you decide to become a client?* It might help you to be aware that some firms have professional salesmen who introduce you to the company, convince you of their 100% integrity and charm, secure your decision, get you to sign the contract—and then you never see them again. You work with someone entirely different (or a whole team). *Ask the man or woman you are talking to, if he or she is the one (and the only one) you will be working with, should you eventually decide to become a client.* If he or she says No, ask to meet those who would be actually working with you—even if it's a whole battery of people. When you actually meet them, there are three considerations you should weigh:

(1) *Do you like him, her or them?* Bad vibes can cause great difficulties, even if this person is extremely competent. Don't dismiss this factor!

(2) *How long has he or she been doing this?* Ask him, her, them! And what training did he or she have for it? (Legitimate questions; if they get huffy, politely thank them for their time, and take your leave gently *but firmly.*) Insiders allege that some agencies hire former clients as new staff. Such new staff are sometimes given "on the job training." Since you're paying for Expertise, already acquired, you have *a right* to ask about this before making up your mind.

(3) *How much time will he or she give you?* Each of them, if it is a team. As a minimum? As a maximum? (There's got to be a maximum, no matter what they may at first claim. Every agency runs into extremely-dependent types as clients, who would be there all day every day if the agency didn't have some kind of policy about maximum. *Press* to find out what it is, just so you'll know.) Over how long a period can you use their services? And, will they put all this in writing? (That's the question that separates the men from the boys, and the women from the girls.)

● *What is the cost of these services? Are there any additional costs for additional services (like printing and sending out resumes)? If so, what are those services, and how much do they cost? Also, do you have to buy the whole program or will they sell you their help for just parts of it, where you need help the most? What provisions are there about payment?* These are questions to ask while you are still doing comparison shopping, before your mind is closed and your wallet open. Clues: fees will range from $200 on up to $3000 if you're talking to some of the large-volume agencies out there in Secularland. Whether you choose *any* of these places or not, will probably depend on whether you're a high school or college student, say, looking for your first job (in which case, forget it!) or an executive or professional in mid-career crisis, looking for top-flight help (in which case, *maybe*).

● *What does the contract state? What does it bind them to? What does it bind you to? What provision is there for rebate of part of the fee if you become unhappy with their help? After what point will no rebate be given? (Crucial.)* Ask to see the contract (a legitimate request on your part). Study your notes to see what they promised that is important to you: are these all included in the contract? If not, ask if they can be. If the answer is no, ask Why? With some firms, the promises that attract the client to choose that particular firm, turn out—upon inspection—to be all verbal, none of them spelled out in the actual contract of promised services. Hello, sucker.

Having gotten the information *you* want, and therefore having accomplished *your* purpose for this particular visit, you politely thank them for their time and trouble, and depart. You then go on to two other places, and ask the very same questions, please! There ought to be no charges involved for such comparison-shopping visits as this, and if they subsequently bill you, inquire politely whether or not a mistake has been made by their accounting department (good thinking). If they persist, pay a visit to your local friendly Better Business Bureau, and lodge a nice unfriendly complaint against the firm in question. (BBB's serve some useful functions.) You'd be surprised at how many firms experience *instant repentance* when the Better Business Bureau phones them. They don't want a complaint on their BBB record.

6. Back home now, after visiting the three places you chose for your comparison shopping, you have to decide: a) whether you want none of the three, or b) one of the three, and if so, which one.

Time for thought, maybe using some other people as a sounding board (wife, husband, professor, placement center, friend, buddy, business friend, consultant friend, or whoever) and time for some thoughtful meditation. What's at stake is a lot of *bread*, as they say, and you ought not to spend it casually—even if you have managed some savings, and are feeling rather desperate.

Look over your notes on all three places. Compare those

places. Study your notes. Ask yourself two final questions:

What am I looking for—friends, or experts? Not so silly a question as at first appears. W. A. Schofield views psychotherapy as a way that someone who is in distress can *purchase friendship.* The same might be said for almost any kind of consulting, including career consulting and job-hunt consulting. Professor David McClelland says that indeed some people faced with choosing between friends or experts to help them with a problem they are working on, will prefer friends *if their strongest need is that of affiliation with other people.* He says they will only choose experts, over friends, *if they have a strong need to be Achievers.* Of course, you are an Achiever, so you are going to look over your notes to see which consultants will prove most expert—right? and not just which ones you *liked* because they would make good friends. Rapport, as we said earlier, is important; but not $1000 important. For that kind of bread, a little expertise would help, too.

If I conclude I really do need friendship during this whole process (call it A Support Community if you want to use current favored phrases), are there other places to get it? Good thinking. Lou Albee, in his book *Over Forty—Out of Work?*[2] (borrow it, from your local library) has an excellent

chapter (Face Your Family Problem) on how you can include your family in the whole job-hunt process. Indeed, he argues it is essential. In his book, p. 127, he suggests other ways of building community,—like contacting other job-hunters who are in a similar boat. You can form a sort of "Job-hunters Anonymous." No need in the world to go about this whole process Alone; and highly undesirable that you should.* But choosing a career consultant and paying his or her fee *just in order to purchase friendship* needs looking at.

Well, having weighed these two questions, discussing, and tossing it about with friends, you make a decision. You're going to do this on your own. OR you can decide help is essential for you, so you choose the consultant you like best, go back, get their contract, *take it to a lawyer* and then if he sees nothing wrong, sign it.

You haven't got a job yet, but hopefully you've gotten what *you* wanted: *expert coaching.*

But, we repeat, this should only be your last resort, after you've first read this book from cover to cover, and done your darnedest to follow the process in Chapters 5-7 by yourself (or with a mate, friend, or like that). If then, you still need help, you'll at least feel good about how hard you tried.

---

*We would suggest you find other job-hunters to band together with, if it is humanly possible. A most interesting experiment was conducted in Illinois, comparing the job-finding experiences of those who banded together with others (in a "job-finding club") vs. the job-finding experiences of those who hunted all by themselves. This is how it went:

Members of the behavior research laboratory at the Anna State Hospital in Illinois formed a job-finding club in a small college town with a long history of unemployment above the national average. Unemployed clients were gathered through newspaper ads, the state unemployment service, personnel departments of businesses, and by word of mouth. They were matched in terms of "employability" determined by such factors as their race, sex, age, education, marital status, and former salary levels. Sixty of the clients then set out to seek jobs on their own while a comparably employable 60 took part in the job-finding club.

Each client in the club was urged to attend sessions every day until he found a job. The group setting allowed for a buddy system in which members offered one another mutual assistance in their search. They shared job leads, reviewed and criticized one another's resumes, role-played through practice interviews, and provided peer-group advice and encouragement. In addition, clients were counseled in virtually every conceivable skill thought to be helpful in securing employment.

Going on the theory that employers often hire as much on the basis of social and personal attributes as on strict sets of qualifications, the researchers encouraged their job seekers to assume stated job prerequisites to be flexible, and to follow up every possible newspaper ad or other lead. Their resumes emphasized their personal and social attributes as well as their vocational skills and included a photo to help fix their identities in the employer's mind.

The job-finding club seems to have been highly effective. Half the group found jobs within two weeks. Two-thirds of its members found employment within one month compared with one-third of those in the control group. At the end of two months, 90 percent of the counseled job seekers were employed compared with only 55 percent of those not counseled. All the clients who loyally attended the sessions eventually found employment. And the average starting salary for the club members was 36 percent higher than the beginning wage for those who found jobs on their own.

The name of Nathan H. Azrin, from the Center for Human Development, in Carbondale, Illinois has become widely known as the pioneer in this sort of job-hunting club idea. His work has been described in the *Journal of Applied Behavioral Analysis;* and widely written up, elsewhere.

1 *The Wall Street Journal*, p. 1, October 11, 1968: "Raising False Hopes?"
2 This has been also issued in paperback, with a different title: *Job-Hunting After Forty* (New York: Arco Publishing Company), 1971.

The Inquiring Reporter
asked the young woman why
she wanted to be a mortician.
Because, she said, *I enjoy
working with people.*

The San Francisco Chronicle

CHAPTER FIVE

Only *You* Can Decide:

What Do You Want To Do?

)oint we've told you what to avoid. We've taken you on a guided tour of the primrose path that so many job-hunters and career-changers before you have innocently walked down, and we've shown you all the things to avoid: the banana peel here, the thorns behind the roses there, and so forth. X marks the spot. If you've *hung in* all the way, so far, you now realize that there is *a veritable army* of people who are thriving on the *anxiety, naivete* and *vulnerability* of the would be job-hunter. Your sole defense against this army is to sit down and do your own homework. *You have got to know what it is you want, or someone is going to sell you a bill of goods somewhere along the line that can do irreparable damage to your self-esteem, your sense of worth, and your stewardship of the talents that God gave you.*

That is true for those just starting out; it is even more true for those who are changing careers, and those who have been "phased out": ex-buffalo skinners, ex-buggy whip makers, ex-blacksmiths, ex-railroad men, ex-Hollywood actors, ex-airline pilots, ex-military, ex-stock brokers, ex-aerospace engineers, ex-defense workers, ex-scientists, ex-marketing executives, ex-employment agency staff, ex-technicians, ex-personnel executives, ex-public relations men, ex-teachers, and ex-practically everything.

Changing careers because you have to? You are joining a flood of vocations that are in the same pr dicament. It begins to look as though every man and woman is going to have to learn how to go about identifying a viable second career for himself and herself. And maybe even a third. Indeed, some social scientists who count themselves futurists have said as much. Workers must be prepared to change careers several times during their lives, says the Advisory Centre for Education in England. That means thinking about it *now*!

It is, unhappily, taking our educational system (particularly higher education) a painfully long time to become aware of this. We train people to do just one thing, we encourage them to become specialists—and then we wonder at their agonized cry when they discover, one day, that their specialty is no longer needed. Our only solution for them, at that moment, is to suggest that they go back and get retrained all over again for another specialty. Never mind how much time it takes, or how much money must come from somewhere to retrain them. And never mind how short-lived this *new specialty* of theirs may turn out to be, in terms of demand in the marketplace. This is the route that our country typically takes (from Congress on down) when faced with growing unemployment in a number of fields. Band-aid after band-aid. A crisis solution that is short-lived, and only leads to another crisis—in the lives of countless individuals and professions.

CAREER AND LIFE PLANNING: AN OVERVIEW OF THE ART

In protest against this, there has grown up a field called by many names, but known generally as *career and life planning*. The purpose of this new "art" (for that is what many regard it as being, at this present time) is to take a longer view of a person's life—so that one can avoid short-term, band-aid thinking. It involves building in Alternative Options, from the beginning. Like, in high school or college.

You can find this new art being practiced in a number of places: in books, at conferences, at human growth centers, in management consultant seminars—not to mention in the quiet of people's own individual craniums.

Career and life planning is something we are *all* going to have to do quite a bit of. Because if you go about identifying *what it is you want to do*—not only for the immediate present, but also for some steps beyond that—you *are* doing life planning. The minute you think or write down some short term goals and some long term goals for yourself, you are into it.

But we must be very clear about this: *there is no magic in the name.* Some of our people have gone away to seminars billed as "long range life planning," and have come back "happy"—but just as confused and uncertain about what they wanted to do, as they were before they went. The name "long range life planning" can get tacked on (and has) to some pretty disorganized and generalized vague long range "dreaming."

Since it is the purpose of this section of our manual to be immensely practical, and *teach you how to do career and life planning for yourself,* we begin with this one immensely practical goal:

> For us, career and life planning is useless, unless at the end of this part for our homework, we are very definite about exactly what we want to do—for now, and beyond.

Given this criterion, you can—as a matter of fact—call it almost an infinite variety of *names* (and people have):

> long range career development
> long term help in career planning
> full career planning
> studying your career patterns
> full career program
> long range action planning
> self-counseling and planning
> critical assessment of oneself and one's future
> self-confrontation and design
> dealing with what I will become as well
> as with what I will do.
> human resources planning
> vocational development process
> long range life planning

CAREER AND LIFE PLANNING DEALS WITH ALL TWENTY-FOUR HOURS

Regardless of its name (and we will, for the sake of simplicity, call it career and life planning), it should be noted that this activity is not *restricted* just to the question of vocation, or what one does between nine and five, weekdays.

Career and life planning deals with more than that: ideally, it deals with one's whole life mission, one's life role, and one's life-long identity (or identities). It deals with identification of one's goals, calling, values, priorities, and so forth.

On the other hand, career and life planning which *omits* exact identification of *what it is you want to do* is foolishness, because you live half your life at your job—whatever it may be. God's world already has more than enough people who can't wait for five o'clock to come, so that they can now go and do what they really want to do. It doesn't need us to swell that crowd. Us . . . or anyone else. It needs people who know what they really want to do, and do it *at* their place of work, *as* their work.

CAREER AND LIFE PLANNING INCLUDES PLANS FOR A SECOND CAREER, MAYBE A THIRD

Can you really sit down and actually figure out an alternative career for yourself, based on what you really enjoy doing—without going back to school for a million years of re-training? Or figure out a first career, systematically? You bet you can.

Then why is this whole country in general, and our personnel system in particular, baffled as to how to go about this whole process?

Now, that is a *very* good question, particularly when the creative minority has been crying out for years that it could be done and has been done by countless numbers of ordinary people from all walks of life. It's all very simple, they have been saying . . . and saying . . . and saying.

There are only four things that hold people back from completing this personal homework exercise successfully:

1. *Lack of Purpose.* People trying to identify a first or second career for themselves are not sure what kind of things they need to be looking for.

2. *Lack of tools or instruments.* People know what kind of things they are looking for, perhaps, but they have nothing to help them go about it systematically and comprehensively.

3. *Lack of Motivation.* People know what kinds of things they are looking for, and they have helpful instruments so

that they can do it, but the *internal push* to get at it and keep at it until it is done, is inadequate. This is usually *the* major roadblock of the four.

4. *Lack of time.* Purpose is grasped, tools are in hand, motivation is just great, but they have waited to get at this exercise until they are actually living in Desperation Gulch (just on the outskirts of Panic City)—and the amount of time needed to do this properly just does not seem to be there. So of course the exercise is done joylessly and, often, without much profit. Food meant to be savored cannot be wolfed down, without the danger of acute indigestion. Likewise, career and life planning meant to be done with much time for reflection, cannot be telescoped without the danger of erroneous judgments and conclusions.

WHAT'S GOING TO PUT YOU AHEAD

You can sit down and work out exactly what it is that you want to do once you resolve that *you* will not and do not lack the four prerequisites for this kind of work:

Time
Motivation
Purpose
Tools & Instruments

We will consider each of these, in turn.

● TIME: TWENTY THOUSAND HOURS OR MORE ARE AT STAKE

When you sit down to try to identify what it is that you want to do for your life ahead, you are planning an awful lot of time ahead. A forty-hour a week job, done for fifty weeks a year, adds up to 2000 hours per year. How long are you going to be doing it? Ten years? 20,000 hours. Fifteen years? 30,000 hours. *It is worth spending two weeks of your life, or two months, or whatever it takes to plan well—so that what you do those 20 or 30 thousand hours is something you enjoy and something you do well and something that fits in with your life mission.*

Needless to say, if you've got 25 to 50 years ahead of you before retirement, your task is even more awesome and worthwhile. What a lot of hours you have still to put in. In enjoyable, productive, helpful activity just at your job—*not to mention your leisure time and what it is you will be doing after retirement, which should also be a part of your thinking and planning.*

You aren't going to get this done just by sitting up late one or two nights. It takes longer than that. You need to make up your mind to that, before you even begin. Thoughts, like soup stock, often need to simmer for awhile—on the front burner, or on the back.

● MOTIVATION:
$250,000 OR MORE IS AT STAKE

If you're currently unemployed, you are highly motivated to sit down and figure out exactly what you want to do— short-range and long-range. You may want to get it over with, fast—and that way lies madness (frustration, ineffectiveness, *under*employment)—but at least you *are* motivated.

What if you are still employed? Face it, it's harder, but it can still be done *provided you want to do it enough.*

Of course, the temptation is to procrastinate. And procrastination, as my grandfather used to say, has sent more men to hell than whiskey.

What are you waiting for? Well, if you're like the rest of us, you're waiting until you are actually staring down the muzzle of the gun called "Unemployment."

"What do you want to do, for the rest of your life?" "Oh, I don't know; I'll figure it out when I have to."

I hate to tell you this, but the time to figure out where your parachute is, what color it is, and to strap it on, is *now*—and not when the vocational airplane that you are presently in is on fire and diving toward the ground.

But most of us typically wait until we are unemployed. Bad! None of us are fools. We all know that we may have to become self-supporting, with very short notice. We are poor stewards indeed of the talents God has given us if we relegate this task to about twenty-fifth priority in our lives.

As we said earlier, he who waits usually waits *until* he is unemployed. That's not only bad for figuring out what you really want to do, it's bad for job-hunting. *Like it or not, your value automatically drops if you have to admit that you hold no job. The world is just conditioned to that idea, and they are not likely to be able to switch gears just because you say, "Oh, I'm changing careers." If you're employed, somebody wants you—and values you enough to say so, in the coin of the realm. If you're unemployed, there is just the breath of suspicion that perhaps no one wants you. And faced with this suspicion, many employers will choose to make no decision about you (i.e., not hire you) rather than take a gamble.* This is as true for women as for men.

Talk with other job-hunters and they'll all, virtually, tell you the same thing: stay with it as long as you can, and don't make a move until you've got another job nailed down. If the choice is yours.

Of course, the choice may not be yours. All of a sudden you're out. You didn't see it coming. There was no warning. Or maybe there was, and you just didn't see it. Well, no sense kicking pebbles and wishing you had been wiser. You *are* unemployed. And that just means you've joined a lot of other company. You can still do the whole process right; it's just going to be that much harder, that's all. You may want to, for starters, read some of the books (in your library) that are listed at the end of this manual in Appendix B. Specifically, try Kent (pp. 11ff, 43, 181ff), Albee (pp. 1-35, 58, 109, 124) and Miner (pp. 114, 131, 167). They have been able to suggest some helpful pointers for the person who is engaged in career planning/job-hunt, and is already out of his or her last job. . . voluntarily or involuntarily.

Employed or unemployed, you *can* find the motivation, my friend. Figure out what is important to you, and then see how this kind of planning can be related to it.

Just in case money is *one* of the things that is important to you, for example, let us point out that if you've still got 20,000-60,000 hours (or more) of "working time" ahead of you, you're automatically talking about $150,000-500,000 of potential income, or more. So, how carefully would you plan if someone offered you up to half a million dollars? Yet, that is exactly the case you are in.

Now, hopefully, all this splendid allusion to your stewardship of time and to your stewardship of "unrighteous mammon" (money) will have galvanized you out of your chair while your need to find other employment is *still a long way off*. And you will say, "No matter what other things I have to get done during these next few weeks, *now* is the acceptable time, *now* is the day when I must do some long range planning—because I owe it to myself, I owe it to my loved ones, and I owe it to my Creator." *And you will give this first priority.*

If, however, you know yourself terribly well, and you know that this task is liable to be procrastinated and procrastinated to death, then we have a very practical exercise for you.

Practical Exercise (Warmup)

Decide who you know (wife, friend, etc.) that you can take into your confidence about this. Tell them what you need to do, the hours it will take, and how much you need *them* to keep you at this task. Then put down in your appointment book regular weekly dates when he/she will *guarantee* to meet with you, check you out on what you've done already, and be very stern with you if you've done little or nothing since your previous meeting. The more a taskmaster this confidante is, the better. Tell them it's at least a 20,000 hour, $250,000 project. Or whatever. It's also responsible, concerned, committed *Stewardship*.

A final thought about motivation: You're not just doing this for yourself. Your long range life planning means greater happiness for your loved ones, and (unless you are planning on fleeing to a desert island) for countless other people who will be affected and helped by your First, Second or Third Career—or, if you prefer, by this new form of your service to God and to Man.

Practical Exercise (Cooling Down?)

If two weeks after putting down this manual, you pick it up again, and realize you still haven't even begun this first step of sitting down and deciding what it is that you want to do; and you haven't enlisted anyone else to help you either, then face it: you're going to *have to* pay someone to aid you. Too bad, because you could do it just as well or better yourself. But: better this way than no way: turn to Appendix C, choose three possible professional places, go ask them some questions, and then choose one. Pay them, and *get at this.*

For, the truth is that people prefer to wait, in these matters, until the hour is very late. As we said earlier, procrastination sent more men to hell than whiskey.

● PURPOSE:
TO DISCOVER GOALS, SKILLS, TIME LINES, AND WHO'S IN CONTROL

Okay, let us assume you are motivated enough to want to do this task *yourself.* Even so, maybe you can find a friend who must also go through this same task (sooner or later) and is willing to do it at the same time you do. If so, we recommend it. If you paid somebody, you already have that partner.

Now, on your own—or with a *planning partner*—what is it that you are looking for, during this process? We have already indicated the over-all purpose. It's worth repeating:

> Career & life planning is useless, unless at the end of the process we are very definite about exactly what we want to do—for now, and beyond.

74

But let's be even more specific than this. Any career and life planning that is worth its salt should help the person who is engaged in doing it (namely, You) to do the following things:

1. You need to become more aware of your goals in life. **GOALS** What do you want to accomplish before you die? What is your life's "mission," as you perceive it?

You may revise this list ten more times, as life goes on *(Career and life planning is, ideally, an on-going process—not a single event, done once and for all)* but as you perceive it now what are you trying to accomplish, what are you trying to become? What's unique about *you*?

2. You need to inventory what skills you presently have— **SKILLS** things you do well and enjoy. This inventory needs to be taken in terms of basic units—*building blocks, if you will*—so that as time goes on, these basic units can be arranged in different constellations. The creative minority insists this is the very heart of planning for first, second, etc., careers.

3. After identifying your long- and short-range goals, and **TIME** inventorying your skills in terms of basic units, you need to **LINES** consider and identify what Peter Drucker calls the *futurity of present decisions.*

Considering where you would like to go, and what you would like to do, what time spans are built in to present decisions (e.g., if school is demanded, how many years before you get out?), and what risks are built into present decisions? The purpose of your planning is not to eliminate risks (there can be no movement forward without them) but to be sure that the risks you take are the right ones, based on careful thought.

4. You need to basically decide who (or what) is control- **WHO'S** ling your career planning: accident, circumstance, the stars, **IN** the system, Providence, God (how?), your family, other **CONTROL** people or—forgive us for mentioning this possibility—You. You see, ultimately, this comes down to a question of how passive you want to be about it all. (Life, career, where you

work, the whole bag.) We have, admittedly, an axe to grind here: we believe you will improve your effectiveness and your sense of yourself as a person 300% if you can learn to think (or already think) of yourself as *an active agent* who helps to mould his present environment and his future; rather than as a passive agent, who waits for his environment to mould him. (Or her environment to mould her.)

But, to say that your purpose is to find your goals, skills, time lines, and who's in control, is not enough. Your real purpose is to identify the core of your life, the constant thread, the constancy in you that persists through all the changing world around you. As we all know from Alvin Toffler (Future Shock) now, change is coming at us so fast that many people are going into shock (marked by apathy, withdrawal, paralysis or galloping nostalgia).

The planning outlined above helps you to deal with change by identifying what in your life is unchanging: your sense of life "mission," your basic skills etc.—the things that continue relatively unchanging at the core of your *inner nature*. A base of constancy is necessary in order to deal with the bombardment of change that has become the hallmark of this world in which we presently live.

You build this base of constancy by: identifying the goals, values, priorities, etc., that you already have; inventorying the basic building blocks of your skills that you already have; identifying the time spans and risks that you must deal with in making your present decisions; and exercising your present identity as one who moulds his fate rather than letting fate mould him (or her).

The secret of dealing with the shock that lies in the future for you is not that you should try to nail down that future— every plank of it—as though it were possible to spell it out and then stick to it, no matter what . . . (This is what it is going to be like, and this is what I am determined it shall be. On March 4, 1982, I will be doing exactly thus and so.) Ridiculous, even as "the Now Generation" has been so quick to point out.

The secret of dealing with the future is to nail down what you have in this present—and see the different ways in which

the basic units of that can be rearranged into different constellations, consistent with the goals and values that direct
the inner nature which the Creator has given you, as you
perceive them.

You are aiming at being able to fill in this chart:

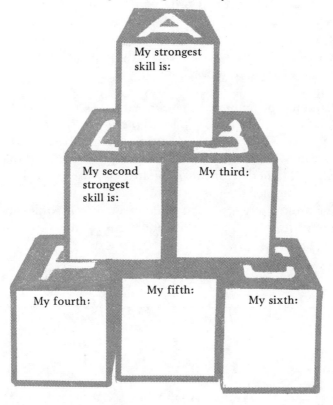

My strongest skill is:

My second strongest skill is:

My third:

My fourth:

My fifth:

My sixth:

THAT BOGEY-WORD — Skills

Now many people just "freeze" when they hear the word
"skills." It begins with high-school job-hunters: "I haven't
really got any skills," they say. It continues with college
students: "I've spent four years in college. I haven't had time
to pick up any skills." And it lasts through the middle years,
especially when a person is thinking of changing his career:
"I'll have to go back to college, and get re-trained, because
otherwise I won't have any skills in my new field." Or: "Well,
if I claim any skills, I'll start at a very nominal kind of level."

All of this fright about the word "skills" is very common, and stems from a total misunderstanding of what the word means. A misunderstanding that is shared, we might add, by altogether too many employers, personnel departments, and so-called "vocational experts."

By understanding the word, you will automatically put yourself way ahead of most job-hunters. And, especially if you are weighing a change of career, you can save yourself much waste of time on the (currently popular) folly called "going back to school for retraining."

So, here we go:

According to the *Bible* of vocational counseling,—the third edition of the *Dictionary of Occupational Titles,* Vol. II (Washington, D.C.: U.S. Government Printing Office, 1965)—Skills break down, first of all, into three groups, according to whether or not they are being used with Things or Data or People.

Thus broken down, and arranged in a hierarchy of less skill (at the bottom) to higher skills (at the top), they come out looking like this:

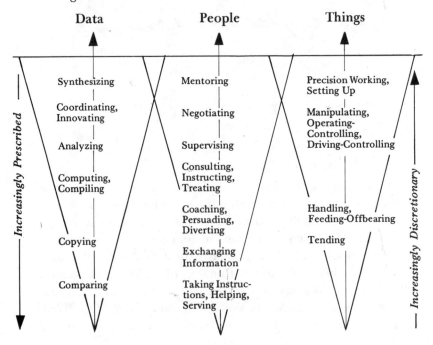

Before we explain these skills in more detail, let us look at the *most startling fact about all these skills*. It is, simply, this:

> If you graded all these skills in terms of how many of their duties are prescribed in detail vs. how many are discretionary, i.e., left to the discretion of the employee, you would discover that the lower the skill, the more its duties are prescribed, with comparatively little discretion left to the employee; but, the higher the skill, the less its duties are prescribed, and the more that is left to the discretion of the employee.

This almost paradoxical meaning of the word "skill" can be easily illustrated from any, or all, of the three hierarchies on the previous page. For the sake of comparative brevity, we will take just one, namely, those which deal with people. (You know, today most people when asked what they want to do out in The World, will almost always answer, "I want to work with people." Might as well show those of us who say this, just how varied Work with People can be.) Note, as we progress to higher levels of skills, *how it becomes harder and harder for a prospective employer (say) to draw up a job description for this skill.*

The People Functions Scale on the following page is from the *Dictionary of Occupational Titles*, Vol. II, pp. 649-50, as modified and adapted by Dr. Sidney A. Fine of the W. E. Upjohn Institute for Employment Research (see Appendix B).

Each higher skill level usually or typically involves all those which preceded it.

Level	Definition
1A	**TAKING INSTRUCTIONS—HELPING** Attends to the work assignment, instructions, or orders of supervisor. No immediate response or verbal exchange is required unless clarification of instruction is needed.
1B	**SERVING** Attends to the needs or requests of people or animals, or to the expressed or implicit wishes of people. Immediate response is involved.
2	**EXCHANGING INFORMATION** Talks to, converses with, and/or signals people to convey or obtain information, or to clarify and work out details of an assignment, within the framework of well-established procedures.
3A	**COACHING** Befriends and encourages individuals on a personal, caring basis by approximating a peer or family-type relationship either in a one-to-one or small group situation, and gives instruction, advice, and personal assistance concerning activities of daily living, the use of various institutional services, and participation in groups.
3B	**PERSUADING** Influences others in favor of a product, service, or point of view by talks or demonstrations.
3C	**DIVERTING** Amuses others.
4A	**CONSULTING** Serves as a source of technical information and gives such information or provides ideas to define, clarify, enlarge upon, or sharpen procedures, capabilities, or product specifications.
4B	**INSTRUCTING** Teaches subject matter to others, or trains others, including animals, through explanation, demonstration, practice, and test.

Level	Definition
4C	**TREATING** Acts on or interacts with individuals or small groups of people or animals who need help (as in sickness) to carry out specialized therapeutic or adjustment procedures. Systematically observes results of treatment within the framework of total personal behavior because unique individual reactions to prescriptions (chemical, physician's, behavioral) may not fall within the range of prediction. Motivates, supports, and instructs individuals to accept or cooperate with therapeutic adjustment procedures, when necessary.
5	**SUPERVISING** Determines and/or interprets work procedure for a group of workers, assigns specific duties to them (particularly those which are prescribed), maintains harmonious relations among them, evaluates performance (both prescribed and discretionary), and promotes efficiency and other organizational values. Makes decisions on procedural and technical levels.
6	**NEGOTIATING** Exchanges ideas, information, and opinions with others on a formal basis to formulate policies and programs on an initiating basis (e.g., contracts) and/or arrives at resolutions of problems growing out of administration of existing policies and programs, usually after a bargaining process.
7	**MENTORING** Deals with individuals in terms of their overall life adjustment behavior in order to advise, counsel, and/or guide them with regard to problems that may be resolved by legal, scientific, clinical, spiritual and/or other professional principles. Advises clients on implications of diagnostic or similar categories, courses of action open to deal with a problem, and merits of one strategy over another.

In the D.O.T. (as the "in crowd" calls the *Dictionary of Occupational Titles*) Vol. II p. 649 you can find similar lists for Data and Things, if you think that you prefer to work with them, rather than with people. (At your local public library.)

The point of all this for you, the career-changer/job-hunter, is:

1. The lower the level of your skills that you claim, the more the skills can be prescribed and measured and demanded of you. You'll have to fit in. Conversely, the higher the level of skills that you can legitimately claim, the less the skills can be prescribed and measured, and the more you will be free to carve out a job in the shape of *you*—making the fullest use of the special constellation of abilities that are you.

2. The higher level of skills that you can legitimately claim, either with people, or data or things (or, in varying degree, with all three)—depending on what *you* want to do,—the less these kinds of jobs are advertised or known through normal channels; the more you'll have to find ways of unearthing them—which is what the next chapter is all about.

3. Just because the opportunities for the higher level jobs (or careers) are harder to uncover, the higher you aim, the less people you will have to compete with—for that job. In fact, if you uncover, as you are very likely to, a need in the organization (or organizations) that you like, which you can help resolve, they are very likely to create a brand new job— for you, which means—in effect—you will be competing with practically no one, since you are virtually the sole applicant, as it were.

The Paradoxical Moral Of All This

The higher a skill level you can legitimately claim, the more likely you are to find a job. Just the opposite of what the typical job-hunter or second careerist starts out believing.

So, now that you know what you are looking for, on with the job:

● TOOLS & INSTRUMENTS:
MEMORIES, FEELINGS, AND VISIONS

What is needed, at this point, are some practical—some *very* practical—tools or instruments. We are going to list a lot of them. Some of you may want to try every one. Most of you will want to approach them as a kind of smorgasbord, picking and choosing from among all those that are offered. How to know which ones to choose?

If you have a reflective-type mind, it will have struck you that long range planning must include past, present and future.

The kinds of exercises available correspond to these three divisions of time.

To be sure, there is overlapping, but in terms of their major emphasis, we can categorize the exercises as follows:

YOUR MEMORIES (OF THE PAST):
Exercises No. 1, 2, 3, and 4.

YOUR FEELINGS (ABOUT THE PRESENT):
Exercises No. 5, 6, 7, and 8.

YOUR VISIONS (OF THE FUTURE):
Exercises No. 9 and 10.

If, because of pell-melling change or great stress, your memory has just taken a holiday, then we suggest you forget about the exercises that deal with your past. If you are deep in apathy (literally, *lack of* feelings; lack of *consciousness* of feelings would be a better description) the exercises dealing with the present aren't likely to be of too much help. And if you have what the Johnson O'Connor people call "low foresight," then the exercises that deal with the future aren't likely to be too fruitful.

Naturally, if your whole mind is having trouble, we suggest you go get a *good* rest before you tackle *any* of these exercises. Otherwise, choose the ones you like best, and can best use. Or, do them all.

Exercises 1, 2, 3, and 4— involving
YOUR MEMORIES OF THE PAST

Career and life planning involves the past, as well as the present and future, because:

1. You are being encouraged to develop a holistic (rather than atomistic) approach to life, that builds upon previous experiences rather than rejecting them.

2. You are being encouraged to see that the drives which will dictate your future course have not been inactive up until now, but have been continually manifesting themselves in what you have done best, and enjoyed most.

3. You are being encouraged to see that your life is a continuum, with a steady continuing core, no matter how the basic units or building blocks may need to be rearranged. The change lies in *the varying constellation* that these basic units are constructed in, (see page 71), but everything you enjoy most and do best will use the same building blocks that your past activities have.

Therefore, we need to look back, and see when we were (and are) enjoying life—and precisely what activities we were doing at that moment, what skills or talents we were employing, what kinds of tasks we were dealing with, what kinds of accomplishments were being done, and precisely what it was that was "turning us on."

Here, then, are some exercises and instruments designed to assist you in doing this:

Practical Exercise No. 1

A. Write Your diary of your entire life. An informal essay of where you've been, what you've done. Where you were working, what you did there (not in terms of job titles—forget them—but in terms of what you achieved).

B. Boast a little. Boast a lot. Who's going to see this document, besides you, God, and any twenty people that you choose to show it to? Back up your elation and sense of pride with concrete examples, and figures.

C. Describe your spare time, in each place that you were. What did you do? What did you enjoy doing? Hobbies? Avocations? Great. What skills did they use? Were there any activities in your work that paralleled the kinds of things you enjoyed doing in your spare time?

D. Concentrate both on the things you have done, and also the characteristics of your particular surroundings at each point in your career that were important to you, and that you really enjoyed: green grass, the theater, golfing, warm climate, skiing, or whatever?

E. Keep your eye on that "divine radar": enjoyable. It's by no means *always* a guide to what you should be doing, but it sure is more reliable than any other key that people have come up with. Sift later. For now, put down anything that helped you to enjoy a particular moment or period of your life.

F. Don't try to make the diary very structured. You can bounce back and forth (free associate) if that's more helpful; then go back later, and use the questions above (and others later) to check yourself out. If you need further help with how you go about writing a diary like this, by all means get your hands on *Where Do I Go From Here With My Life?* by that genius, John Crystal (Appendix B, at the back of this book for details). Of course, not everyone is helped by any one approach. So, if you want different ways of writing the diary, see Ira Progoff's very helpful *At A Journal Workshop* (at your local library, or from Dialogue House Library, 45 West 10th Street, New York, N.Y. 10011; $12.50), or the more general *Telling Your Story: A Guide to Who You Are and Who You Can Be,* by Sam Keen and Anne Valley Fox (Signet Books, New American Library, P.O. Box 999, Bergenfield, N.J. 07621; $1.50).

G. When your diary is all done, you may have a small book—it can run 30-200 pages. (My, you've done a lot of living, haven't you?) Now to go back over it, take a separate sheet of paper, and put two columns on it:

Things Which, On The Basis of Past Experience, I Want To Have Or Use In My Future Career(s)	Things Which, On The Basis of Past Experience, I Want To Avoid In My Future Career(s)

As you go back over the diary, each time you come to something you feel fits in the first column, put it down there. Each time you come to something that you feel fits in the second column, put that there.

H. Note particularly that when you come to a skill that you a) *enjoyed* and b) *did well* (in *your* opinion), put it down in the first column and underline it twice.

I. When this is all done, choose your most important skills (*to you*—again, only your opinion counts)—choose 10, 9, 8, 7, 6, 5, but not less than five. Underline these three times.

J. Now rank them in order of decreasing importance to you. You can use the chart on page 77. Fill it in. Now you have your basic units.

K. What this exercise has left you with (hopefully) are: a) six or more building blocks that (when woven together) will form one coherent job description for you; b) a couple of lists which list (for your own private thinking, at the moment) some other things you want to have, or avoid, in your future employment.

So much for this exercise. If it helps, great. But maybe you want more help. Or, if you are a high-school or college student or housewife, who feels you haven't done enough yet (vocation-wise) for the exercise to be very profitable, try this one:

Practical Exercise No. 2

Analyze your hobbies (after listing all the ones you have done over the years, and then organizing them in terms of greatest enjoyment, on down) to see what you were doing, what skills you were using, and what results you were accomplishing. Here is a clue to what skills you enjoy using the most.

You can do this same exercise, of course, with your courses in school, etc. All of which is to say, what you are doing when you are *not* working (allegedly) may be even more revealing of your skills and interests, than what you do "on the job." Try it!

The above exercises, to be sure, leave you a lot of freedom to go about them however you want. But perhaps you want a little more direction and help; maybe a more systematic printed-type thing.

There are, surprisingly, quite a few such instruments floating around. They have various names (and copyrights): *Success Factor Analysis, Career Success Inventory, SIMS (System to Identify Motivated Skills), Vocational Interest Profile, Experience and Capability Inventory, Functional Self-Analysis, Inventory of Meaningful Abilities,* and a number of others. New ones will appear tomorrow or the day after, because this whole science is not yet a science but only an art. You need not take our word for this. Read Crites or Holland (see Appendix B).

Consequently, the search for more perfect (i.e., helpful) instruments will be continuing for a long time. And each inventor of a new instrument will claim *his* or hers is more effective, scientific, objective, definitive, helpful and what-have-you, than anyone else's. The truth is:

Certain people are more helped by one device,
and certain other kinds of people are
more helped by other devices.
You have to hunt (some)
until you find the one that helps
you
the most.

One systematic printed-type thing you may like, is:

Practical Exercise No. 3

Bernard Haldane in his books (Appendix B) presents a helpful instrument for analyzing your skills. The technique, which he was a pioneer in, consists in choosing two achievements which pleased *you* immensely from each five-year period of your life, then arranging the ten most important (to *you*) in decreasing priority, proceeding to say (about each of the ten) *why* it gave you satisfaction, *what* you did, *and results* therefrom, finally yielding a chart in which the ten most satisfying achievements are going across the top, and then a list of *functions* or *skills* (running down the side) being checked off, to see which occur most often among the ten achievements.

We end up, as you can see, in the same place that we did on page 77. You should, that is, end up with building blocks for a job description.

Incidentally, if there are any Puritans left among our readers (and there are a surprising lot of them around, these days) you may be "hung up" over the idea of bragging about your successes, as in the previous instrument. Time for

"A SPECIAL WORD FOR PURITANS"

Puritans come in all sizes, shapes, genders, ages, and colors. Puritans allegedly believe in God; but, what a god! A Puritan believes that God didn't intend us to enjoy anything. And that if you enjoy it, it's probably wrong for you. Let us illustrate:

Two girls do babysitting. One hates it. One enjoys it thoroughly. Which is more virtuous in God's sight? According to the Puritan, the one who hates it is more virtuous.

Two Puritans met on the street. "Isn't this a beautiful day?" said one. "Aye," said the other, "but we'll pay for it."

A Puritan will talk about his failures, but hardly ever about his or her successes — and even then, always with a feeling that "God is going to get me, for such boasting." It's too enjoyable!

Given the Puritan's belief in God, what the Puritan fails to recognize is that enjoyment, in human life, isn't a fluke. It's part of God's plan. He wants us to eat; therefore He designs us so that eating is enjoyable. He wants us to sleep; therefore He designs us so that sleeping is enjoyable. He wants to have us procreate, love, and make love; therefore He designs us so that sex is enjoyable, and love even more so. *He gives us unique (or at least unusual) skills and talents; therefore He designs us so that, when we use these, they are enjoyable.*

That is, we gain a sense of achievement from them.

So, Puritans arise; if you believe in God, believe in One who believes in you. Downgrading yourself is out—for the duration.

Practical Exercise No. 4

When you are through with all of the above exercises, you may have a lot of data about your past life at your fingertips, but be puzzled with how you now go about making decisions concerning it. Indeed, one of the skills some of us never got any help with when we were going through our country's vaunted school-system, is that of how you go about making decisions. To meet this need, the College Entrance Examination Board has published a most useful study on how to make decisions, which you can get for $2.50. It is entitled *Deciding*, and may be ordered from Publications Order Office, College Entrance Examination Board, Box 592, Princeton, New Jersey 08540. (And if, by any chance, this is used in a group, there is also *Deciding: A Leader's Guide*, free with each ten copies ordered of *Deciding*.) Let us also note, that while this guide was designed for students, it is highly useful to anyone of any age who feels he or she would like to sharpen his or her decision-making ability.

Exercises 5, 6, 7, and 8— involving
YOUR FEELINGS ABOUT THE PRESENT

Maybe your memory isn't so hot, lately. If so, of course the previous exercises aren't going to be very useful to you, whatever help they may be to others. Sooooo, we press on to the present. No need for memory, here; just feelings.

But what use, you may ask, are feelings, in trying to determine what kind of work one should do? Aren't we interested only in skills, talents, and all that? Well, not exactly. You see, studies have revealed that:

1. Your interests, wishes and happiness determine what you actually do well more than your intelligence, aptitudes, or skills do. This is the conclusion of numerous vocational psychologists (Holland, Mierzwa, Clark, Crites) and personnel people (Snelling, and others). Strength of desire outweighs everything else, they say. (Crites, pp. 26-33) see Appendix B.

Maybe the word "feelings" or "wishes" sounds just too erratic, in your ears. OK, then borrowing a word from biology, let's speak instead of "tropisms"; things which living creatures instinctively go toward, or away from. Man is no exception, and in addition each one of us has his own personal, unique tropisms. You must know: what do you feel drawn toward, what do you instinctively go away from? Your own personal tropisms are determinative for your first, second (third, or fourth) career.

2. If you do work you really enjoy, and at the highest level that you can legitimately claim, you are bound to do an outstanding job, and be of genuine help to others—as the creative minority (Crystal, and others) have long been maintaining.

3. No tests or other instruments have been devised yet, that measure what you want so effectively as just *asking you* or having you *ask yourself.* As Holland says:

> "Despite several decades of research, the most
> efficient way to predict vocational choice is
> simply to ask the person what he wants to be;
> our best devices do not exceed the predictive
> value of that method."[1]

And now, to our exercises in this section. The first one, naturally enough, simply takes Holland at his word:

Practical Exercise No. 5

This exercise consists of a very simple question indeed; write out your answer to the question: If you could have any kind of job, what would it be? (Invent your own, if need be.) Never mind what you *can* do; what do you *want* to do?

Sometimes the question is put in other forms, or with time sequences: a year from now, ten years from now, twenty years from now? Try them all.

Exercise No. 5 presumes you know what makes you happy. Maybe, however, you have a much clearer idea of what makes you unhappy (a list, as it were, of "negative tropisms"— things you instinctively want to avoid). Okay, this exercise thrives on that:

Practical Exercise No. 6

Write a detailed answer to the question: What are the things which make me unhappy?

Analyze what you have written (afterwards) in terms of two columns, with the first one sub-divided:

THINGS THAT LIE WITHIN THE CONTROL OF MYSELF		THINGS THAT LIE WITHIN THE CONTROL OF OTHERS, OR FATE, OR CIRCUMSTANCE
Things which I could change thru a change of environment (my job, or place where I live)	Things which I could change thru working on my interior life (what's going on inside me)	

Check it over, when you are done, by reviewing the second list to be sure these things are *really* beyond your control or power to alter. Then go over the first list and decide whether the priority for you is to work on your *external* furniture (environment, work, etc.) or your *internal* furniture (personal growth, emotions or spiritual factors), or *both*. List concrete resolutions, with time goals beside them.

If you come down, very heavily, in the previous exercise, on the need to deal with your *internal* furniture, then we suggest you read Appendix C, section E, and go deal with that first off.

Jobs, after all, are primarily a question of what should your *external* furniture be. They are questions of environments, which are mostly "people environments," and the issue of how well these correspond to, and are compatible with, your internal furniture. In the past, our society has insisted that when your external furniture and your internal are "out of sync," that you go get your internal furniture "rearranged," as it were. A lot of people, especially the young, are getting very impatient with this "solution." But not just the young. The increased interest in second careers these days, among those who served "honorably" in their first—clergy, doctors, aerospace engineers, physicists, executives, etc.— may be traced in large part to a decision that where the external and internal are out of synchronization, it is easier by far (and more sensible) to alter the external. To make the environment conform to you, rather than you to the environment. (A few religious souls among you may recognize this is a paraphrase of something Jesus said; about the Sabbath. But, ah, never mind. It is splendidly self-evident anyway.)

If you want to take a good look at the external environments that are most compatible with your internal furniture, there is an exercise you may like (and a book you *must* read):

Practical Exercise No. 7

Holland's *"The Self-directed Search"* in his *Making Vocational Choices: a theory of careers* (Prentice-Hall, 1973) helps to identify particular occupations you might be interested in, defined in terms of your preferred people-environments. Tremendously useful. If you want *"The Self-directed Search"* all by itself, this is available to professionals only (get your clergy person, counselor, or placement officer to order it for you, if you yourself don't qualify) from Consulting Psychologists Press, 577 College Avenue, Palo Alto, CA 94306, for around a dollar. (If you are already familiar with this popular instrument, you may want to know that it has been rather substantially revised, in the 1977 edition. One hundred and thirty-nine changes have been made, together with the elimination of all graphs from the main instrument. The auxiliary "Occupations Finder" now has 500 occupational titles in it. And a complementary guide "Understanding Yourself and Your Career", by John L. Holland, has been issued for use with *"The Self-directed Search."*) These materials are especially useful if you are a high-school student; but are helpful with older ages too.

If in opposition to external environments you want to do some hard thinking about the internal "You" that—hopefully —your work environment has got to be compatible with, in order for you to be happy, then we suggest you try the following exercise:

Practical Exercise No. 8

1. Take ten sheets of paper. Write on the top of each one the words: Who am I?
2. Then write, on each sheet, *one* answer to that question. At the end of the ten sheets, you'll have the same question written, but ten different answers.
3. Now go back over the ten again, and looking at each answer, write below it on each sheet *what turns you on* about that particular answer.
4. Now go back over the ten sheets, and arrange them in order of priority. Your most important identity goes on top. Then in order, on down to the identity that is *to you* of least importance, among the ten.
5. Finally, go back over the ten sheets, looking particularly at the answers you wrote (on each page) to *What turns you on?* and see if there are some common denominators.
6. If so, you have begun to put your finger on some things

that your career (calling, vocation, job or whatever) *must use* if you are to be truly happy, fulfilled, used and effective—to the height of your powers.

Since this can be an eye-opening exercise, if you possess some degree of self-knowledge, but difficult if you don't, let us show how one person filled it out. This is not in any way to suggest the kind of answers you should give, but only to flesh out the instructions above—with an example from one completed exercise:

Part 1: Who Am I?
1. A man
2. An urban dweller (and lover)
3. A loving person
4. A creator
5. A writer
6. A lover of good movies and music
7. A skilled counselor and teacher
8. An independent
9. An executive
10. An enabler

Part 2: What Turns Me On About These?
1. Taking initiative, having inner strength; being open, growing, playful
2. Excitement, variety of choices available, crowds, faces
3. Feelings, empathizing, playfulness, sex, adoration given, happiness
4. Transforming things, making old things new, familiar wonderous
5. Beauty of words, variety of images, new perspectives, new relationships of ideas, words, understandings
6. Watching people up close, merging of color, photography, music
7. Using intuition, helping, seeing totalities of people, problem solving, long-term close helpful relationships
8. Making own decisions, carrying out own plans
9. Taking responsibility, wise risks, using mind, seeing totalities of problems overall
10. Helping people to become freed-up, to be what they want to be.

Part 3: Any Common Denominators? Variety, totalities, rearranging of constellations, dealing with a number of different things and showing relationships between them all in a new way, helping others.

Part 4: What Must My Career Use (and Include) For Me To Be Truly Happy, Used and Effective? A variety of different things that have to be dealt with, with people, where seeing totalities, rearranging their relationships, and interpreting them to people in a new way is at the heart of the career.

This is but one illustration. There are many other ways, and many other levels that the exercise can be done at. Be as wild, imaginative, creative as you want to be with it.

And when it is done, here are some check-back questions, to be sure you have gotten all that you can out of the exercise:

Checkback: Practical Exercise No. 8 concluded

7. What is it (or what are they/them) that, if I lost it, life would have no meaning? Is it included in the exercise above? If not, why not? (Think hard, and revise your answers, in the light of this new insight; or old.)
8. Out of the ten identifications of myself, and the ten lists of things which turn me on, which of these must be included in any job I have? *Remember the world is already filled with people who are trying to use their time after 5 p.m. to do all the things they really enjoy.*

Members of the counter-culture who feel there is too much emphasis on *doing* in our society, and not enough on *being*, should find the above exercise particularly up their alley.

Exercises 9 and 10 — involving
YOUR VISIONS OF THE FUTURE

If your memory groans at the idea of trying to remember the past, and if your feelings about yourself at the present are difficult for you to put into words, there is still another family of exercises available to you—which may help you pinpoint just exactly what it is that you want to do with your life. And that is, of course, those exercises which deal with the future.

The future. It sounds far away, mystical, and mysterious. But, as someone has said,

> "We ought to be interested in the future, for
> that is where we are going to spend the rest of
> our lives."

Well, of course, we *are* all interested in the future. Even the "now generation" which makes its chief value that of "living in the present" dreams its dreams of the future. If nothing else: "How long will I be able to continue to live like this?"

Most of us have our visions and dream our dreams. It's only when we come to our job, and what we want to do with the rest of our lives, that we think our visions and dreams must be shelved. In career planning there is a certain group of professionals, here and there, who love to play the game of getting you to say just what you want to do, and then "bringing you down to earth" by saying, "All right; now, let's get realistic." What they should ask is, "Are you *sure* this is what you really want?" because if it is, chances are you will find some way to do it. Remember the man who was called "The Great Imposter." Whatever he wanted to do badly, he found a way to do. Something of him lives in us all.

Never mind "being realistic." For every person who "over-dreams"—of doing more than his merits would justify,—there are four people who "under-dream," and sell themselves short. (According to the experts, 80% of the workers in this country are "under-employed," as we have said.)

You are not going to do this task well if you keep one eye fixed on what you *think* you know about the job market, when you try to draw up what you would like to do at your job, e.g., "I'd like to be able to do this and that at my job, but I know there is no job in the world like that."

Granted, you may not be able to find a job that has all of that. But why not aim for it, and then settle for less if and when you find out that you simply have to? But don't foreclose the matter prematurely. You'd be surprised what you may be able to turn up (see our next chapter).

Dreams may have to be taken in stages. If you want to be president of a particular enterprise, for example, you may have to work your way toward it through two or three steps. But it is quite possible you will eventually succeed—*if your whole heart is in your dream.*

Here, then, are some exercises to dust off some of those visions and dreams you may have shelved awhile back.

Practical Exercise No. 9

Spend as much time as necessary writing an article entitled "Before I die, I want to . . . ." (Things you would like to do, before you die.) Confess them now, and maybe they'll happen.

Or you may prefer to write the article on a similar topic: "On the last day of my life, what must I have done or been so that my life will have been satisfying to me?" When it is finished, go back over it and make two lists: Things Already Accomplished, Things Yet To Be Accomplished. Then make a third column, beside the one called Things Yet To Be Accomplished, listing the particular *steps* that you will have to take, in order to accomplish these things that you have listed.

1	2	3
Things already accomplished.	Things yet to be accomplished. *(Then number them in the order in which you would like to accomplish them.)*	Steps needed in order to accomplish the things in column 2

As you get involved with these exercises you may notice that it is impossible to keep your focus only on your vocation, occupation, career or whatever you call it. You will find some dreams of places you want to visit creeping in, some experiences you want to have, that are not on-the-job, etc. *Don't omit these.* Be just as specific as possible.

Incidentally, you don't have to do the above exercise just once and for all. Some experts in career and life planning suggest making the previous exercise into a continuous one, with a list posted on your office or kitchen wall—crossing out items as you accomplish them, or do them, and adding new ones as they occur to you from month to month.

Turning from dreams (albeit, concrete, solid dreams) to visions, let us talk of goals and purposes—for these are the visions of the future which cause men and women to set their hands to present tasks. Here is an exercise to deal with the goals that drive you (and there always are such, however undefined):

Practical Exercise No. 10

Think of some practical concrete task or project in your life (hopefully in the present) that you are a) doing successfully and b) enjoying immensely. (Well, besides that!) It could be at work, at school, or in your spare time. But it must be one which really "turns you on." Put down this task in the center of a blank piece of 8½x11 paper turned on its side, then take the following steps:

1. Begin at the lower left hand side of the page, and write the word "why?" (do/did you want to do this), and on the line above it, indented, write that reason, goal, or purpose.
2. Then write "why?" after this answer, too; and on the line above *it*, indented even more, see if you can write an even more basic reason, goal or purpose.
3. Then write "why?" after it, and on the line above . . . etc. Continue this exercise up the paper, until you think you have reached a basic purpose or goal, that is rather ultimate. (You cannot think of any "why?" behind it.)
4. Now, take that most basic goal (the topmost one on the paper), and draw an arrow from it, down to the part of the paper that is beside the "task" with which you began. There write the words "how else?", and think of what other tasks or projects would accomplish the same ultimate goal (the topmost one on your paper). In the end, your exercise will look something like this:

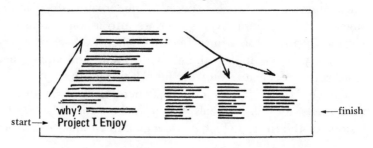

5. Repeat it with other projects or tasks that have really "turned you on," a new piece of paper for each one. See if you begin to see what turns you on about life, and some alternate strategies (or jobs) that could accomplish the same goals. If you "run out of gas" by step four, consult with some wise friend or vocational counselor (at school or whatever).

IN SUMMARY: CHECK BACK

So much for our exercises. You've read them over. Please try them. One or two. Or (if you're the really thorough type) all. Until they achieve your purpose: knowing exactly what you want to do, you aren't through with them. And if you draw a blank with all of them, you obviously are going to have to turn to someone for professional help. (See the chapter "What About Help?")

Let's assume you've tried some of the exercises. Here's a check list of questions to help you see how well things are going for you thus far:

Check-Back Questions:
1. Have you identified the basic building blocks (and filled the chart in, on page 77) of your strongest skills and interests? (strongest=done best *and* enjoyed *and* feel confident about, in your opinion).

   Do you prefer most to be related to people, data, or things? Or all three? In what priority?

   Have you avoided putting a definitive (restricting) job title on what you want to do? (There are many different titles for the same job, and many different jobs for the same title—don't build a box for yourself by means of a title.)

2. Are you getting locked in, in your thinking, to just one route to go in the future, or are you trying to preserve alternative options, so that you see different ways your basic skills could be utilized, and not just *one* way?

What risks are there: a) in the kind of job you might be working towards and b) in the route you are taking thereto? Have you provided for alternative procedures, techniques and goals if the risks materialize?

When all is said and done, are you planning for a changing world, or are you assuming the world will stay still while you move? (As the experts say, *Planning without planning for change is planning for nothing but trouble.*)

3. What time spans are *built in* to the route that you have decided (or think) you ought to take?

If you decide you simply *have to have* credentials, what date will you need them on, how long will it take to get them; and, when—therefore—should you start working on this? If you decide you need experience, where, how, and how long? When will you need it, how long will it take to get it, when should you start?

(If time is a continuing problem or hangup for you, you may wish to get your hands on: Drucker, Peter F., *The Effective Executive*, New York: Harper & Row, 1967, 178 pages. Excellent on time-use.)

4. Do you know what questions of life you are most earnestly seeking answers to?

Do you know now what you are after in life? Your needs? Your values? Your tropisms—the things that you instinctively (or otherwise) go *toward*, and the things you instinctively go *away from?* The things that make you happy and the things that make you unhappy?

Which values actually hold the most attraction for you (not *should* but *do*): service, security, status, popularity, recognition, approval, affection, belongingness, acceptance, power, achievement, authority, glamour, wealth, etc.? Which rewards hold the most meaning for you?

5. In terms of the goals you are moving toward will a change in externals (your environment, job, place of work, and so forth) be sufficient? Or do you feel that you also need some internal movement and growth?

To the extent that you can put a label on what is bothering you in your career/life at the moment, would you characterize it basically as Conflict or Frustration? (Or both? Or neither? What, then?) Frustration is between an individual and his environment, and would point to the need for a new work environment. Conflict is within an individual, and points to the need for personal help and personal growth.

6. Do you feel that all planning of this nature is just too much work? Too long and lonely? (How about involving your loved ones in it with you?—you might be surprised at the increased communication and its helpful benefits!)

If you don't do any planning, what will rescue you (or who) if you reach a dead-end in creativity, work and happiness? (As Ezra Pound said, *A slave is one who waits for someone else to come and free him.*)

PUTTING THE BUILDING BLOCKS TOGETHER

Okay, let's assume you pass all the above "check-backs." You know what the basic building blocks of your skills are. Now, how do you arrange them into different constellations or careers? (Good question.)

We ought to begin with some basic vocabulary.

Jobs, positions, work, careers are used by some people to mean different things and by other people to mean essentially the same thing. The Distinguishers vs. The Synonymists. The former generally tend to regard the word "job" as a dirty word. By job, they mean *just a job.* The Distinguishers are exquisitely careful about their vocabulary, and may look down on the Synonymists—who are not so precise. The latter feel that the framework of thinking within which a man uses particular words is of more significance and importance than the particular words he may or may not use.

Tasks, functions, aptitudes, abilities, skills—another group of words used by some people to mean very different things, and by other people to mean essentially the same thing. The Distinguishers can give carefully differentiated meanings, which are all supported completely by Webster's Unabridged. The Synonymists, on the other hand, can take you by the hand out onto the street and bid you listen to Everyday Man's conversation—whereupon you discover that Everyday Man makes no such careful distinctions between the meanings of these words, much of the time.

If you want to know the jargon, technically, *a job is a flexible combination of tasks*—which can be arranged and rearranged in a number of different tantalizing ways. *A career is a flexible combination of skills*—which can be arranged and rearranged in a number of different tantalizing ways.

Now, beyond vocabulary:

Researching your skills involves trying to discover what different kinds of careers (i.e., constellations of skills) are open to you, and then arranging these in order of priority *according to what you enjoy most.*

How do you go about nailing this down?

Here are some *beginning* suggestions:

**PRACTICAL
AID
NUMBER**

The Dictionary of Occupational Titles Vols. I, II, and III. Third Edition: Washington, D.C.: Superintendent of Public Documents, 1965. Based on concept of *functional job analysis,* the outgrowth of research directed by Sidney Fine,[2] 1948-1959, this "Bible" of the vocational field lists some 35,000+ job titles, covering 23,000 occupations. Called by experts either "the greatest single source of occupational information in the world" or "an unwieldy mishmash,"[3] you can locate occupations (careers) by a) physical demands, b) individual working conditions, c) interest, d) aptitude, e) educational requirements, f) vocational preparation, and so forth.

Each occupation has been given a six-digit code number. The first three digits are called *the occupational group* and describe The World of Work.

The second three digits describe what workers do with data (the fourth digit, Vol. II, p. 649), with people, (fifth digit, Vol. II, p. 649), and with things (sixth digit, Vol. II, p. 650).

You are encouraged to go to your library, get Vol. II and browse in it for quite a while, to get the feel of it. Note particularly pp. 217-529, which lists worker-trait groups, within various areas of work, and then related occupations (classifications) that use similar skills.

You will also want to notice pp. 3-24, which list various fields that may not have occurred to you, where possibly your skills could be well used and enjoyed.

The point of all this research is to *be sure that you do not get prematurely locked into one field or occupation, but that you see some of the alternative options that are open to you.*

Caution: "Training and Methods of Entry" on pp. 217-529 (wherever it occurs, in various fields) needs to be confirmed by your own research before being accepted as the only way. The method(s) described is/are often only the most common entry(ies).

Incidentally, a new edition (by definition, The Fourth) of the D.O.T. has just been published. There have been changes in sexist titles (of course), elimination of outdated titles and skills (after two hundred years, it's probably time to drop "Skilled at riding through countryside, yelling 'The British are coming' "), and the like.

Our Canadian readers (or job-hunters in the U.S.A. who want a slightly different perspective) will want to look up in their library the *Canadian Classification and Dictionary of Occupations,* 1971. Vol. I and II. Published by Manpower & Immigration, available from Information Canada, 171 Slater Street, Ottawa, Canada if not your library.

PRACTICAL
AID
NUMBER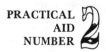

A Handbook for Job Restructuring, Washington, D.C. 20402: Superintendent of Documents, U.S. Government Printing Office, 1970. If your library does not have this, then I'm afraid you're out of luck, because it's out of print. Has interesting section (pp. 30-42) on "benchmarks" of various skills or aptitudes. "Benchmarks" are typical situations where, at various levels, the skill is used. Very valuable.

PRACTICAL
AID
NUMBER 3

Occupational Outlook Handbook, Bulletin No. 1700, U.S. Department of Labor, Washington, D.C. Get this in your library (it's $6.50 if you buy it). It gives an outline for 700 (or so) occupations: what its future looks like, nature of work, usual training required, employment outlook, earnings and working conditions—for each occupation. Helpful if you don't just want to get into occupations that're closing out; but its prophecies should be taken with a large barrel (not just "grain") of salt. There is also an *Occupational Outlook Handbook for College Graduates,* ($2.95).

The very word "outlook" (occupational or employment) ought to make you beware. "A good outlook" for a particular industry only means, if you will stop to think about it, that there is relatively little competition for the openings that exist; i.e., there are more openings than there are bodies to fill them. On the other hand, "a bad outlook" for a particular field, or a prediction that it is going to be 'crowded' is only another way of saying, there is going to be a lot of competition. That just means you will have to follow the techniques described here more faithfully, that's all. Remember, time and time again, men and women have gotten positions in a place where everyone told them there was No Employment At All; and they did it by following the techniques in these chapters.

PRACTICAL
AID
NUMBER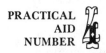

In the course of researching your skills, we urge you to consult with one or more of the following persons, to ask them: What occupations use these skills that I have?

Your *librarian* (or business librarian); *counselors* at the appropriate department of your local State Employment office; *friends,* knowledgeable in the fields that interest you; *consultants* to the fields you are interested in (see *Consultants and Consulting Organizations,* First Edition. A Reference Source and Directory of Concerns Engaged in Consultation for Business and Industry. Paul Wasserman with Willis R. Greer, Jr. Graduate School of Business and Public Administration, Cornell University, Ithaca, New York—for a list of possible people you can consult. Lists them by state, field of interest, and alphabetical order).

> Remember, in doing research through interviewing (just as with reading) it is *essential* that you have clearly in your own mind what questions you are trying to find answers to. Essentially what you are looking for, at this point, is an answer to the question: *What occupation or occupations will use as many of my strongest skills, and on as high a level, as possible?*—So that—*at my work*—*I am doing what I enjoy most, and not just waiting until I get home from work to start enjoying what I am doing.*

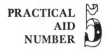
In the course of researching your field we urge you to consult with a number of people who are already active in it. You should not be hesitant about asking for the time of important men, even heads of companies or corporations. *If they really like their own vocation,* they should be very receptive to your desire to know more about that vocation: what they do, the various kinds of tasks and skills required, and the aspects of it that they particularly enjoy.

You say you freeze at the very thought of tackling interviews (even interviews *only for information*) with people — afraid you'll botch it all, through shyness or nervousness? Not if it's YOUR enthusiasm you're exploring — the thing in this world you're dying to know more about. But you still want some brush-up pointers on how to go about this whole business of interviewing — like, what do you do the first four minutes that you're in the room with that guy, or gal? Okay, pick up a copy of *Contact: The First Four Minutes* by Leonard and Natalie Zunin (in your library, paperback bookstore, or directly from Ballantine Books, 201 East 50th Street, New York, N.Y. 10022; published 1972; $1.75). That should help. After all, the harder you work on this, now, the more it's going to repay you later.

Remember, it's 10,000 hours—on up—of your time that you are trying to plan. Remember also, that you *may* be coming back to some of these men in a different role later on (if they are in the area you want to work in), so it would be helpful to leave a good impression behind you. In other words, dress well and conduct yourself *as quietly confident that you will be an asset to any organization which you ultimately decide to serve in.*

**PRACTICAL
AID
NUMBER**

The D.O.T., Volume II (see page 97) will repay extensive browsing, on pages 531-639, and elsewhere. For example, if your skills seem to indicate management level work, you will find not only listings of various industries which could use this, but also nonprofit organizations (p. 599) and other fields which might not have occurred to you. *Make a list of the possible fields that look interesting to you.*

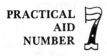

**PRACTICAL
AID
NUMBER**

Many (if not most) fields have professional journals. Ask your local librarian to assist you in getting your hands on these. Follow all leads that they may suggest to you, as your reading of articles and ads uncovers these, for additional information.

Again, many if not most fields have professional, trade, or union associations. Your public library has all kinds of listings of such associations—yours for the asking. So does Biegeleisen's book (in Appendix B) in its Appendix: "Where to Get Additional Information: Books, Pamphlets, Professional and Trade Associations."

Your Chamber of Commerce may have a library on various fields; try to see what other resources there are, in the place where you are: University libraries, etc. Libraries at appropriate businesses, etc.

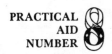

**PRACTICAL
AID
NUMBER**

If you decide that what you want help in researching is something that fits You, within the alternative forms of vocation these days, then we suggest you look at some of the counter-culture directories; such as:

People's Yellow Pages. Box 31291, San Francisco CA 94131.
$1.50.

Source Catalog. No. 1, Communications; No. 2, Communities/Housing. Chicago, The Swallow Press, Inc. 1971, 1972.
No. 1, $1.50; No. 2, $2.95.

To find what there is in your own community, visit the
college book store, the counter-culture 'head shop' downtown, or the American Friends Service Committee (which
usually knows the resources on alternative forms of careers,
quite well).

**PRACTICAL
AID
NUMBER**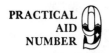

We have placed a number of notes on pp. 180 ff of this book,
summarizing *some of the things* that other people have discovered (why shouldn't *you* benefit from their research?)
about various fields. So,

If you're interested in:
    business and management, turn to page 180,
    social service or change, turn to page 183,
    the education field, turn to page 186,
    working in government, turn to page 188,
    self-employment (counseling, consulting, writing,
    owning your own business, etc.), turn to page 190,
    going back to school, turn to page 193,
    going overseas, turn to page 197.

None of this is intended to replace your own research.
Remember, if you will, that the *woods are alive* with people
who will solemnly tell you *something that ain't true* as
though they were sure of it with every fibre of their being.

Check and cross check and cross check again the information that books, people, and experts give you. Let no one build any boxes for you; and watch that you don't hand them any wood with which to build one, either.

There is virtually no information you want to know, that you cannot find out. This is a *knowledge society,* and the only limits — really — lie within you, as to the amount of commitment, diligence and perseverance you want to lavish on all this. If you feel you're not cut out for this sort of research, an absolutely invaluable book is *Finding Facts Fast: How to Find Out What You Want to Know Immediately,* by Alden Todd. And subtitled: *A handbook for high school, college and graduate students, political activists, civic leaders and professionals. . . based on methods used by reference librarians, scholars, investigative reporters and detectives.* (See your library, bookstore, or write directly to the publisher: William Morrow and Company, Inc., 105 Madison Avenue, New York, N.Y. 10016. It was published in 1972, first paperback printing 1974, which costs $2.45 — and worth ten times that much.)

When you are through with all this research (written and oral) you ought to have a very clear idea of what it is you would be most fulfilled doing.

Typically, this process takes two weeks to two months. But it is essential for you to know what you want to do *before* going looking for a job.

PUTTING A PRICE TAG ON YOUR LIFE STYLE

You need to know what your minimum salary requirements are going to be, before you ever start looking around to see where you want to use your talents.

If you are a part of the youth counter-culture, and very big on "subsistence type living," this is going to be simple. Just figure out how much you need for subsistence. Housing, food, school, household, furnishings, clothing, medical—and car, gas, and insurance (yes, most of the subsistence people

I've met seem to have a car, for some reason or other; it boggles the mind). Things like recreation, gifts, personal stuff and—like that—are probably academic, in your case.

If you're not into 'just subsistence,' then we suggest you make up two budgets. First: the 'rock-bottom need' budget —what do you need to just survive, if you found yourself (and your loved ones) between a rock and a hard place? Second: the 'I hope' budget—what do you hope you will have to live on? The categories, for both budgets, of course, include: Food—at home; Food—away; Housing—rent/mortgage, tax, insurance; Housing—furnishings; Housing—utilities and household supplies; Transportation—car payments, insurance, parking, gas, other maintenance; public transportation; Clothing—purchases; maintenance; Hairdos, toiletries; Medical—insurance, physicians visits, other, including dental; Education—tuition, books, loan repayment; Recreation; Gifts, contributions; Life insurance; Union dues; Savings; Payments on debts; Pension contribution; Social Security; Federal/state income taxes.[4]

To the two budgets add 15% more, because people habitually underestimate their needs. Now you have your range: the amounts between which you can bargain, at the conclusion of a hopeful job interview.

If you're already out into the world of work, and have been for some time, you may want to fool around with making a graph of your salary history, over the years (yearly salary, plotted against time in years). If you're real good at graphs, you may want to make an overlay, of the inflation rate at the same time—that'll send you into a Depression! It may also give you the impetus to think seriously how long you want to stay where you are, without a decent further raise.

The point is, if you use the methods in these chapters, you start here—*before* you ask your librarian to help you figure out what the average salaries are in your field, to find out if you're in the right ball park.

Now, *if* you have done all the exercises in this chapter, and are still very hazy about what you want to do, you need a more detailed step-by-step plan. Fortunately, such is available in a detailed Life-Planning Manual, written by John C. Crystal (and a "ghost"). You can obtain it by writing the publisher: Seabury Press, 815 Second Avenue, New York, N.Y. 10017. Ten Speed Press, Box 7123, Berkeley, California 94707 also carries it. Its title: *Where Do I Go From Here With My Life?* (1974). It deals also with the material covered in the next two chapters in this manual, in greater step-by-step detail.

If you want a faster way of getting more details, there is my "Quick Job-Hunting Map," which may be found in Appendix A at the back of this book. (If you want it in larger or separate form, it is available in 8½ x 11" size from Ten Speed Press, Box 7123, Berkeley, CA 94707. $1.25 plus postage.) This Map was invented, incidentally, in response to insistent demands from our reader(s) in Oblong, Illinois.

---

1   Reprinted by permission of the publisher, from J. L. Holland: THE PSYCHOLOGY OF VOCATIONAL CHOICE (Waltham, Massachusetts, Ginn and Company, 1966.) Now out of print.

2   Fine, *Guidelines*, p. 7 (see Appendix B for detail).

3   Fine, *1965 Third Edition*, etc., p. 13 (see Appendix B for detail).

4   Military are advised by the creative minority not to include their retirement pay in any way in their computations. That's extra, for emergencies. Clergy are advised that they probably make $11,500 to $15,000 — on the average — although this is hard to comprehend, until you add in all the perquisites, etc., or ask the thought-provoking question: how much would they have to pay in order to hire a layman to do my work, after I leave?

"Students spend four or more years learning how to dig data out of the library and other sources, but it rarely occurs to them that they should also apply some of that same new-found research skill to their own benefit—to looking up information on companies, types of professions, sections of the country that might interest them."

Professor Albert Shapero
University of Texas at Austin
Management Department

CHAPTER SIX

Where Do You Want To Do It?

t took you two weeks or two months,

it was done easily or only with much blood, sweat

whe er you did it all on your own, or only with professional help, you now have identified *which skills you have
that you enjoy most and do best.*

Your *priority skill*—the one you gave first place to (like, on
page 77) will dictate the general kind of thing that you will
be doing. Hopefully. Your *secondary skills*—the ones you
gave lesser rank to (page 77, again) will help determine the
more specific thing you will be doing within your general
field, and perhaps give some clue as to where.

Naturally, you'll want to be narrowing this down, and also
determining *at what level* your skills should (and can) be
defined. But before we show you how the creative minority
suggests you go about doing just that, let us look at the
Second Key to your job hunt . . . career search program . . .
or whatever you would like to call this whole process.

WHERE, OH WHERE

*You have to decide what city, or what part of the country
(or the world) you would like to work in.*

You probably have one of four answers immediately
trembling on the tip of your tongue:

*1. I want to continue to work right where I am, because I
just love it here. OR*

*2. I want to work in _____, because it is my favorite
spot in this country of ours. OR*

*3. I haven't got the foggiest idea; I don't really care,
either. OR*

*4. This is a silly exercise. Where I want to work, and where
the jobs are, may be two entirely different subjects. So, why
get my hopes all up, for nothing?*

Since that last answer, if true, effectively wipes out the first
three, let us deal with No. 4 right off the bat—and at some
length—so that we understand this whole business of what is
(*laughingly*) called

114

The Job Market

Upon hearing this very misleading term, one has visions—instantly—of some central place, like the Stock Exchange say, where every job opening and every job-hunter can meet each other. Such a vision may dance, like a sugar plum, in the job hunter's head; but the reality is quite different. And, much more jolting.

When he/she starts into the *supposed* single job market, to conduct his/her own job-search campaign, the job-hunter sooner or later discovers that he/she actually faces *seventy million (or more) separate job markets* (or however many million individual businesses, organizations, agencies, and foundations that there allegedly are in this country). Every business or organization has its own way of going about the process of hiring—separate, independent of, and uncoordinated with, other businesses or organizations.

THE SOURCE OF THE MYTHOLOGY

What deludes people into thinking of the whole country as a vast single job market? Two factors, at least:

First of all, the term itself. *Market* is a metaphor, at best. By analogy with the market where we shop, we have come to speak—in the world of business—of three *markets* today:

a) The market for goods and services; b) the market for capital, money, investment; c) the market for labor.

Whatever usefulness the term may have in the hands of genuine experts, as it has come to be commonly bandied about in everyday language it often means little more than *demand*. e.g., "How's the labor market this month?" It certainly does delude the job-hunter. There is no such central market—and the generalizations made about it are downright demonic and soul-destroying to unwary and naive job-hunters.

The second factor which has deluded people into thinking of the country (as a whole) as though it were one market is the statistics that appear in the paper each month. You recall, of course, how an English professor once conjugated the word "lie":

LIES, DAMN LIES, AND STATISTICS

In any event, once a month (the first Friday of the month, usually, and published in Saturday's papers—if you care) the nation is alternately comforted or terrorized by *One statistic for the whole country.* It is published (naturally) by the U.S. Government (its Bureau of Labor Statistics, or BLS). And it is (naturally) the unemployment figure.

To understand it, you must be aware that there are actually three basic figures that are of interest:

1. *The total number of people in the nation who want to work: e.g., 94,643,000 for June 1976.*
2. *The total number of people in the nation who are actually employed that month: e.g., 87,500,000 for June 1976.*
3. *The difference, e.g., 7,143,000 for June 1976.* The last figure is the number of people who are unemployed, *as best the government can estimate*, across the entire country.

INTIMIDATING FIGURES

Prominent press coverage is always given to *this one statistic for the whole country: the unemployment figure.* The human mind is staggered by the thought of almost five million people being out of work. It would be even more staggered if it realized that there is good evidence that actual unemployment may be up to three times the government figure. The human tragedy that this represents, to each of us in the imagination of our hearts, is overwhelming.

But the press does not leave it to the imagination. Continuously, throughout the rest of the month, we are given details. Recently, for example:

College placement offices reporting their graduates were facing the toughest job market in thirteen years, with those who would have gotten five to six job offers in previous years being lucky now if they got one.

New Ph.D.s having rough going in finding jobs, and the prediction that the going is to get rougher in the decade ahead.

The teaching field glutted, with some cities (such as Boston) having as many as 3500 applicants for 350 vacancies. White collar unemployment at a ten-year high, with 1,114,000 persons (or 2.7% of the entire potential white collar labor force) being out of work—compared with only 873,000 a year earlier.

The demand for engineers and scientists hitting a ten-year low.

Extensive dismissals in aerospace industries, and electronics, and television manufacturers, and construction companies, and advertising agencies, and clothing manufacturers, and chemical producers, and in public relations, security sales, industrial psychology, and what have you.

Then, if the contemporary situation isn't bad enough, there are always some handy, long-range predictions about what technology, automation, the computers, and such, will do to various industries within the coming decade.

By the time that *Mr. Newspaper Reader* is ready to become *Mr. Job Hunter* and venture out into the so-called Job Market, he or she is convinced there isn't a job left out there.

IS NO ONE HIRING?

But then, the unemployment figure doesn't really tell us anything about vacancies—as, upon sober reflection, we must realize. It only tells us how many people we are competing with (sort of) for whatever vacancies exist. That is, *assuming we all possessed the skills that the vacancies call for.*

But, how many vacancies are there?

It's a relatively easy formula to figure out.

First of all, you need to take the total number of jobs in one year as compared to the previous year. For example, in October, 1971, 79.8+ million people were employed. In October, 1970, that figure stood at 78.6.

From this, we may safely conclude that a minimum of over one million new jobs were created, over a twelve-month period, sometimes by businesses, and sometimes by individuals going out and inventing their own job or starting their own business.

But of course if during that period let us say five million

old jobs were phased out in various manufacturing plants and private businesses (and no one seems to know the actual figure), then actually six million new jobs would have had to have been created in order to preserve the net rise of one million. So, we must add to the minimum of one million however many old jobs were phased out.

We must also add the number of jobs which fell vacant during the year at one time or another, due to the mobility of the employed, who leap from one job to another at a prodigious rate—something like 800,000 each month.[1] (The turnover rate for office employees averaged out to 26% in 1969.[2]) We have, then, revolving unemployment—much like a game of musical chairs. And, of course, while the chair is empty, *you* can compete for it as well as anyone.

What does this all add up to? It adds up to what one member of the creative minority estimates are one million job openings each month[3] —not counting sales or latent jobs. About which, more as we go on.

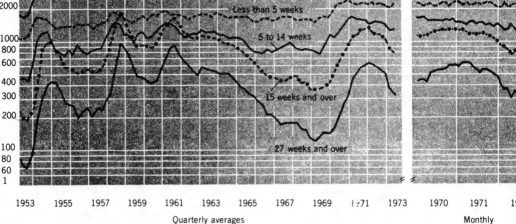

DURATION OF UNEMPLOYMENT, 1953 TO 1973
(Seasonally adjusted)

NUMBER OF WORKERS UNEMPLOYED

HOW MANY WANT THE JOB THAT I WANT?

Are 7.1 million people, then (or whatever the unemployment figure is, in a given month) competing for these one million job openings each month? Well, of course you know they are not. And, for the following reasons:

1. *Musical chairs:* A lot of vacancies never have a chance to get publicized, because as soon as they exist some employee recommends a relative, or else someone (by accident or design) walks in off the street, is interviewed, and straightaway hired.

2. *Stiff demands:* A lot of jobs call for very special skills which just may not exist in sufficient abundance, and so the jobs stay vacant for long periods of time.

3. *Low visibility:* There are a number of vacancies for which any number of qualified applicants could be found if only we had some way of getting the information *out.* But, particularly for jobs that are at all decent, many employers prefer not to advertise the vacancy, since they are very particular about whom they hire. Not long ago, it was estimated that there are 750,000 management vacancies each year, only 250,000 of which are filled by the end of the year.[4] The same goes for other levels.

4. *Shying away:* Some job-hunters want relatively unskilled work, for which vacancies there are any number of

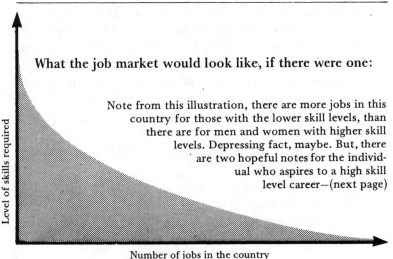

What the job market would look like, if there were one:

Level of skills required

Note from this illustration, there are more jobs in this country for those with the lower skill levels, than there are for men and women with higher skill levels. Depressing fact, maybe. But, there are two hopeful notes for the individual who aspires to a high skill level career—(next page)

Number of jobs in the country

applicants competing with them. These include job-hunters who are new to the job market such as unskilled teenagers, housewives, grandmothers, retired persons looking for part-time work, etc.

5. *Fictitious job-hunters:* Some people who are collecting unemployment insurance (and therefore listed by the U.S. Government as job hunters, which *in theory* they must be in order to collect) actually have no interest in competing for any of the one million vacancies that month. They are such persons as students between semesters, seasonal workers, production workers on temporary layoff, singers, actors and dancers awaiting a call, etc.

Recalling from our previous chapter, the paradoxical nature of the word "skills" (pages 77 ff), this means for the job-hunter of today (whether student, housewife, or second careerist):

1. The higher level of skills that you can legitimately claim, either with people, data or things (or, in varying degree, with all three) the less these kinds of jobs are advertised or known through normal channels; the more you'll have to find ways of unearthing them—which is what this chapter you are now reading is all about. It is written for *You!*

2. Just because the opportunities for the higher level jobs (or careers) are harder to uncover, the higher you aim the less people you will have to compete with—for that job. In fact, if you uncover, as you are very likely to, a need in the organization you like (or organizations), which you can help resolve, they are very likely to create a brand new job for you, which means—in effect—*you will be competing with practically no one, since you are virtually the sole applicant,* as it were. Even if you're young, or whatever. To repeat:

The Paradoxical Moral Of All This

The higher a skill level you can legitimately claim, the more likely you are to find a job. Just the opposite of what the typical job-hunter or career-changer starts out believing.

JOB MARKET DIAGRAMS NEVER INCLUDE
JOBS FOR WHICH NO VACANCY EXISTS

The average job-hunter—left to his own devices—is almost sure that his job-hunting task consists—in one way or another—of unearthing *jobs which someone held before, and which are now vacant. So he searches classified ads, employment agencies, etc. (Women do the same.)*

It rarely occurs to him or her that if, instead, he selects the organizations or companies that interest him, and does enough research to unearth their problems (and how he can help solve them) that they will be perfectly willing to create a new job, for which no vacancy exists just because they will ultimately save money by doing so. (Problems always cost a lot more.) Heaven knows, there are enough insiders who have said—in print—that this hidden job market is what the job-hunter ought to be aiming at. Creation of new positions is the key to the professional job market, the creative minority have said again and again and again. One third of today's jobs didn't exist ten years ago.[5] This is particularly true when the economy is going through a paroxysm, like "the energy crisis" of 1974. New positions *must* be created.

Certainly, a little reflection will tell you why all of this is so. Pretend, for a moment, that you are an executive of some company or organization. Your organization exists in order to get a certain job done, or product produced. And it's doing a pretty good job. But *naturally* you've also got problems; who doesn't? Some of them are just minor, of longstanding, and probably just something you live with. Others are major, maybe even with a sense of a *time bomb*—if you don't solve these, they're going to break your back. All of them are costing you money.

Now, naturally your employees are aware of these problems—and some at least are trying to solve them. But, for one reason or another, they haven't succeeded. Then, into your office one morning comes someone who knows an amazing amount about your company or organization, including some of the major problems that you are facing. He has analyzed them, and has skills which he (or she) believes can help solve them. Very soon, you believe he or she can too, but *there is*

*no vacancy in your company. Will you go and create a new
job, in order to get your hands on this guy or gal? Regardless
of age, background, or whatever?* Provided you have the
authority (and our man or woman won't be talking to you if
you don't) *you bet you will.* In fact, you may have been
thinking you needed a new position, anyway.

KNOWLEDGE IS POWER

These facts about the nature of the "job market," the
meaning of "skills," and the availability of "high level positions" are very strange.

They are also contrary to what many people, posing as
experts, will tell you.

They are also (nonetheless) true.

And (consequently) they work.

Time after time, again and again, men (and women) who
have comprehended the true nature of what they were facing
in the matter of "the job market"—so called—have successfully found their first job, or made the transition from one
career to another (without re-training or further post-graduate courses), in the area of the country that *they* chose.

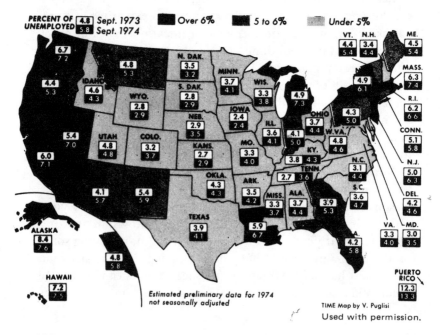

TIME Map by V. Puglisi
Used with permission.

122

And this, in spite of the fact that often the area they wanted to live and work in was designated as virtually a disaster area, unemployment-wise and job-wise.

They realized, as we said earlier, that all the unemployment figures tell you is how many people are competing with you for whatever vacancies there are, or for whatever new positions there could be.

But, the vacancies (or potential new positions) *are there no matter how bad the economy is.* People get promoted; people move; people die; executives get tired of dealing with the same old unsolved problems and resolve to hire *anyone* capable of solving them. Young or old; male or female.

Since the vacancies or potential new jobs are there—wherever in the country one turns—you must choose where it is you want to focus.

That means: the place where you already are (if you love it) or the place where you've always wanted to be or if you are absolutely without any preference, it means something like pinning up a map of the U.S. and throwing darts (one guy actually did this).

But one way or another *you* have got to do the choosing.

You should not ask another man or woman to make that decision for you, nor should you ask external events (fate, coincidence, or where the "job market" is alleged to be favorable) to decide for you.

It's your move. *Your* move.

JOB MARKET FOCUSING
(THE LASER BEAM APPROACH)

Job-hunters begin by thinking there are too few job markets (and therefore, too few jobs) "out there." Thus far, in this chapter, we have argued just the opposite. There are too many. If you try to hit them all (shot-gun style) you will only diffuse your energies and your effectiveness. Better, far better, to try concentrating your energies and effectiveness. Rifle style. (For peace lovers, a non-military? image would be the laser beam.) The whole process might be compared to a funneling:

79,000,000 JOB MARKETS IN THE UNITED STATES (THAT'S THE TOTAL NUMBER OF NON-FARM PAYROLLS),including 19,400,000 Manufacturers' Job Markets. • You narrow this down by deciding just what area, city or county you want to work in. This leaves you with however many thousands or millions of job markets there are in that area or city. • You narrow this down by identifying your Strongest Skills, on their highest level that you can legitimately claim, and then thru research deciding what field you *want* to work in, above all. This leaves you with all the hundreds of businesses/ community organizations/agencies/schools/hospitals/ projects/associations/foundations/institutions/firms or government agencies there are in that area and in the field you have chosen. • You narrow this down by getting acquainted with the economy in the area thru personal interviews with various contacts; and supplementing this with study of journals in your field, in order that you can pinpoint the places that interest you the most. This leaves a manageable num- ber of markets for you to do some study on. • You now narrow this down by ask- ing yourself: *can I be happy in this place, and, do they have the kind of prob- lems which my strongest skills can help solve for them?* This leaves you with the companies or organizations which you will now, carefully plan how to approach . . .

THE CRUCIAL MATTER: WHAT WILL GET YOU A JOB?

Suppose the time has come when you will need an alternative career. As you think about the job-hunt, very well-meaning people will tell you that the only route is to go back to college: go learn some skill or profession other than the one you had, *they say*. Go back to school. Get re-trained. Get your doctorate. *They say*.

The government, personnel experts, and many others think along these same lines: *retraining* always seems to be the answer, even to many well-meaning people, trying to give helpful advice. As you will discover, when that time comes.

There is, of course, a reason for this:

People think there are only two things that you can get a job with: experience, or credentials. They figure you've got to have one or the other.

1. Experience. If you want to be a machinist, and you've done it for ten years, you have convincing experience. If you want to be a teacher, and you've taught for ten years, you have convincing experience. If you've done it long enough, many people don't care *how* you picked up the skill in the first place. But many people, after they have identified a (second) career that they would enjoy, have to admit they have no convincing experience to prove they are good (or would be good) in that career. And since all their friends tell them their *only two means of getting a job is either experience or credentials,* the poor souls assume they therefore must go and get:

2. Credentials. Now, to be sure, there are certain fields, such as law or medicine, where the aspirant is simply going to have to go back to school and get the requisite training and resulting credentials, before he can practice. So if you have settled upon this kind of career for your *second* or even *third* transition, there is not likely to be any way you can avoid the credentialing route.

With most careers, however, this is not true. No matter what others may tell you. (It is amazing how much bad advice is dispensed in our society with the sound of certainty by people who have depended either on outdated data, or on scanty sampling, or on rumor and hearsay—rather than going

EXPERIENCE

CREDENTIALS

and doing their own research before they solemnly tell you what you must do.) Maybe you do need credentials—if you are going to set yourself up in private practice as a marriage counselor, or consultant or such; maybe. But you ought to reach this conclusion as a result of your own intensive research first, if you reach it at all. You will discover that people have gotten jobs as full professors at Universities when they did not possess a doctorate or any other credential that everyone told them they *had* to have. Likewise with other fields. And all of this because these men and women carving out a second career for themselves just didn't believe there were only two things with which to get a job. There has got to be a third thing, they reasoned, that doesn't depend on the past at all; and that is, to give a demonstration of your skills right in front of the prospective employer. Impossible, you say? Not at all. You can show him/her right in his/her own office that you have the skill he/she wants more than anything: the skill of

PROBLEM-SOLVING

3. Problem-solving. No matter how much different kinds of work may vary upon the surface, underneath they have this common base: they deal with one kind of problem-solving or another. Universities, community organizations, businesses—all require people good at problem-solving *no matter what title may be tacked on the man (or woman) they hire in order to justify his/her salary.* Problem-solvers get hired, whether they are fresh out of college, or in later life.

Now, how do you prove you are a problem-solver right before the very eyes of a prospective employer? Forget about producing convincing Experience from the past, or producing credentials from the past. Just do the most thorough-going research imaginable of the particular company(ies), university(ies), organization(s) or other "job markets" *that you have chosen as most interesting to you,* before you ever go into the office to seek the job.

Now we said this third pathway is the key to getting a job when changing careers. But it is just as important when you are setting out to find your first job, or staying in your own field for your job-hunt. Therefore, we urge this path all job-hunters through your own most thorough-going research; we don't mean just an hour or two in the library. This is not what we are talking about, here.

> We are talking about the most thorough-going research that you have the patience and determination to do. Hour after hour; day after day. Phew! Lots of work. But the rewards: Wow.

DON'T PAY SOMEONE TO DO THIS RESEARCH FOR YOU, WHATEVER YOU DO.

There are a number of reasons why *no one else* can do your research for you, in this whole process.

1. Only *you* know what things you are looking for, what things you want to avoid if possible; in a word, what your *tropisms* are.

2. You need the self-confidence that comes as you practice this skill of researching *before* you go after the organizations that you have chosen.

3. You will need to use this skill after you get your job, so the time spent practicing it before you get the job will pay off directly.

Can you do it?

Of course you can.

If you went to college or even post-graduate school, which over half of the high school graduates today are doing, you know exactly how to go about Researching—since you did lots of it there. (Or did you patronize one of those term paper places? Tsk. Tsk.)

If you only went to high school, you still did source papers and maybe even term papers. Anyway, you'd be surprised how this kind of skill can come back, once you try to revive it.

It consists, in essence, of a skillful blend of :

WRITTEN STUFF, AND PEOPLE

In researching any part of this whole process: a) your skills; b) your field; c) your geographical area; or d) your chosen places to approach for a position, you will probably be dealing *alternately* with written material (books, journals, magazines, and other material librarians and such can direct you to) and with people, who are experts in one aspect or another of the subjects you are researching. YOU READ UNTIL YOU NEED TO TALK TO SOMEONE BECAUSE YOU CAN'T FIND MORE IN BOOKS; THEN YOU TALK TO PEOPLE UNTIL YOU KNOW YOU NEED TO GET BACK AND DO SOME MORE READING. And much depends, in the end, on which you are more comfortable with.

Essential to your research (in either form) is that you know: **WHAT IT IS THAT YOU ARE LOOKING FOR**

When You Are Reading or Interviewing About	Among the Things You May Be Looking for Are:
your skills	what kind of work uses *most* of these skills *together*
fields of possible work	which ones you will be happiest (and therefore most effective) in, because they fit in with your total Life Mission as you perceive it
geographical area that you have chosen	the kind of places that might need your skills, in the field you have chosen
places where you might want to work	to find out if there is any reason why you might *not* want to work there; to find out what problems they have *and* which problems are most urgent ("time-bombs") and which ones your skills can help solve.

Beyond mechanics, it is essential for you to remember who you are, as you are going about this whole business of researching and interviewing *for information only.* The whole process will divide into two parts. Let us make clear what they are:

Part I. You are the screener. The employers and organizations are the *screenees.* You are looking them over, trying to decide which of these pleases YOU. This is for information, building of contacts, and tracking down places that interest you *only.*

During Part I, you can even take others with you (especially if you are in high school or college and this is all new to you, or if you are a housewife coming into the marketplace for the first time). After all, you are going out only to find information. You are not yet job-hunting, in this Part of the Process. Therefore, it's perfectly okay to take someone with you, if you want to.

Part II. Having narrowed down the possibilities to four or five that really fascinate you, you now return to them in the fashion we shall describe in the next chapter, to seek an actual job there (doing the thing you have decided you would most like to do). At that point *and only at that point,* you now become the Screenee, and the employers or organizations, or funding-sources, or whatever, become the Screeners. Though, of course, you are still keeping your eyes and ears open in case you see something dreadful that will put you abruptly back into the role of Screener and cause you to say, to yourself at least, I have just learned this place really isn't for me.

In any event, this first part of the research is Part I —where you are the Screener; and is not to be confused with Part II (next chapter) where you become the Screenee. If you *feel* as though you are the Screenee in this first part of the research we are presently describing, you're doing something wrong — even if you have all the mechanics down pat. You've got rights: to go look at places and decide whether or not they interest you, and whether or not you could do your most effective work there, because you like what they're doing.

FOCUSING DOWN:
TO A GEOGRAPHICAL AREA

RESEARCH AID NUMBER 1

If the area you would like to live and work in is *not* the place where you presently live, you will need to do as much research of the area, at a distance, as you can. Writing to the Chamber of Commerce to ask them what information they have on the area, and doing research in some of the books listed on pages 149 and 150, will begin to suggest *some of the places* you are interested in seeing first hand.

Also, your local library has a yearbook of newspaper advertising, put out by *Editor & Publisher,* which contains a handy profile of *major* U.S. communities, at least.

RESEARCH AID NUMBER 2

It will ultimately be *essential* for you to visit the place you want to work in (if you do not already live there). You will want to talk to key individuals *who can suggest other people you might talk to, as you try to find out what organizations interest you.*

You will want to define these key individuals ahead of time, and let them know you are coming. Your list may include: friends, college alumni (get the list from your college so you can find out who lives in that area), high school pals, church contacts. Chamber of Commerce executives, city manager, regional planning officers, appropriate county or state offices in your area of interest, the Mayor, and high level management in particular companies that look interesting from what you've read or heard about them.

When you "hit town," you will want to remember the City Directory, the Yellow Pages of your phone book, etc. Some experts call this your personal economic survey.

If going into a strange new geographical area is a totally new experience for you, and you have no friends there in your chosen target area, just remember there are various ways of meeting people, making friends, and developing contacts rather quickly. There are athletic clubs, Y's, churches, charitable and community organizations, where you can present yourself and meet people from the moment you walk in the doors. You will soon develop many acquaintances, and some beginning friendships, and the place won't seem so lonely at all.

Also, visit your high school or college before you set out for this new town and find out what graduates live in the area that you are now visiting for the first time: they are your friends already, because you went to the same school.

Since you are job-hunting, you may want to put a modest-sized advertisement in the paper, saying you would like to meet with other people who are following the job-hunting techniques of *What Color Is Your Parachute?* That way you'll quickly form a kind of 'job-hunters anonymous', where you can mutually support one another in your hunt.

You will want to follow the same process, even if you already live in the area you are interested in working in. Your search: for places that need your skills. Your purpose: not to find out primarily if *they* want you, but rather, whether or not *you* want them, as we said before.

FOCUSING DOWN: TO KINDS OF PLACES IN THAT AREA

Suppose, now, you've decided that, say, being a consultant uses more of your skills than anything else. The question you then face is: should I be a consultant in education, in business, in non-profit organizations, in fund-raising, or what? It is important, as you are identifying what you like to do, that you also identify in what kinds of places you might enjoy doing this.

It is the same with every other career or occupation. You want to be a teacher, let us say. Do you want to be one at a university, a college, a junior college, a business school, in private industry (some corporations, such as IBM for example, make large use of teachers), or where? The purpose of this section of your research and interviewing, is to look at *all the options,* so that you can choose the one you prefer the most; *and* alternatives.

You are looking for the organizations or places (colleges, institutions, agencies, etc.) where you would be *happiest* working. Because the more you enjoy *what* you are doing and *where* you are doing it, the better you are going to use the talents which God gave you.

Here are the kind of questions about yourself that you are (hopefully) trying to find the answers to (as you do your research and interviewing):

Do I want to work for a company, firm, agency, college, association, foundation, the government, or what?

Do I want to work for an older and larger organization, or get in on the ground floor of a new and smaller one, with growth possibilities?

Do I want to advance rapidly? If so I need an organization with solid plans for expansion—overseas or at home.

Do I want to work for a "going concern" or for "a problem child" type of operation. As the experts say, *a company in trouble* is a company in search of leadership. Same goes for foundations, agencies, etc. If that is your cup of tea, (well, is it?) you can probably find such places without too much investigation. Some experts say if you go for such a challenge, give yourself a time limit (say 3-5 years) and then if you can't solve it, get out.

Other questions: *your own personal ones*—what do I want to accomplish? what working circumstances do I want? what opportunities? what responsibilities? kinds of people to work with? starting salary? salary five years from now? promotion opportunities? (Keep these always in mind.)

It all looks, at first sight, as though this whole process were an awful lot of hard work. And, at first, it certainly is. Self-inventory, meaningful skills, career and life planning, job markets—there were times when we were tempted to forget the whole thing, and just go about the transition process and job-hunt in the haphazard way so many others do it. But, we told ourselves, *that way lies madness.* So, we kept at it. And now, we've begun to notice something: we're enjoying it. No telling just when it happened. But, we began to notice it was *fun* to travel around and talk to people. Maybe because they weren't on the spot (yet), and neither were we. And we began to notice it was *fun* to do the research too, in our local library, college, or whatever.

Maybe a detective hides within the breast of each one of us. Maybe we enjoy talking to high level management and finding out that it isn't so difficult as the books (*with their long chapters on the art of conducting interviews*) make interviewing out to be. Maybe we enjoy the renewed sense of self-confidence that we are picking up, in non-stress situations. This isn't as hard as I thought it was going to be.

Well, you with the soul of a detective, you *are* solving a mystery. In what environment will this hardy plant called *you* thrive, grow, and bloom the best? Or: if you're instinctively religious, a better form of the question for you might be, in what place can your service to the Lord best continue —without the danger of burying your talents in the ground?

That's the mystery you are unraveling.

Sure, it's fun. It's you. And by focusing down, in this fashion, you are increasingly able to concentrate your energies.

You are acting as though the organization that gets you will be darned lucky. You are right.

AND JUST HOW DO YOU GO ABOUT
YOUR PERSONAL SURVEY?

In visiting the geographical area where you most want to work, and conducting your own personal and organizational survey of the area, you are trying to go from one person to another, building a chain of links in which each person you see refers you to another (and hopefully sets up the appointment for you, or at least allows you to use his name).

Let's listen to an actual job-hunter describe the process:

"Suppose I arrived cold in some city, the one place in all the world I want to live—but with no idea of what that city might hold as a match and challenge for my personal talent bank. I have an economic survey to make, yes; but I also have an equally or more important personal survey to accomplish.

Can this city meet my peculiarly personal needs? To find out, I meet Pastors, bankers, school principals, physicians, dentists, real estate operators, et al. I would be astonished if opportunities were not brought to my attention together with numerous offers of personal introduction to key principals. All I would be doing is forging links (references) in a chain leading to my eventual targets. *The reference is the key.*"

People who haven't tried this are understandably afraid: afraid important men won't have time to see them, afraid they won't be able to get past the secretary, etc. But, as was said above, referral is the key.

Well, suppose you just can't find a reference to a particular man you want to see?

Let's listen to John Crystal, a master in this field, describe the process:

"If you really are interested in highway carrier operations and really do know quite a bit about it, for instance, and you get to Charlotte, N.C., where you learn that one small, new company is doing something really innovative and intelligent in *your* field I would guess that the chances are that its President is just as fascinated by that subject as you are. And if you called him up—Oh, yes, the secretary, well this goes for her too—and told him the simple truth about that shared interest—if he asks if you are job hunting tell him the truth, *No*—but that you are *in truth* impressed by what you have heard about his bright ideas, and that you want to hear more about them, and that you just might possibly have a suggestion or two based on your own experience which he might find useful—Well, he just might invite you to lunch. And if he wants to offer you a job after a while, and many do, it's strictly *his* idea. And you do not accept it although you are always polite enough to say that you will be glad to consider it and perhaps talk it over with him again later on, after you have decided precisely what you want to do, where, with whom, etc. The key to the whole thing is this: treat the other guy just as you would like to be treated yourself."

If this process has been followed religiously (so to speak) you will have at the end of your initial survey:

1. A *list* of places in your chosen geographical area *that interest you, and that look as though they have problems your skills can help solve.*

What you then want to do further research about is:

2. *Identifying in detail what those problems are,* for the manageable number of organizations you have now identified in list No.1 above.

There are resources to help you at this point, but resources are useless, unless you keep firmly in mind what kinds of questions you want the resources to help you with. So, let's list a few *samples* of the kinds of questions:

SUPPOSE YOU ARE TRYING TO SURVEY A FAR-AWAY PLACE?
The Principles of Information-Searching
At a Distance (Or Up Close)

1 *Be clear about the different kinds of information you are going to need for your job-hunt.*

You are going to need information about the following (use this as a check-list):

a. *What your skills are (1) that you have already demonstrated; (2) that you enjoy.* This list must be in detail, *and* clustered into families, *and* prioritized in terms of your six or so favorites. If you failed to do any of these three steps (in detail, clustered, and prioritized) you will seriously hamper your subsequent information-search.

b. *Where you want to use these skills.* Someone who has the skill of welding can use that skill to weld the casing for a nuclear bomb, or to make a wheel for a cart. What do you want to use your skills with? In the service of what? To accomplish what? Simply to say you want to do welding (or whatever) is not sufficient, and will seriously hamper your subsequent information-search.

c. *What kinds of organizations (1) that you like; (2) either already do use people with your skills in the service of your goals; or, (3) ought to, and perhaps could be persuaded to; (4) in the* geographical area (or areas) *you have focussed on.*

The last step above is the pre-condition for answering the other three. An overseas soldier—for example—cannot do an information-search about corporations' department of mental hygiene, until he has *first* selected at least an area of the country, and preferably two or three cities in that area, by name.

d. *What the names of such organizations are, in the cities you have focussed upon.* The more specific and detailed you have been in step "c." above, the easier this step "d." will be. The more general you have been, the harder this step will be, e.g., "Corporations" is too general. In a particular city, that will turn out to be a very long list. But (for example) "Corporations with not more than 200 employees, which produce some product" is a much shorter list, in any particular city (or country-area). Likewise, "non-profit organizations" is too general. That again will produce a long list, if your information-search is thorough. "Non-profit organizations dealing with. . . ." what? health services, consumer protection, or what? The more detailed you are, the easier to do the information-search.

e. *What are their problems, as organizations—and, particularly, "in the areas where I would be working?"* A lot depends on the level at which you want to work. If at the clerk or secretary level, the problems are pretty predictable: absenteeism, too-long coffee or lunch breaks, not caring about the subject-matter, not accepting the supervisor's priorities about which work needs to get done first, etc. If you want to work at a higher level, the problems are likely to be more complex.

f. *Who there has the power to hire (it's not likely to be the Personnel Department) for the level of job you are aiming at?*

2 *Set down on paper which of the above information-searches you can do where you are, and which you need others' help with in the cities of your choice.*

Normally, you can do the information-search on "a." and "b." above, right where you are, since this is potentially a self-directed information-search. To aid you in doing that part of the information-search, there is the Quick Job-

Hunting Map; Beginning Version, for high school students and others who are entering the world of work for the first time. Advanced Version, for those who have had considerable experience in the world of work, or who wish to change careers. (The Advanced Version is in Appendix A, page 198.)

If, even with the Map, you have difficulty identifying your skills or where you want to use them, you may then: (1) Recruit your mate, or a friend, or business acquaintance there in your city where you presently are, to help you work through the map; OR (2) Use a professional career expert such as your college career-planning or placement office; or one of the two hundred professionals who have been trained by the National Career Development Project in a two week workshop (name of the person(s) nearest you upon request, by writing to: Referrals, NCDP, P.O. Box 379, Walnut Creek, CA 94596, and enclosing a stamped, self-addressed return envelope, with a $1 cheque for postage and handling.)

Now, once this is done, you are ready to go on to the other information searches listed on the previous page. IF there is a really good library where you are, or if that library (however small and limited) is on an inter-library loan system, you can do *some* research on "c." on the previous page, *some* research on "d." and some also on "f."

So, your two lists will *probably* come out looking like this:

Searches I Can Do Here	Searches Others Must Do There
a. in detail	
b. in detail	the rest of
c.	c.
d. some	d. in detail
f.	e.
	f.

3 *Determine how much time you have before you* **absolutely** *have to find a job.*

Yes, of course it would be just dandy if you could conclude your information-search—successfully—within the month. But it is not at all unusual for a job-hunt to take nine months (something symbolic about *that*) or longer. Soooo, how much time *do* you have? At the outside limit? The earlier you can get started, the more lead-time you can give yourself, the better.

4 *Figure out if there isn't* **some way** *during that time that you could go visit the city or cities of your choice.*

Does a vacation fall within the time period you have between now and when you must finally have that job? Could you visit it on vacation? Could you take a summer job there? Go there on leave? Get sent to a convention there? Get appointed to a group or association that meets there? Think it through. You will *have* to go there, finally (in almost all cases) for the actual job interview(s). If worse comes to worst, go there a week or so ahead of that interview. Better late than never, to look over the scene in person.

5 *Until you can go there, use every resource and contact you have in order to explore the answers to "c. d. e. and f." on page 135-136.*

It will be doubly-apparent by now, to one and all, how crucial it is for you to choose *by name* two or three cities or towns where you are going to (a) focus your information-search; (b) at least initially. And if it's a country-area that interests you, then at least identify that area, and then the name of the nearest city or town(s). And then, starting with the city or town that's on the top of your list, use the following resources in your information-search:

a. *The local daily or weekly newspaper.* Almost all papers will mail to subscribers anywhere in the world. So: subscribe, for a six month period, or a year. You'd be surprised at what you can learn from the paper. Some of the answers to "c.", "d.", "e." and "f." will appear there. Additionally, you will note businesses that are growing and expanding in that city you are researching.

b. *The Chamber of Commerce, and City Hall (or the Town Hall).* These are the places whose interest it is to attract newcomers, and to tell them what kinds of businesses there are in town—as well as some details about them. So: write and ask them, in the beginning, what they have about the city or town in general. Then, later, don't hesitate to write back to them with more specific questions.

c. *The local library or reference librarian, if your target-city/town has one.* Yes, of course it is perfectly kosher to write to the library of your target city, asking for information that may be only there. If the librarian is too busy to answer, then use one of your contacts to find out. (See below.) "Bill (or Billie) I need some information that I'm afraid only the library in your town has. Specifically, I need to know about company x." Or, whatever.

d. *Your contacts.* Yes, of course, you know people in whatever city or town you're researching during your job-hunt-as-information-search. For openers, write to your old high school and get the alumni list for your graduating class. Then write to your college—if you went to college—and ask for the alumni list for your class, also. Subscribe to your college's alumni bulletin for further news, addresses, and hints. If you belong to a church or synagogue, write to the church or synagogue in your target city, and tell them that you're one of their own and you need some information. ("I need to know who can tell me what non-profit organizations there are in that city, that deal with x.") Or, whatever. ("I need to know how I can find out what corporations there are in town have departments of mental hygiene.") For further contacts, ask your family and relatives who they know in the target city or town of your choice. You know more people in that city, who could help you, than you think.

e. *The appropriate state, county, and local government agencies, associations, etc.* Ask your contacts to tell you what that appropriate agency might be.

6 *Regard the city or town where you presently are, as a replica of the city or town you are interested in going to (at least in some respects)—so that some of the information-search can be done where you are, and then its learnings can be transferred.*

Suppose, for example, you know that you are skilled in counseling people, particularly in one to one situations, that you are knowledgeable about—and well-versed in—psychiatry, and that you love carpentry and plants. You are (obviously) at stage "c." on page 135.

What kinds of organizations does this point to?

To get at this, first translate all of your above interests into people (counseling = counselor), (psychiatry = psychiatrist), carpentry = carpenter), (plants = gardener).

Next, ask yourself which of these persons is most likely to have the largest overview? This is often the same (but not always) as asking: who took the longest to get his or her training? The answer here: psychiatrist.

In the place where you presently are, then, go to see a psychiatrist (pay him, or her for fifteen minutes of their time —if there is no other way) or go see the head of the psychiatry department at the nearest college or university, and ask them: Do you have any idea how to put all the above together in a job? And, if you don't, who might?

Eventually, you will be told by him or her: Yes, there is a branch of psychiatry that uses plants to help heal people.

Having found this out in the place where you live, you can then write to your target city or town to ask, What psychiatric facilities are there, there, and which ones—if any— use plants in their healing program?

Thus can you conduct your research where you are, and then transfer its learnings to the place you want to go.

For further information on how to conduct this information search more thoroughly, see *Where Do I Go From Here With My Life?* (op. cit.) and especially pages 102-112, 120-148, even-numbered pages particularly.

WAYS OF FINDING OUT WHAT
AN ORGANIZATION'S PROBLEMS ARE

All organizations have money—to one degree or another. What I am looking for are *problems*—specifically, *problems that my skills can help solve; what problems are bugging this organization? Ask; look. (If you are talking to men within a company or organization that looks as though it might be interesting to you, ask them:* What is the biggest problem you are encountering here?)

The problem does not have to be one that is bothering only that organization. You may want to ask what problem is common to the whole industry or field—low profit, obsolescence, inadequate planning etc.? Or if there is a problem that is common to the geographic region: labor problems, minority employment, etc. All you really need is one major problem that you would delight to help solve.

How does this organization rank within its field or industry? Is this organization family owned? What effect (if so) on promotions? Where are its plants, offices or branches? What are all its projects or services? In what ways have they grown in recent years? New lines, new products, new processes, new facilities, etc? Existing political situations: imminent proxy fights, upcoming mergers, etc.? What is the general image of the organization in peoples' minds? If they have stock, what has been happening to it (see an investment broker and ask).

What kind of *turnover of staff* have they had? What is the attitude of employees toward the organization? Are their faces happy, strained, or what? Is promotion generally from within, or from outside? How long have chief executives been with the organization?

Do they encourage their employees to further their educational training? Do they help them pay for it?

How do *communications* work within the organization? How is information collected, by what paths does it flow? What methods are used to see that information gets results— to what authority do people respond there? Who reports to whom?

Is there a "time-bomb"—a problem that will kill the organization, or drastically reduce its effectiveness and efficiency if they don't solve it fast?

Some of these questions will be relevant, for you; others will not be. *If you are "going after" a college, for example, some of these may have to be ignored, and some adapted.*

Some of these questions are general in nature, and you will try to answer them about *any* organization you approach. Other questions are very specific, requiring detailed research, and you will have to keep at it, searching, digging, interviewing, until you find out. But the skills you are sharpening up will more than repay you the time spent, a thousandfold.

So much for the general principles. Now, here are some more detailed rules.

RULES FOR FINDING OUT
THE NEEDS OR PROBLEMS
OF AN ORGANIZATION

Rule No. 1: *You don't need to discover the problems of the whole organization (unless it's very small); you only need to discover the problems that are bugging the-man-or-woman-who-has-the-ultimate-responsibility (or power)-to-hire-you.* The conscientious always bite off more than they can chew. If they're going to try for a job at the Telephone Company, or IBM or the Federal Government, or General Motors or— like that—they assume they've got to find out the problems facing that whole organization. *Forget it!* Your task, fortunately, is much more manageable. Find out what problems are bugging, bothering, concerning, perplexing, gnawing at, the-man-or-woman-who-has-the-power-to-hire-you. This assumes, of course, that you have first *identified* who that man or woman is. If you did a thorough information search, of course, you probably have already met that man or that woman, in the course of gathering your information. So he or she is more to you than just a name. If it's a committee (of sorts) that actually has the responsibility (and therefore Power) to hire you, you will need to figure out who that one individual is (or two) who *sway* the others. You know, the one whose judgment the others respect. How do you find that out? By using your contacts, of course. Someone will know someone who knows that whole committee, and can tell you who their *real* leader is. It's not necessarily the one who got elected as Chairman or Chairperson.

Rule No. 2: *Don't assume the problems have to be huge, complex and hidden. The problems bothering the-man-or-woman-who-has-the-power-to-hire-you may be small, simple and obvious.* If the job you are aiming at was previously filled by someone (i.e., the one who, if you get hired, will be referred to as "your predecessor") the problems that are bothering the-man-or-woman-who-has-the-power-to-hire-you may be uncovered simply by finding out (through your contacts, etc.—who know your prospective boss) what bugged him or her about your predecessor. Samples:

"S/he was never to work on time, took long lunch breaks, and was out sick too often"; OR

"S/he was good at typing, but had lousy skills over the telephone"; OR

"S/he handled older people well, but just couldn't relate to the young"; OR

"I never could get him/her to keep me informed about what s/he was doing"; Etc.

In your research you may be thinking to yourself, Gosh, this firm has a huge public relations problem; I'll have to show them that I could put together a whole crash P.R. program. That's the huge, complex and hidden problem that you think the-man-or-woman-who-has-the-power-to-hire-you *ought to be concerned about.* But, in actual fact, what s/he *is* concerned about is whether (unlike your predecessor) you're going to get to work on time, take assigned lunch breaks, and not be out, sick, too often. Don't overlook the Small, Simple and Obvious Problems which bug almost every employer. (For boning up, browse through *Management: Tasks, Responsibilities, Practices* by Peter F. Drucker, Harper & Row, 1973; and *Work in America,* Report of a Special Task

Force to the Secretary of Health, Education, and Welfare, M.I.T. Press, 1973; also, *Jobkeeping; A Hireling's Survival Manual,* by David Noer, Chilton Book Company, 1976—at your local library.)

Rule No. 3: *In most cases, your task is not that of educating your prospective employer, but of trying to read his mind, or her mind.* Now, to be sure, you may have uncovered—during your information search—some problem that the-man-or-woman-who-has-the-power-to-hire-you is absolutely unaware of. And you may be convinced that this problem is *so crucial* that for you even to mention it will instantly win you his or her undying gratitude. Maybe. But don't bet on it. Our files here at the National Career Development Project are filled with sad testimonies like the following:

"I met with the V-P, Marketing in a major local bank on the recommendation of an officer, and discussed with him a program I devised to reach the female segment of his market, which would not require any new services, except education, enlightenment and encouragement. His comment at the end of the discussion was that the bank president had been after him for three years to develop a program for women, and he wasn't about to do it because the only reason, in his mind, for the president's request was reputation enhancement on the president's part. . ."

Inter-office politics, as in this case, or other considerations may prevent your prospective employer from being receptive to Your Bright Idea, or educable. In any event, you're not trying to find out what *might* motivate him or her to hire you. Your research has got to be devoted rather to finding out what *already does* motivate him or her *when s/he decides to hire someone for the position you are interested in.* In other words, you're trying to find out What's Already Going On In His (or Her) Mind. In this sense, your task is more akin to a kind of mind-reading than it is to education. (Though *some* people-who-have-the-power-to-hire are *very* open to being educated. You just never know.)

Rule No. 4: *There are various ways of finding out what's going on in his or her mind: don't try just one way.* We will give a kind of outline, here, of the various ways. (You can use this as a checklist.)

A. *Analyzing the Organization at a Distance and Making Some Educated Guesses.*
1. If the organization is expanding, then they need:
   a. More of what they already have; OR
   b. More of what they already have, but with different style, added skills, or other pluses *that are needed;* OR
   c. Something they don't presently have: a new kind of person, with new skills doing a new function or service
2. If the organization is continuing as is, then they need:
   a. To replace people who were fired (find out why, what was lacking?); OR
   b. To replace people who quit (find out what was prized about them); OR
   c. To create a new position (yes, this happens even in organizations that are not expanding—due to
      1) Old needs newly perceived, which weren't provided for, earlier, but now must be, even if they have to cut out some other function or position.
      2) Revamping assignments within their present staff)
3. If the organization is reducing its size, staff or product/ service, then they
   a. Have not yet decided which staff to terminate, i.e., which functions to give low priority to (in which case *that* is their problem, and you may be able to help them identify which functions are "core-functions"); OR
   b. Have decided which functions or staff to terminate (in which case they may need multi-talented people or generalists, able to do several jobs (i.e., functions) instead of just one, as formerly)

B. *Analyzing the problems of the-man-or-woman-who-has-the-power-to-hire-you by talking to him or her directly, during your preliminary information-interviews.*
Why guess at what's going on in his or her mind, when you can find out directly by including him/her in your informa-

tion survey? (*See "The Quick Job-Hunting Map" in* Appendix A on page 198.)

C. *Analyzing the problems of the-man-or-woman-who-has-the-power-to-hire-you by talking to his or her "opposite number" in another organization which is similar (not to say, almost identical) to the one that interests you.*

If, for some reason, you cannot approach—at this time—the organization that interests you (it's too far away, or you don't want to tip your hand yet, or whatever), what you can do is pick a similar organization (or individual) where you are —and go find out what kind of problems are on his or her mind. (If you are interested in working for, say, a Senator out West, you can talk to a Senator's staff here, where you are, first; the problems are likely to be similar.)

D. *Analyzing the problems of your prospective employer by talking to the person who held the job before you—OR by talking to his or her "opposite number" in another similar/identical organization.*

Nobody, absolutely nobody, knows the problems bugging a boss so much as someone who works, or used to work, for him or her. If they still work for him or her, they may have a huge investment in being discreet (i.e., not as honest as you need). Ex-employees rarely have such values or needs. Needless to say, if you're trying to get the organization to create a new position, there is no "previous employee". But in some similar/identical organization *which already has this sort of position,* you can find someone to interview.

E. *Using your contacts/friends/everyone you meet, in order to find someone who*
   1. Knows the organization that interests you, or knows someone who knows;
   2. Knows the-person-who-has-the-power-to-hire-you, or knows someone who knows;
   3. Knows who his or her opposite number is in a similar/identical organization;
   4. Knows your predecessor, or knows someone who knows;
   5. Knows your "opposite number" in another organization, or knows someone who knows.

146

F. *Supplementary Method: Research in the library,* on the organization, or an organization similar to it; on the-individual-who-has-the-power-to-hire-you, or on his or her opposite number in another organization; etc. (ask your friendly librarian or research-librarian for help—tell her or him what you're trying to find out).

Rule No. 5: *Ultimately, this is a language-translation problem. You're trying to take your language (i.e., a description of your skills), and translate it into his or her language (i.e., their priorities, their values, their jargon, as these surface within their concerns, problems, etc.).* You should be aware to begin with that most of the-people-who-have-the-power-to-hire-you for the position that you want DO NOT like the word "problems." It reminds them they are mortal, have hangups, haven't solved something yet, or that they over-looked something, etc. "Smartass" is the word normally reserved for someone who comes in *and shows them up.* (This isn't true of everybody, but it's true of altogether too many.) Since you're trying to use *their* language, speak of "an area you probably are planning to move into" or "a concern of yours" or *anything* except: "By the way, I've uncovered a problem you have". Use the word *problems* in your own head, but don't blurt it out with your prospective employer, unless you hear him or her use it first.

Beyond this, your goal is to be able to speak of Your Skills in terms of *The Language* of Their Problems. We will close with some examples, in order to bring this all home:

He or she who has the power to hire you, was bugged by or concerned about:	You therefore use language which emphasizes that you:
Your predecessor had all the skills, but was too serious about *everything*.	have all the skills (name them) *plus* you have a sense of humor.
This place is expanding, and now needs a training program for its employees.	have the skills to do training, and in the area s/he is concerned about.
All the picayune details s/he has to attend to, which s/he would like to shovel off on someone else.	are very good with details and follow up. (That had better be true.)
This magazine probably isn't covering all the subjects that it should, but that's just a gnawing feeling, and s/he's never had time to document it, and decide what areas to move into.	have done a complete survey of its table of contents for the last ten years, can show what they've missed, and have outlined sample articles in those missing areas.

So much for the kinds of questions. Now, where do you turn for the answers? Okay, here goes:

RESEARCH AID NUMBER 3

Tools for identifying organization's problems.
(Available from your local library, a brokerage
office, bank or the organization itself.)

American Men of Science.
American Society of Training and Development Directory.
    Who's Who In Training and Development. P.O. Box 5307,
    Madison, Wisconsin 53705.
Better Business Bureau report on the organization (call your BBB in the
    city where the organization is located).
Chamber of Commerce data on the organization (visit the Chamber
    there).
College library (especially *business school* library) is there is one in your
    chosen area.
Company /college /association /agency /foundation *Annual Reports*.
    Get directly from company etc. or from Chamber or library.
Contacts Influential
Directory of Corporate Affiliations. (National Register Publishing Co., Inc.)
Dun & Bradstreet's Million Dollar Directory.
Dun & Bradstreet's Middle Market Directory.
Encyclopedia of Associations, Vol. 1, National Organizations, Gale
    Research Company.
Encyclopedia of Business Information Sources (2 volumes).
Fitch Corporation Manuals.
F and S Indexes (recent articles on firms).
F & S Index of Corporations and Industries. Lists "published articles" by
    Industry and by Company name. Updated weekly.
Fortune Magazine's 500.
Fortune's Plant and Product Directory.
The Foundation Directory.
Investor, Banker, Broker Almanac.
MacRae's Blue Book.
Moody's Industrial Manual (and other manuals).
National Trade and Professional Associations of the United States and
    Canada and Labor Unions (Garrett Park Press).
Plan Purchasing Directory.
Poor's Register of Corporations, Directors and Executives (may be
    indexed under "Standard and Poor's"). Key executives in 32,000
    leading companies, plus 75,000 directors.

Research Centers Directory
Register of Manufacturers for your state or area (e.g. California Manu-
    facturers Register).
Standard Register of Advertisers.
Standard and Poor's Corporation Records.
Standard and Poor's Industrial Index.
Standard and Poor's Listed Stock Reports (at some broker's office).
Statistical Abstract of the United States (U.S. Department of Commerce).
Thomas' Register of American Manufacturers.
Value Line Investment Survey, from Arnold Bernard and Co.,
    5 East 44th Street, New York, N.Y. 10017. (Most libraries have
    a set.)
Walker's Manual of Far Western Corporations and Securities.

If all of this seems like an embarrassment of riches to you, and you don't know where to begin, there's even a guide to all these directories:

If you don't know which directory to consult, see
Klein's *Guide to American Directories*,

or

your friendly neighborhood librarian.

Besides the directories, some of these resources may also be worth perusing: Periodicals: *Business Week, Dun's Review, Forbes, Fortune,* and the *Wall Street Journal.*

Trade Associations and their periodicals. Trade journals.

And, of course, you won't just hide yourself away in the libraries all the time. All this information out of books ought to be supplemented with talks with *insiders*—brokers, college alumni, friends, anyone you know who has friends within the particular organizations you are interested in, who can give you helpful insights. Use every contact you know.

No matter how thorough your research, remember when you are finally into the interview at a place that interests you to listen carefully to the employer you are talking to. The greatest problem every employer faces is people who will listen to him and take him seriously. If you listen, you may find he discusses his problems—giving you firmer ground to relate your skills to.

THAT OLD DEBBIL:
THE RESUME

As you do your survey, through interviewing and research, it will become clearer and clearer to you what kind of a position, and at what kind of a place, you are aiming. You are then in a position to write that most formidable of all personal documents: the resume,—if you want one. (Some people prefer to go about this process without one, using themselves instead as "walking resumes.") But, if you want one, there are any number of books that offer samples and suggestions. The best guide, by far, is *Who's Hiring Who*, by Richard Lathrop.

The key to an effective and useful resume is very simple: you must know why you are writing it (to open doors for you, to help people remember you after you've interviewed them, or both), to whom you are writing it (the man who has the power to hire), what you want him to know about you and how you can help him and his organization, and how you can support this claim so as to convince him to reach a favorable decision.

You must know your primary *functional* goal (your strongest skill), plus your primary *organization* goal (where you can do it best).

If you have followed faithfully the techniques suggested by the creative minority (as outlined in these chapters), your resume will show it. Don't, whatever you do, just copy and adapt someone else's resume. It will be self-evident to the reader, that you didn't go through the process in this chapter.

FINAL HINTS

Never put in *anything negative that would cause your resume to be screened out.* Save confessions and excruciating honesty for the confessional. E.g., omit "divorced," if that be your case, because it may imply "quitter" about your future in that organization. (Say "three dependents" or "single" and leave it at that.)

Never lie; but do select your truths carefully. Don't volunteer something negative. Confessions are for the confessional, not for the resume.

And do figure out just exactly why you want a resume in the first place. You got A in Creative Writing? and are dying to use that skill? You should be out seeing people directly instead of inserting a piece of paper between you and them.

Thanks

Hopefully you will remember each night to sit down and write a brief note to each person you saw that day. This is *one of the most essential steps in the whole job-seeking process—and the one most overlooked by job-seekers.* Every professional counsels this step, and yet people overlook it continually. *It should be regarded as basic to courtesy, not to mention kindness, that we thank people who help us along the way.* Call them "bread and butter notes." Or whatever. We all ought to be most serious about this business of saying Thank You. Letters along the way also serve secondary purposes, such as underlining things we said, adding or correcting impressions we left behind us, and confirming our understanding of things the people we talked to said.

Don't forget those secretaries, either. Get their names. Thank them for their help. They will appreciate you, and remember you. If you go to see their boss again; greet them by name (you did jot it down, didn't you?).

After all, you are presenting yourself as one who has one of the most sought-after skills in the world today: Knowing how to treat people as persons. Prove it, please—day by day. You'll get pleasure from it. And, what's more:

It just may get you the job. (According to one survey, job-hunting success was more related to this "thank you note" process than any other factor.) Indeed, we know of one woman who was actually told that she was hired because she was the only interviewee who sent a thank-you note after the interview.

1 Snelling, Robert, *The Opportunity Explosion*. p. 8. (see Appendix A for detail).
2 *The Wall Street Journal*, September 8, 1970.
3 *Who's Hiring Who*, 1977 edition, p. 19.
4 *Dun's Review*, February 1969 issue.
5 According to Vocational Biographies, Sauk Centre, Minnesota.

"You're a bunch of jackasses.
You work your rear ends off in
a trivial course that no one will
ever care about again. You're not
willing to spend time researching
a company that you're interested in
working for. Why don't you
decide who you want to work for
and go after them?"

Professor Albert Shapero
(again) to his students

CHAPTER SEVEN

You must
identify the man
or woman who
has the power
to hire you
and show them
how your skills
can help them
with their
problems

HIRD KEY TO
ᴄAREER-PLANNING AND JOB-HUNTING

As you have gone through all this intensive research concerning the particular places that you have selected as the places you would like to work, you have achieved two deliberate results:

1. *Your list is probably smaller yet,* as you discovered some of the places that interested you (even after visiting them) *did not have the kind of problems or difficulties that your strongest skills could* a) solve; and b) let you enjoy, during the process.

2. You know *a great deal* about the remaining organizations, including—most specifically—*their problems, and what you can do to help solve them.*
You are going to be a very rare bird when you walk in that front door. Organizations love to be loved (so do hospitals, colleges, and everything else). *You know far more than you are ever going to have to use*—in the hiring process anyway. But the depth of your knowledge will show, anyway, in your quiet sense of competence. You know they have problems, and you know you can help solve them.

This fact will be of great interest—most of the time—to the man you go to see, provided you have taken the trouble to identify, learn about, and ask to see *the top executive whose responsibility it is to solve the particular problems that you have zeroed in on.* ("Man" here, of course, embraces "woman".)

That is the man you are going to approach, by name, by appointment: the one man who has the interest, the responsibility and the motivation for hiring *this problem solver: y·o·u·*

You are going to ask to see *him,* and you are going to stay *far away* from

THAT ORGANIZATION'S PERSONNEL DEPARTMENT

This advice is given by just about every book or counselor that you can turn to: Albee, Crystal, Haldane, Harper, Kent, Miller, Miner, Shapero, Snelling, Townsend, and Uris—to name just a few who are listed in our bibliography.

The advice is stated strongly by many experts:

⭐ the personnel department in most companies,
they say, is at the bottom of the social and
executive totem pole; it rarely hears of middle-
high level vacancies even within its own
company; when it does know of the vacancies,
it rarely has power to hire; it can only
screen out applicants, and refer those who
survive, on up to higher executives; therefore avoid this department like the plague.

Professors in some graduate business schools are predicting that personnel departments are either on the way out or on the way to drastic restructuring.

In the meantime, men and women aspiring to jobs above entry-level are advised to go nowhere near these departments. Even executive secretaries would be well-advised to steer clear of the personnel department, and follow these techniques.

Instead, you are going to have to do enough research— using *Poor's Register, Who's Who in Commerce and Industry, Who's Who In America, Who's Who in the East,* and any other resources—such as periodicals—that your friendly neighborhood librarian can suggest, so that in each organization you know who is the *top man responsible for solving the*

problem that you can help solve, at that organization. *If in doubt, go higher, rather than lower.*

And it will help greatly if you know something about that man too, so you don't step on his *known prejudices,* if you can help it. (After all, he's as entitled to his *tropisms—the things we instinctively go toward, or away from—*as you and I are.) If you were referred to him by someone, earlier, that someone may be able to give you some helpful background at this point.

WELL, YOU WANT TO SEE HIM OR HER, BUT DOES HE OR SHE WANT TO SEE YOU?

This is the question that bothers almost everyone new to the job-hunt. We sort of just assume the answer is no. But, on the contrary,

Ten to one the answer is yes. Young or older; male or female.

First of all, you may have already met, during the process of your own personal survey of your chosen geographical area and field.

He or she may have liked you.

He or she may even have offered you a job (this happens many times) during the personal survey process. And, as we said earlier, you told him or her at that time the Absolute Truth: which was that you were flattered, that you would certainly keep it in mind, but that at this point you weren't ready to say yet just exactly where it was that you wanted to work. But now you are ready, and you call to tell him or her so.

On the other hand, maybe the two of you didn't meet before.

Even so, he or she is interested. The odds are 10-1 you've figured out someone who'll refer you, and act as your link to him or her; but even lacking that referral you still can tell him or her that *you want to talk to him or her about some of the problems of the organization, and what you've discovered that might be helpful to him or her.*

That's a switch!

Most of the time, when he or she does interviewing (for hiring, or otherwise) people are there to tell him or her what *he or she* can do for them.

Now, you offer to come in and tell him or her what *you* can do for *him or her.*

Is he or she interested?

Odds are ten to one he or she is.

(If he or she is not, maybe you'd better re-evaluate whether you really want to work for this kind of guy or gal. And if you decide you still do, maybe you're going to have to convince him or her that he or she should hire you—even if he or she has to establish a new function or position, at a senior level, just for you. E. A. Butler, incidentally, tells an interesting story of how he persisted with an employer until he got a job (p. 10 in his book).

THIS GUY OR GAL YOU ARE GOING TO SEE IS JUST LIKE YOU, BUT UNDER REAL STRESS

The creative minority in this field have correctly pointed out that one of the reasons the hiring process in America today (at the above-$10,000 level) is so difficult, is because of the great stress involved.

Let's look at some of those sources of stress:

1. The odds are very great that the executive who does the interviewing was hired because of what he or she could contribute to the company, and not because he or she was such a great interviewer. In fact, his or her gifts in this field may be rather miserable.

2. He or she can't entrust the process to someone else, because he or she has got to live with him/her afterward. So, hiring-interviews for above entry-level positions have a heavy accent of "I wish I could get someone else to do this for me, but I just can't."

3. If the man or woman with the power to hire makes a mistake, he or she is going to rub shoulders with that mistake, chances are. He or she doesn't usually hire someone, and then never see him or her ever again. An executive who has the responsibility of hiring for this position is given (or takes) that responsibility away from the personnel department *because this position is directly under his or her own and he or she is going to have to live with whomever is hired, day by d*⸺

4. If he or she hires a mistake, it's going to make him or her look very bad with his or her superiors, board of directors, stockholders, or whoever it is that he or she reports to.

5. If he or she hires a mistake and he or she isn't the chief executive yet, this could cost him or her a promotion personally —since he or she has proved he or she has bad judgment; and maybe his or her department is getting botched up—to boot.

6. If he or she hires a mistake, it's going to cost money. $30,000 for a top manager, $10-15,000 for a middle manager, $3,500 for a lower-middle manager (according to a study done by R. G. Barry Corporation, of Columbus, Ohio). That's what it costs in "orientation time" for the new exec and those around him or her. And all wasted, if the new employee doesn't pan out; and having to be spent all over again on whoever is hired after him or her.

Not bad. In one twenty-minute interview (or even several of same), the man or woman with the power to hire can botch up part of the organization, cost the organization a great deal of money, lose his or her own promotion, be called to account, and acquire a whole new set of ulcers. No wonder hiring is such a stressful situation.

A man or woman could be forgiven for wanting never to do it. But hiring is unavoidable. Experts estimate a good president spends 25% of his or her time (of necessity) in looking for new talent within his or her own ranks, and outside.

Failing to get rid of the responsibility entirely, a president (or whoever) could be forgiven for praying at least for a new way to do it—*one with much less stress b⸱ilt in.*

YOU OFFER A PLEASANT LOW STRESS INTERVIEW

This is where you come in.

You are following the suggestions of the creative minority, who all are united in this: *create a situation where you and the man or woman with the power to hire you for a position you want, can get a look at each other—without having to make a big decision.*

If the man-or-woman-with-the-power-to-hire met you during your personal survey of the economic picture in the area, or while you were developing "remembrance and referral" contacts, or now—in your role of problem-solver—he or she had a chance to see you in what is—for him or her—a low stress situation. It is a form of talent *window shopping*.

You come into his or her office on one mission—Mr. or Ms. Researcher, or Surveyor or whatever; but the man or woman with the power to hire you has a chance to look at you surreptitiously as Mr. or Ms. Possible-Human-Resource-for-My-Organization.

All the creative minority who have studied the career transition process and the job-hunt are agreed in this: any way you can let an executive windowshop you, without your putting him or her on the spot, will create a very favorable situation for you.

With this clue firmly in your hand, you may be able to think up an even more inventive approach to the man or woman with the power to hire, in each organization. If so, more power to you.

But let's be very clear about one thing: you are going to show him or her how your skills can help him or her with his or her problems *as he or she perceives them*. We cannot stress this strongly enough. You may think you perceive a problem that he or she is absolutely blind to, in that organization, but if so, you are going to have to very delicately and very skillfully explore how he or she perceives that particular problem area, before you hit him or her over the head with your brilliant insight into it all.

We ourselves have had would-be job-hunters approach *us* for a job and confidently tell us that we desperately needed a person with such and such skills (which they just happened to possess) in order to accomplish—and then they proceeded to lay out some goals and priorities for our organization (the National Career Development Project) which we had already consciously rejected as part of our plan. But they didn't know that because they hadn't done their homework.

As you sit across the table from the man or woman you'd most like to work for, it is crucial that you relate your skills to what's going on in their head, not merely to what's going on in yours. If I'm dying for lack of a creative artist in my organization, and you walk in and show me you have genuine skills in that area, you are interpreting your skills in terms of my problems. But if I have long since decided I don't need any more help with art work, and you try to sell me on the idea that I need one (namely, you), you are falling into the pitfall of interpreting your skills in terms of *your* problems, not mine.

DOES THIS ALWAYS WORK?

No one can absolutely guarantee you a job exactly where you want it, doing exactly what you want, at the salary you want. But most people who follow the method set forth in these last three chapters get very close—with perhaps some compromises—and some succeed in virtually every particular.

This method is, in any event, so far superior to the traditional form of the job-hunt, that it ought to be taught to every job-hunter in this country, and especially to those above the most menial level.

With the traditional numbers game, as you will recall, a man had to send out 300-500 resumes, in order to get 3-5 interviews, and one or two job offers—assuming he was lucky.

On the other hand, with this method, you might have the same experience as did one man (among many we could cite): 107 places that looked interesting in the geographical area he chose, 297 letters sent to them (and 126 phone calls) followed by a visit to the area where he had 45 low-stress interviews as part of his personal economic survey, resulting in 35 job offers—including exactly the job he wanted.

For job-hunters in the process of career transition, this method is infinitely superior to any other—particularly if you are trying to avoid not merely un-employment but the even greater danger of under-employment.

INTERVIEWS, RESUMES, SALARY NEGOTIATIONS

Books on the job-hunt often devote the bulk of their contents to these three topics. We have practically ignored them. There are reasons.

First of all, it is perfectly possible for you to get a job without ever being trained in interview techniques, ever getting together a resume, or knowing the art of salary negotiations ... provided you follow the techniques in these last three chapters faithfully, step by step.

Secondly, by following those techniques, you get constant practice in the art of talking with high level management— which is, after all, what we mean by that dreadful word *interviewing*. Your self-confidence improves, which is—after all—the key to successful interviews, for you. You get this practice in low stress situations.

Thirdly, if you pick up the materials we recommend in Appendix B you will find that Lathrop's book gives some helpful instructions about the interview, the resume, and salary negotiations for the reader who feels he or she needs more guidance in these areas; it would be folly for us simply to duplicate here the very things that it explains most carefully.

We will however, give an interview check list here, to be sure you are "up" on what all the books say, as you think through these three special hurdles in the job hunt.

INTERVIEW CHECK LIST

In preparing yourself for an interview, when it comes, you can of course be *really* thorough and try to figure out what is going on in the mind of that guy or gal sitting on the other side of the desk, by reading their own training manuals (like, *The Interviewer's Manual* by Henry H. Morgan and John W. Cogger — available at your local library or from The Psychological Corporation, 757 Third Avenue, New York, New York 10017 — $7.50.) This is, of course, taking the optimistic view, and assuming that your interviewer has had time to read a manual about interviewing.

If you want to take the more realistic view you will assume that every interviewer is a complete individual in his or her own right, and that you don't know anything about that interviewer except that a) he or she has *enthusiasms*. If you've done your homework thoroughly you have some idea what these are. If you haven't done your homework, use the interview to try to discover what they are; b) he or she has *problems*. Again, if you have done your homework, you have some idea what they are. Again, if you didn't do your homework, try to use the interview to discover what *he* or *she* thinks those problems are; c) he or she has certain questions they're dying to ask you. These latter kinds of curiosities are crucial to you, and — as the most expert career counselor in the country, John Crystal, points out — they tend to fall into three major categories:

1. WHY ARE YOU HERE? Why have you chosen this particular place to come to? If you've done all the research recommended earlier in this book, and followed the steps in funneling (p. 124) you'll *know* the answer. If you haven't, you won't.

2. PRECISELY WHAT CAN YOU DO FOR ME? You will talk about his (or her) problems to the degree that you have been able to guess at them, and also listen very carefully to what he (or she) has to say. If new factors are revealed, field them as best you can; all the while showing how your skills can help with those problems. Within this category of questions, be prepared also for the particular form of: after you got this job, if you did, how would you start out?

3. HOW MUCH IS IT GOING TO COST ME? He or she probably has a range in mind (with a two to three thousand dollar variation), if you're seeking a job above the very lowest level. If you have done your research thoroughly, you probably have some idea at least of what that range is. Therefore, you will need to quote it at this point, adding that money isn't everything and you are interested in the opportunity and challenge as well.

As can be seen, the research we have exhorted you to do in these chapters previously, is absolutely key to your successful conduct of an interview, and the fielding of these categories of questions. You will be at a disadvantage precisely to the degree that you have tried to cut corners or short-circuit the whole process described in these Chapters (5-7).

Do remember to look professional. Have a good-looking suit (or dress) on, a decent haircut (or coiffure), clean fingernails, dentally cleaned teeth, deodorant, shined shoes, no smoking or pre-drinking—clean breath. It may seem like a silly game to you, but it's a game with very high stakes, in which you want to be the winner. (Check chart on page 176.)

There are certain questions no employer is any longer allowed to ask you—unless they are BFOQ's— "bona fide occupational qualifications."

Here are some interview guidelines that one major California company has drawn up for its managers and supervisors:

SUBJECT	**CAN** DO OR ASK	**CAN NOT** DO OR ASK
Your sex—	Notice your appearance.	Make comments or take notes, unless sex is a BFOQ.
Marital status—	Status after hiring, for insurance purposes.	Are you married? Single? Divorced? Engaged? Living with anyone? Do you see your ex-spouse?
Children—	Numbers and ages of children after hiring, for insurance purposes.	Do you have children at home? How old? Who cares for them? Do you plan more children?
Physical data—	Explain manual labor, lifting, other requirements of the job. Show how it is performed. Require physical examination.	How tall are you? How much do you weigh?
Criminal record—	If security clearance is necessary, can be done prior to employment.	Have you ever been arrested, convicted or spent time in jail?
Military —	Are you a veteran? Why not? Any job-related experience?	What type of discharge do you have? What branch did you serve in?
Age—	Age after hiring. "Are you over 18?"	How old are you? Estimate age.
Housing—	If you have no phone, how can we reach you?	Do you own your home? Do you rent? Do you live in an apartment or a house?

As a job applicant, what can you do if you are asked one of these illegal questions? The Wall Street Journal pointed out you have three courses of action:

"1. Answer the question and ignore the fact that it is not legal.

"2. Answer the question with the statement: 'I think that is not relevant to the requirements of the position.'

"3. Contact the nearest Equal Employment Opportunity Commission office.

"Unless the violation is persistent, is demeaning, or you can prove it resulted in your not being employed, number three should probably be avoided. The whole area is too new; many interviewers are just not totally conversant with the code requirements.

"Answer number 2 is probably, in most circumstances, the best to give. There are times when it may cost you the job, but are you that interested in working for someone who is all that concerned about your personal life?"

Whatever the interviewer may ask about your past, (like, why did you leave your last job?) remember the only thing he (or she) can possibly be really interested in is the future (under what circumstances might you leave me?).

Never volunteer negative information about yourself.

And now for some final thoughts about this whole matter.

Never accept a job on the spot, or reject one. And, unless you are talking with a very "liberated" employer, do not say, I need to talk with my mate (it implies you are not a decision maker on your own.) Just say, "I need some time to weigh this."

SALARY NEGOTIATION

A woman was once describing her very first job to me. It was at a soda fountain. I asked her what her biggest surprise at that job was. "My first paycheck," she said. "I know it sounds incredible, but I was so green at all this, that during the whole interview for the job it never occurred to me to ask what my salary would be. I just took it for granted that it would be a fair and just salary, for the work that I would be doing. Did I ever get a shock, when my first paycheck came! It was so small, I could hardly believe it. Did I ever learn a lesson from that!" Yes, and so may we all.

AT ITS SIMPLEST LEVEL

To speak of salary negotiation is to speak of a matter which can be conducted on several levels. The simplest kind— as the above story reminds us—involves remembering to ask during the job-hiring interview, what the salary will be. And then stating whether, for you, that amount is satisfactory or not. *That* much negotiation, everyone who is hunting for a job must be prepared to do.

It is well to recognize that you—or the students or clients that you are trying to teach about job-hunting, if you are a career counselor—are at a disadvantage if salary negotiation is

Average hourly and weekly earnings of production or non-supervisory workers on private non-agricultural payrolls, by industry

Industry	Average Hourly Earnings				Average Weekly Earnings			
	Jan. 1975	Nov. 1975	Dec. 1975p	Jan. 1976p	Jan. 1975	Nov. 1975	Dec. 1975	Jan. 1976p
TOTAL PRIVATE	$4.40	$4.68	$4.68	$4.72	$157.08	$169.42	$170.82	$170.39
Seasonally adjusted	4.41	4.68	4.68	4.73	159.64	169.88	170.35	173.12
MINING	5.69	6.11	6.15	6.22	238.98	262.73	265.07	263.11
CONTRACT CONSTRUCTION	7.07	7.45	7.46	7.55	250.99	270.44	275.27	272.56
MANUFACTURING	4.67	4.93	5.00	5.01	180.73	197.69	204.00	199.40
DURABLE GOODS	4.95	5.29	5.38	5.36	195.53	213.72	222.73	215.47
Ordnance and accessories	4.98	5.44	5.54	5.52	207.17	226.85	231.02	230.18
Lumber and wood products	4.05	4.41	4.43	4.39	149.85	172.87	178.53	172.97
Furniture and fixtures	3.64	3.82	3.86	3.83	130.68	150.13	154.79	147.84
Stone, clay, and glass products	4.67	5.06	5.07	5.06	185.87	207.46	209.39	203.41
Primary metal industries	5.93	6.43	6.47	6.44	240.17	257.20	262.68	256.31
Fabricated metal products	4.78	5.22	5.30	5.30	190.24	212.45	220.48	214.12
Machinery, except electrical	5.17	5.54	5.61	5.60	215.07	227.69	236.18	230.72
Electrical equipment	4.43	4.70	4.76	4.76	173.21	188.00	194.21	188.02
Transportation equipment	5.77	6.25	6.40	6.33	223.88	256.25	276.48	258.90
Instruments and related products	4.42	4.64	4.75	4.78	173.71	186.99	194.28	191.20
Miscellaneous manufacturing	3.73	3.87	3.93	3.99	139.88	150.93	155.24	153.62
NON-DURABLE GOODS	4.23	4.45	4.48	4.53	159.05	176.67	179.65	178.48
Food and kindred products	4.42	4.70	4.75	4.79	175.03	189.88	194.28	193.04
Tobacco manufactures	4.34	4.40	4.52	4.79	160.58	178.20	175.83	190.16
Textile mill products	3.29	3.53	3.55	3.56	117.45	145.44	147.68	144.89
Apparel and other textile products	3.14	3.25	3.26	3.31	104.88	118.30	118.66	118.17
Paper and allied products	4.75	5.21	5.22	5.25	193.80	221.95	225.50	222.60
Printing and publishing	5.16	5.47	5.51	5.58	189.89	204.58	209.93	206.46
Chemicals and allied products	5.15	5.56	5.58	5.65	208.58	230.74	234.92	233.35
Petroleum and coal products	5.88	6.66	6.68	7.00	241.67	281.72	279.89	295.40
Rubber and plastics products, nec.	4.23	4.44	4.51	4.53	165.82	178.93	185.36	184.37
Leather and leather products	3.15	3.28	3.30	3.36	111.51	126.61	128.70	128.02
TRANSPORTATION AND PUBLIC UTILITIES	5.67	6.19	6.19	6.24	224.53	245.12	245.74	248.98
WHOLESALE AND RETAIL TRADE	3.65	3.83	3.82	3.90	121.55	128.69	130.64	130.26
WHOLESALE TRADE	4.74	5.02	5.04	5.07	182.49	194.27	197.57	196.21
RETAIL TRADE	3.24	3.41	3.40	3.47	103.03	109.46	111.52	110.35
FINANCE, INSURANCE & REAL ESTATE	3.99	4.24	4.23	4.29	147.23	155.18	153.97	156.59
SERVICES	3.94	4.22	4.24	4.28	132.78	142.21	142.46	144.24

approached on this simplest level, however. A figure may be named, and you are totally unprepared to say whether this is a fair salary for that particular job, or not. You just don't know.

AT ITS NEXT HIGHEST LEVEL

Hence, you may prefer to do a little research *ahead* of time. Before you ever get in there, for that interview. This is taking salary negotiation to its next highest level. Visiting the library in your community, before you interview for hiring.

If it's a non-supervisory job, you can find out what a 'ball-park figure' for a particular industry might be by having the reference librarian, or general librarian, find the following sort of Table for you. (See the Table on page 168.) Just add approximately 7% for each year that has elapsed since January 1976.

If it's a supervisory job, or one at a higher level than non-supervisory, you will find that the College Placement Council, with some frequency publishes reports on salaries being offered in various industries to college graduates. While this is of primary interest to such graduates, the "Salary Surveys" of the Council do give some guidance, at least, to other job-hunters. See your library, or the career counseling and placement office of a nearby college—rather than buying this Survey, as it is available only to members of the Council and/ or to subscribers to their Journal Publications Group.

If the job you're looking for information about is not in either of the above sorts of places, there is always the *Occupational Outlook Handbook* in your local library, which has the best available information on earnings in the most popular occupations. You will discover that the only trouble with such information is that it covers all geographic regions in the U.S., all industries, and all periods of economic fluctuations. In other words, the figures are very general.

Your library may have more detailed information for your particular region, regarding the occupation that you are interested in. Witness the following example:

Average Weekly	$295.00	Detroit, Michigan
Earnings of	226.00	Dayton, Ohio
Lead	215.50	Chicago, Illinois
Draftsmen	206.00	Houston, Texas
	193.00	Seattle, Washington
	189.50	Columbus, Ohio
Surveys were	175.00	Salt Lake City, Utah
made at	173.00	Scranton, Pennsylvania
various times	172.50	Raleigh, North Carolina
in	162.50	Little Rock, Arkansas
1970-71.		

REGION

$213.50	North Central
202.00	Northeast
199.00	West
192.00	South
204.00	United States

The figures show the fluctuation from region to region may be quite wide. Though it is important to remember that this depends on the particular occupation that you are interested in. For lead draftspersons, Detroit pays more than any other city. With regard to other occupations, however, Detroit may be at the bottom of the list.

If your librarian simply cannot find for you, or help you find, the salary information that you want, remember that almost every occupation has its own association or professional group, whose business it is to keep tabs on what is happening salary-wise within that occupation or field. For people interested, by way of example, in the guidance and counseling field, there is the American Personnel and Guidance Association. And it has published a modest volume entitled, "Compen$ation *(sic)* in the Guidance and Counseling Field, 1974." Other associations have similar data (in most cases) at their fingertips. To learn the association or professional group for the field or occupation you are interested in, consult the *Encyclopedia of Associations, Vol. 1,* at your library.

Some job-hunters—you, perhaps, or the clients/students you are helping—may want to get beyond these "ball-park figures" into more detailed salary negotiation. They—or you —may want to walk in on an interview knowing exactly what That Place pays for a job. Why? Well, for one thing, it may be too low for you—and thus you are saved the necessity of wasting your precious time on that particular place. Secondly, and more importantly, many places have—as John Crystal has so insistently pointed out—a *range* in mind. And if you know what that range is, you can negotiate for a salary that is nearer the top of the range, than the bottom.

So, let us say that you have done some extensive home-work—such as is represented by *The Quick Job-Hunting Map* or by the process described in *Where Do I Go From Here With My Life²*. And you have gotten it down, by means of the Information Survey, to three or five places that really interest you. You know in general what sort of position you are aiming at, in those particular places—and you are ready to go back and visit them in The Interview for Hiring—*as soon as you know what the salary range is, that they probably have in mind for the position that interests you* (whether that position already exists, or is one you are going to ask them to create). How do you find out what the salary is, or should be, by way of range?

It's relatively easy to Define, as—again—John Crystal has taught us all. The rule of thumb is that you will, generally speaking, be paid more than the person who is below you on the organizational chart, and less than the person who is above you. There are—needless to say—exceptions to this rule: people who don't quite fit in the organizational chart, such as researchers financed by a grant, or consultants, and who—consequently—may be paid much more than the people who are theoretically above them. But In General, the Rule of Thumb is true.

This makes the matter of salary *research* (which precedes salary negotiation) relatively (I said "relatively") simple. If through your own information search you could discover who is (or would be) above you on the organizational chart, and who is (or would be) below you, and what they are paid, you would know what your salary range is, or would be.

It works out like this:

IF THE PERSON BELOW YOU MAKES:

| $6240 | $10,000 | $22,000 |

AND THE PERSON ABOVE YOU MAKES:

| $7800 | $13,500 | $27,000 |

YOUR RANGE WILL BE SOMETHING LIKE:

| $6400– | $10,500– | $23,000– |
| 7600 | 12,500 | 26,000 |

So, how do you find this information out?

For openers, you do all the kind of library research that I alluded to, above. Then you go to work on your contacts: you know, everybody who knows you well-enough even to misspell your name. And, you pick up a copy of the annual report and any other literature available on that company or organization. Your goal, of course (to go into Overkill) is to discover:

The Names of the people above and below you, if you were to be hired at that organization. And:

What they make.

You will be surprised at how much of this information is in the annual report, or in books available at your library. When those sources produce all they can for you, and you are still short of what you want to know, go to your contacts. You are looking for Someone Who Knows Someone who either is working, or has worked, at that particular place or organization that interests you.

If you absolutely run into a blank wall on that particular organization (you know, everyone who works there is pledged to secrecy, and they have shipped all their ex-employees to Siberia), then seek out information on their nearest competitor in the same geographic area (e.g., if Wells Fargo is inscrutable, try Bank of America as your research base).

But you will be surprised at how well perseverance and leg-work pays off, in this. And if your enthusiasm flags along the way, just picture yourself sitting in the interview for hiring, and now you're at the end of the interview (the only proper place for discussion of salary to take place, anyway). The prospective employer likes you, you like her or him, and then s/he says: "How much salary were you expecting?" (Employers *love* to toss the ball to you.) Because you have done your homework, and you know the range, you can name a figure near or at the top of the range—based on your anticipated performance in that job: i.e., "Superior."

But suppose you *didn't* do your research. Then you're Shadow-Boxing in the Dark—as they say. If you name a figure way too high, you're out of the running—and you can't backtrack, in most cases ("Sorry, we'd like to hire you, but we just can't afford you.") If you name a figure way too low, you're also out of the running, in many cases ("Sorry, but we were hoping for someone a little more, ah, professional.") And if you're in the right range, but at the bottom of it, you've just gotten the job—*and lost as much as $2,000 a year that could have been yours.*

So, salary research/salary negotiation—no matter how much time it takes—pays off handsomely. Let's say it takes you a week to ten days to run down this sort of information on the organizations that interest you (three to five). And let us say that because you've done this research, when you go in for an interview for hiring, finally, you are able to ask for and obtain a salary that is $2,000 higher in the range, than you would otherwise have known enough to ask for. In just three years, you'll have earned $6,000 extra, because of that research. Not bad pay, for ten days work!

AT ITS MOST SOPHISTICATED LEVEL

Job-hunters with incredibly-developed bargaining needs, always ask how salary negotiation is conducted at its most sophisticated level. It is my personal conviction that Most Job-hunters will not operate at this level, and therefore do not need this sort of information. But in case you do, or in case you are simply dying out of curiosity, it is completely described in *Where Do I Go From Here With My Life,* pp. 140-142. As honed to a fine point by John Crystal, the most sophisticated salary negotiation goes like this:

You do all the steps described immediately above: i.e., you discover what the range would be. Let us say it turns out that the range is one that varies two thousand dollars. You then "invent" a new range, for yourself, that "hooks" on the old one, in the following fashion:

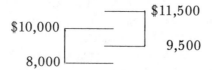

And when the employer says, "What kind of a salary did you have in mind?" you respond, "I believe my productivity is such that it would command a salary in the range of $9,500 to $11,500." This keeps you, at a minimum, near the top of his or her range; and, at a maximum, challenges him or her to go beyond the top that s/he had in mind, either immediately —or in terms of *promised* raises. (Don't be afraid, even as Elwood P. Doud was not, to ask "When?")

FRINGES

In all your research, and ultimate negotiation, do not forget to pay attention to so-called "fringe benefits". In 1974, such 'fringes' as life insurance, health benefits or plans, vacation or holiday plans, and retirement programs, added up to 25% of manufacturing-workers salary, e.g., if an employee received $800 salary per month, his or her fringe benefits were worth another $200 per month. So, if the employee who is beneath you on the organizational chart gets $700 plus benefits, and the employee who is above you gets $1100 plus benefits, while you during the hiring interview are offered $800 *and no benefits,* you will need to negotiate for more than $1000 salary, in order to make up for that lack of benefits.

Of course, if you don't need that extra money—or you couldn't care less that the person below you makes more than you do,—great! But just in case you do, keep this in mind.

FINALLY, THE MATTER OF THOSE RAISES

Salary negotiation, during the hiring interview, ultimately is more than just a matter of negotiation for your Starting

Salary. It is ultimately a matter of negotiating for your Yearly or Semi-yearly Raises, as well. "When, and under what circumstances, can I expect to have my salary raised?" needs not only to be asked, but to be put in writing—if there is a letter of agreement, or any kind of contract forthcoming from your would-be employer. The Road to Hell is paved with Promises that are unwritten, and which employers *conveniently* forget once you are hired. Moreover, employers Leave, and their successor or their own boss may disown unwritten promises ("I don't know what caused him or her to say that to you, but s/he clearly exceeded his/her authority, and we can't be held to that.")

Against That Day, it will pay you to keep a diary, weekly, of your achievements at work, so that when time for discussing raises comes around, you can document—with a one or two page summary—just exactly what you have accomplished there, and why you deserve that raise. . . as Bernard Haldane explains in his classic *How To Make A Habit of Success* (Warner Books, P.O. Box 690, New York, N.Y. 10019. $1.95 plus 35¢ postage and handling must accompany order).

PROMOTION

We hope *promotion* is not for you a distasteful concept. After all, it means wider responsibility (hopefully), and not just more prestige. It means a widening scope for your desire to be truly helpful to people, and not just (hopefully) an illustration of *The Peter Principle*. Women, in particular, should remember that they are generally so much more underpaid than men, that the average woman would require a 71% pay raise, to bring her up to the level of a similarly qualified man.[5]

Do not forget also, that in only twenty five of the last one hundred years has the cost of living declined and the U.S. dollar gained in buying power. The annual rate of inflation lately has been from 5-15% annually. But even if it remained steadily at that lowest figure, prices ten years from now would still be 50% higher than they are today. A person who made $10,000 in 1970, would need to make $57,435 in

2000 a.d. in order to have exactly the same buying power. That's not all that far away!

What our society calls "promotion" is necessary *just in order to stand still.* Lack of promotion automatically means going backward—in terms of purchasing power for you and your loved ones.

And this says nothing of opportunities for you to operate in increasing spheres of influence and helpfulness.

The end of the matter is this: if you negotiate only for your initial position and salary, you are likely to lose a great deal.

When and only when you're sure he or she wants you, and he or she has made a firm offer, negotiate. And when (and if) it's resolved to your satisfaction, *get it in writing, please.*

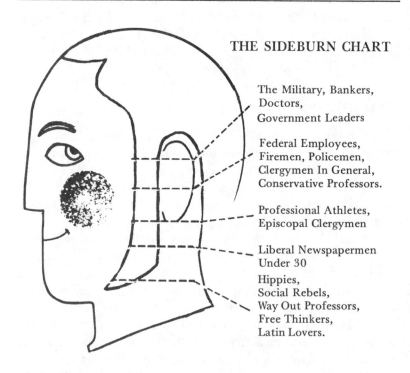

THE SIDEBURN CHART

The Military, Bankers, Doctors, Government Leaders

Federal Employees, Firemen, Policemen, Clergymen In General, Conservative Professors.

Professional Athletes, Episcopal Clergymen

Liberal Newspapermen Under 30

Hippies, Social Rebels, Way Out Professors, Free Thinkers, Latin Lovers.

By permission, from *The Missionary*, Episcopal Diocese of Northern California

FOR THOSE WHO LOVE TO COVER EVERY BASE

If any reader is uncomfortable with the approach given in these last three chapters (and only that approach), feels instinctively that he or she wants to give some time to covering classified ads, visiting agencies, etc., you may perhaps be interested in the advice of the agency set up by Bernard Haldane, which recommends that 20% of one's time (at most) be allocated to these other methods, in view of the fact that only 20% of the jobs over $600 per month are filled through these other methods. *Many going through the job-hunt prefer, however, to give all their time to the method set forth in these pages—with great success; you may want to take this into account in planning your own strategy.*

Remember, in going about all this, you have a tremendous advantage over other job-hunters—and this whole process is, sad to say, at the present time a very competitive business.

You know how to get hired.

In Candide's world, it may be otherwise. But, in this world it remains true:

> He or she who gets hired
> is not necessarily the one
> who can do that job best;
> but, the one who *knows*
> *the most about*
> *how to get hired.*

All men dream... but not equally.
They who dream by night in the dusty recesses
of their minds wake in the day to find that
it is vanity; but the dreamers of the day are
dangerous men, for they act their dream with
open eyes, to make it possible.

T. E. LAWRENCE

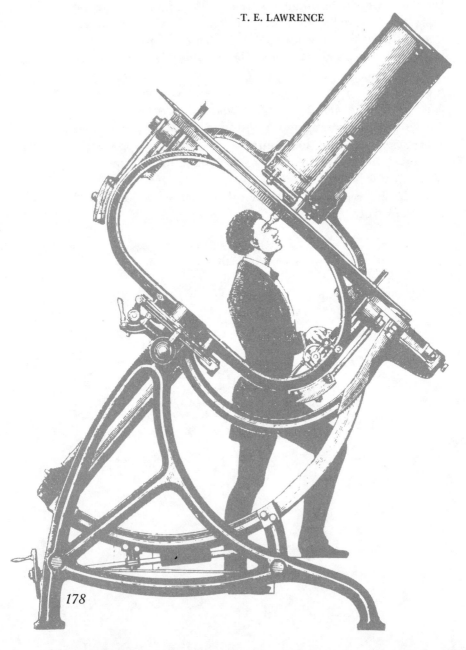

CHAPTER EIGHT

Supplement:

Research Notes for Career Changers (and Others)

People who change their careers have gone into just about every field of endeavor that you can name—including being a politician, doctor, psychiatrist, lawyer, and so forth.

But, there are certain fields of work that career-changers (esp. professionals) seem to choose more often than others, for understandable reasons:

business

social service or change

education

government

self-employment

We are therefore including special notes about these fields and one or two others that people have asked frequently about. *These notes are intended as merely primers for your own research (pump). Most of the research you are still going to have to do yourself.*

SOME RESEARCH NOTES
ABOUT THE FIELD OF BUSINESS

Career-changers who aspire to management positions in the business world usually despair of their unfamiliarity with the business world, and wonder if anyone wants them. Isn't the field crowded already?

Mason Haire, professor of organizational psychology and management at M.I.T. says that before the end of this decade there will be a 40% shortage of people needed to fill management positions that will exist at that time.[1]

In filling management positions, most companies have a penchant for *generalists* who can see "the whole picture" rather than for *specialists* who may suffer from "tunnel vision."

What the businesses need are executives with *people skills.* First of all, this is the way history has moved. The history of the industrial enterprise has focussed successively on Production, Marketing and Distribution, and finally (these days) on the needs of the people making up the organization or being served by the organization.[2]

Most of the problems that an organization faces today are *people problems.* A survey revealed that, in 177 organizations, for every manager who failed to make the grade because of insufficient knowledge, seven failed because of personality problems.[3] Or, as we might prefer to say, because of a lack of "adaptive skills" for that particular environment.

The higher position a man or woman holds, the more he or she has to deal with people. A top executive's major job is to organize resources for the accomplishment of goals. Two-thirds of the average company's resources are *human resources,* i.e., people. It is hardly surprising, therefore, that experts say top executives rarely have more than five minutes to themselves in between their dealing with *people,* and their major task is—in the end—passing judgment upon people.

The qualities being looked for in new executives or managers are:

▶ *authority*—the only authority which succeeds, today, being comprised of (overall) competence + compassion
▶ *ability to work with others*
▶ *communicative skills*—studies[4] have shown that effectiveness is directly correlated with the extent to which a man or woman can express his or her own convictions and feelings and at the same time also express consideration for the thoughts and feelings of others
▶ *intelligence and ability to solve problems*
▶ *perseverance*—the ability to deliver continuously, and not just in spurts; inner motivation
▶ *character, dependability, integrity, maturity*

In other words, intangible assets rather than technical knowledge. Career changers lacking business experience nevertheless offer what business needs in these areas, as *The Wall Street Journal* observed (April 28, 1969).

Ex-pastors, for example, are *generalists,* and they usually possess *people skills* in abundance. If they come out of parish backgrounds, they are accustomed to exercising authority, working with others, and certainly, *communicative skills.* They also usually have intelligence, perseverance and character.

Above all else, they have *clear thinking* and the ability *to get others to accomplish results*—which, as experts like John Crystal have observed, are the only skills really needed at more senior levels in management.

These are the assets all career-changers should stress (assuming you possess them indeed) when it comes time to zero in on the organizations you *want* to work for.

There are few, if any, management positions that are closed. General administration, community relations, man-power development, industrial relations are just some of those that, in the past, career-changers have aimed at, and gotten, in the business world.

Cautions: Career-changers who have been through the mill caution men and women just beginning the process not to be taken in by the title: Executive. That can mean anything from $10,000 to $100,000, with or without a private office, with or without a private phone, with or without a secretary, with or without supervisory powers. *Titles are meaningless.*

For additional research, read Jennings, Eugene E. "Mobicentric Man" in *Psychology Today,* Vol. 4, No. 2, July 1970.

Also: Levinson, Harry, *The Exceptional Executive: A psychological conception.* Cambridge, Mass: Harvard University Press, 1968. $7.25. And: Archer, Jules, *The Executive "Success,"* New York: The Universal Library, Grosset & Dunlap, 1970, $1.95. A description of the executive "rat race" for any dreamers who think the world out there is that much different.

Coming Attractions: in case you want to get into fields or industries that look big, do some research on the energy field, the pollution field, the field of privacy (making it possible to ignore one's neighbor), the field of protection (against burglary, invasion, etc.), the field of leisure and the field of release from personal tension. But take all such predictions with a large grain (not to say, barrel) of salt.

Also Coming: experts prophesy, more hopefully than realistically, in view of women's liberation movements more women in management (30% by 1980, some insiders predict).

SOME RESEARCH NOTES ABOUT THE FIELD
OF SOCIAL SERVICE OR CHANGE

There are the obvious old-time occupations in this field, such as *social work, case work,* etc. There is also a whole new concern, in this country, for what are called *public service careers* or *human service occupations.*

Community colleges are spearheading this concern, since the concern is focussed upon minorities and the disadvantaged. Information, consequently, can often be procured from the Community Colleges division of your State Department of Education.

Public service careers may be with government (Federal, or state, or local), with nonprofit organizations, with agencies (independent of State or local government, but often cooperating with them), with colleges (particularly community colleges), etc.

Public service careers include such varied occupations as *Community Services Officer* at a Community College, *recreation educator, city planner, social service technician* (working with any or all agencies that deliver social services), *welfare administration, gerontology specialist* (for further information, contact—among others—your State Commission on Aging).

Other careers: *Workers with the handicapped, public health officials* (see your State Department of Public Health, or the Chief Medical Doctor at the county Public Health Agency—the Doctor being the best informed person about *opportunities*), *officials dealing with the foster parent program for mentally retarded persons, workers in the child welfare program,* and so forth.

If you are interested in this general field of social service, you ought to do extensive research, including talking with national associations in the fields that interest you, State departments, county, city. And do not forget college people. They have a whole bag of positions, themselves, such as: *Division Director in Human Service Careers, Director of the Department of Human Services* (write Vermont College's Department of Behavioral Science, Montpelier, Vermont, for further information).

Do not overlook the fact that it is very possible to create your own job. For example, in California, for several years now, the State of California has collected an override tax of 5¢ per person, which is designated for the one or more community colleges that are in each particular county, *to be used for community services.* Many of the one hundred Community Colleges in that State could be approached by career changers who could sell themselves for the job of Community Services Officer at that college, a new job to be paid for out of these designated tax funds.

Thorough research on your part will often reveal other ways in which *funding can be found for positions not yet created if you know exactly what it is you want to do,* and find out who knows something about this.

Potential employers for social or public service occupations include social welfare agencies, public health departments, correctional institutions, government offices, Economic Opportunity Offices, hospitals, rest homes, schools, parks and recreation agencies, etc.

As a research aid, there is *Human Service Organizations: A Book of Readings.* Ann Arbor, Michigan: The University of Michigan Press (615 East University, Ann Arbor, Michigan 48106). Paper, $7.95. Deals with an analysis of the structure of schools, employment agencies, mental health clinics, correctional institutions, welfare agencies and hospitals. If you're thinking about going to work in one of these human service organizations, this could help your research.

For those interested in working in State and local government, a most helpful resource is the Western Governmental Research Association, 109 Moses Hall, University of California, Berkeley, CA 94720. They have monthly compilations of employment opportunities in *The Jobfinder,* as well as much other helpful material. They are trying to attract people with integrity into local government.

Now, for those interested more particularly in *working for social change,* your first and most helpful resource has got to be Vocations for Social Change, 5951 Canning St., Oakland, CA 94609, who publish a newsletter called *Work Force* (no charge, but a donation as generous as possible would help

VSC in its unique mission... They also publish a journal for middle-aged dropouts, entitled "The Yin Times" of Black Bart. (Irv Thomas, Editor, Box 48, Canyon, CA 94516).

If you are interested in social change *personally*—that is to say, you are interested in exploring Alternatives not merely in your choice of Work, but also in your lifestyle, choice of technologies, use of resources, etc., there are—as you may be aware from visiting any "Alternatives Bookstore" or "Headshop"—a whole library of helpful books and catalogs to help you out. A comparatively new one is *Rainbook: Resources for Appropriate Technology,* published by a group of people in Portland, Oregon who have been experimenting with "living better with less," for some years now. It costs $7.95, paper, and is available from RAIN, 2270 N.W. Irving, Portland, OR 97210 (503) 227-5110. They also publish a magazine called RAIN, which updates the book.

But if it's more specifically in the area of your work, that you are interested in social change, there are resources to help you do your research *before* you come down to that more immediate decision as to which places interest you the most. One such resource is *Profiles of Involvement* (Human Resources Corporation, Philadelphia, Pa. 1972. $50) which describes and evaluates the social involvement of corporations, organizations, government agencies, banks, non-profit organizations, etc. Very helpful to anyone doing research on the social involvement of potential employers. See your local library.

There is also the *Corporate Action Guide* published by the Corporate Action Project, 1500 Farragut St., N.W., Washington, D.C. 20011 (1974) which is an information guide about corporate power and how it works. ($2.95 with postage).

Finally, there is: *What's Happening To Our Jobs?* by Steve Babson and Nancy Bingham, published by Popular Economics Press, Box 221, Somerville, MA 02143, 1976. $1.45 paperback. An anti-establishment radical analysis of the job-market in toto.

SOME RESEARCH NOTES ABOUT THE FIELD OF EDUCATION

Types of positions typically sought by job-hunters who are new to this field—whether fresh out of college or coming to it later in life—are in the traditional teaching positions in school situations, etc. This is especially true of Ph.D.s. When they run into a tight labor market, as has been the case thus far in the '70s, they often quickly conclude they must abandon their desire to teach, and go hunting for some other kind of employment altogether.

You would do well not to make this error. The range of places that use people with teaching skills is mind-boggling: but as just a sampling, there are—as experts like John Crystal point out—training academies (like fire and police); corporate training and education departments; local and state councils on higher education; designers and manufacturers of educational equipment; teachers associations; foundations; private research firms; regional and national associations of universities, etc.; state and congressional legislative committees on education; specialized educational publishing houses; professional and trade societies. An indication of some of the possibilities you may want to research, can be found in *Education Directory: Education Associations 1974.* It's available in your local library, or from the Superintendent of Documents, U.S. Government Printing Office, Washington D.C. 20402 — $1.50. Stock Number: 1780-01279.

Moreover, the range of jobs that are done within the broad definition of Education are multitudinous and very varied;

186

just for openers, there is: *teaching* (of course), *counseling* (an honorable teaching profession, where it isn't just used by a school system as the repository for teachers who couldn't 'cut it' as teachers), *general administration, adult education programs, public relations, ombudsman,* and such.

All of which is to say, just because you have defined your dream of life for yourself as "teacher" doesn't mean you have even begun to narrow that down sufficiently to go looking for a job. You still have more research, and information gathering to do, before you have defined exactly what kind of teaching, with what kind of groups, in what kind of place. In other words, Chapters 5-7 in this manual apply to you as much, or even more, as to anyone else.

To get you started, there is the dated but suggestive *New Roles for Educators: A Sourcebook of Career Information* prepared for the Harvard Graduate School of Education Placement Office, by Rita E. Weathersby. (Available from Harvard Graduate School of Education, Publications Office, Longfellow Hall, Appian Way, Cambridge, MA 02138. $3.50, prepaid). Or, on a somewhat more elementary level, there is *New Careers for Teachers* by Bill McKee (Henry Regnery Company, 180 N. Michigan Avenue, Chicago, IL 60601, 1972, $4.95).

Along the way in your research, if you are particularly interested in Community Colleges (which in many ways are good places for career-changers to begin), you will want to order a copy of the fact sheet "Teaching in the Community-Junior College" from the American Association of Community and Junior Colleges, One Dupont Circle, N.W., Washington, D.C. 20036. It lists a number of places to pursue in your research. If you want to know what community colleges are in your chosen geographical area, ask the AACJC for their Community, Junior, and Technical College Directory. ($7.00).

If you are interested in working abroad, the states of Victoria, Queensland, Tasmania or West Australia (at this writing), have had a great need for teachers, and Dr. C. N. Pederson operates a selection program from Burwood State College, Burwood Road, Burwood, Victoria, Australia: you may wish to contact her. The Department of Education,

No. 30 Bridge Street, Sidney, New South Wales 2000 sometimes recruits candidates for that State. You can write either
or both of these offices, to find out what the present
situation is.

SOME RESEARCH NOTES ABOUT
THE FIELD OF GOVERNMENT

The diversity of jobs in government (or public service) is
very great. You must decide, first of all, whether you want to
work for *Federal, State, County, Municipal* or *Other Agencies
of a quasi-governmental nature* (redevelopment agencies, regional councils of governments, special district governments,
etc.).

Each of these employs personnel in a great variety of occupations, including *administrative assistant, human relations
specialist*, and others.

All government budgets today are suffering from tight con-
straints, the like of which have not been encountered for many
years. To the extent that you go through traditional routes
to governmental positions (Civil service examinations, etc.)
you are going to face stiff competition. If you go this route,
find out all you can about it first (Warren Barker in *Bearings*

Washington office has pointed out that there are special things that ex-clergy in particular should know: e.g., "How many people were you in charge of?"—*put down total number of volunteers, and not just paid full-time staff under you*).

If you have identified your skills at a high enough level, however, and go to see the one person who has the power to hire you (Chapter Seven), you may avoid all of this level of competition, examinations, etc. Many *have* done this, successfully.

INFORMATION SOURCES (AMONG MANY):

United States Civil Service Commission, *Guide to Federal Career Literature*. Washington D.C.: U.S. Government Printing Office (Superintendent of Documents, U.S. Government Printing Office, Washington D.C. 20402) 1975. $1.00.

Federal: Your nearest Civil Service Commission Office; pamphlet entitled *Working for the USA*, from the above office.

State: Contact your State Personnel Board for beginning clues for your research. Do your research extensively. Follow the techniques of Chapter Six.

County: Personnel departments of the individual counties, again for beginning clues. Lots of interviewing, done by you, to find out what you want to know, is essential before deciding what field you want to aim at and *campaign for.*

Municipal: Personnel departments of individual cities. Also your State may have some association of them (California has the League of California Cities, 1108 "O" Street, Sacramento, CA 95814—for example), where you can pick up clues.

Some regions have organizations or "house organs," for municipalities, e.g., the Western part of the country has *Western City Magazine*—see your local library or 702 Hilton Center Bldg., Los Angeles, CA 90017 ($2/yr.).

Government fields include antipollution enforcement, education, welfare, day care, beautification, probation and parole, public works, recreation and parks, health and hospitals, urban renewal, and countless others.

SOME
RESEARCH
NOTES
ABOUT THE
FIELD OF
SELF EMPLOYMENT

The idea of going the self-employment route is exceedingly attractive to many job-hunters and career-changers. If you are presently employed, and can move gradually into moonlighting—testing out your own enterprise, as you would a floorboard in a very old house, stepping on it cautiously without putting your full weight on it at first, great.

If you are not presently employed, and it will be your only means of support, beware. Many men and women have starved very slowly (or not so slowly) in this kind of activity. Others have done quite well. Odds against new businesses remain depressing; 51% fail during the first five years. And some claim that figure is quite conservative.

You will do well to do as much reading-up on running your own business as possible. See Peter Weaver's *You, Inc. A detailed escape route to being your own boss,* (Doubleday, 1973). Other materials are listed in Appendix B, in the section "On Your Own." This will give you a helpful background.

You will want to decide exactly what you want to do. And this may mean putting several different activities together: for example, if your skills are in helping people, this might mean *private practice, teaching* at the nearby community college, or university extension division, *consulting,* etc.

Your dream, of course, may be to avoid this sort of smorgasbord, and go find funding (somewhere) that will enable you with singularity to do the one thing you most want to do. We're talking about foundations, chiefly; and your problem, of course, is how to research these foundations. One help (among others) is the *1978 Foundation 500,* which hopefully your local library has (otherwise it's $34.50 —ouch!) It's published by Foundation Research Service, 39 East 51st Street, New York, N.Y. 10022. It tells you which foundations give what to what sort of concerns.

If in preparation for this kind of "self-employment" you yourself want to go back to college to get additional training, see page 193.

If you need to get accredited, licensed or whatever, do *intensive questioning* of others in your kind of work.

If your interest is in *sensitivity,* etc., you should include the Association for Creative Change, and the Association for Humanistic Psychology (addresses Appendix C) as contacts to make along the way, in your research. The latter has a newsletter with listings of growth centers (possible leads on employment) and Positions Wanted. Dues: $15. a year.

There is also the *Journal of Humanistic Psychology,* which you can search through at your local library, or get a subscription to (325 Ninth St., San Francisco, CA 94103; $10/yr.).

If your idea of self-employment runs in the direction of *the arts (writing, etc.)* you may be interested in an $8.95 listing of operating foundations, businesses, unions, associations, educational and professional institutions, which give support (thru grants or other kinds of aid) to *writers, painters, filmmakers, musicians,* etc.: "Grants and Aid to Individuals In the Arts" from *Washington International Arts Letter,* 115 5th St., S.E., Washington, D.C. 20003. They have other lists (private foundations active in the arts, federal monies available, etc.) and their *Letter* itself is $10/year (or see your local library to see if it has it).

On the other hand, if you've always dreamed about being a consultant, there are books about consultancy in your library, or at your bookstore; but our readers have found them singularly unhelpful. We recommend, instead, that you go talk to some consultants of the type which interests you (see the yellow pages in your phone book) to see what they regard as the virtues and pitfalls of your intended profession.

IF YOU WANT TO BUY IN ON YOUR OWN BUSINESS, there is an endless number of franchises (you put up $x of your own, and in return you get equipment, know-how, and—sometimes —national advertising campaigns to help you). *You can also get taken to the cleaners by supposedly reputable companies.*

For a sampling of the kind of franchises available you may want to get your hands on *Franchise Company Data for Equal Opportunity in Business,* a United States Department of Commerce Publication, 1970. A good explanatory, introductory text.

Somewhat more detailed is *A Business of Your Own: FRANCHISE OPPORTUNITIES,* from Drake Publishers, Inc., 381 Park Avenue South, New York, N.Y. 10016. (1974; $4.95) For each franchise listed, it gives a lot of detailed information—a great research aid.

There is also the *Franchise Digest Ltd.,* Dept. IJA, P.O. Box 56, Ryder Station, Brooklyn, N.Y. 11234, $5 for three-month trial subscription. Details companies and length of time one must wait before he or she starts to see a return on his or her investment.

Business Opportunity Service, 512 Washington Bldg., Washington, D.C. 20005 provides listings for those wishing placement with a small business or venture capital firm.

Caution: Albee, p. 149 (see Appendix B) warns that the successful entrepreneur and the successful organization-person are two entirely different breeds of cat, and the longer a man or woman has been at one, the less likely he or she will succeed at the other.

Butler, on the other hand (see Appendix B) has a good word for franchises and running your own business. In any event, you had better be aware of the fact that businesses are failing at the rate of 900-1000 a month (33% higher than a year previous). "A Franchise Is a Hard Way to Get Rich," as Michael Creedman said in MONEY magazine September 1973 (see your local library, to get a look at this very apt warning).

To repeat, the odds against new businesses are very depressing: 51% fail during the first five years.

Conclusion: *Be sure you're not tempted to go this route just because you can't stand the job-hunt process. (Say it again Sam.) If you decide to go this route, have a lawyer at your elbow constantly, have enough cash for the first five years to tide you over, and be sure to hire people who have the expertise in areas you lack.* In other words, for most of us: forget it.

SOME RESEARCH NOTES ABOUT THE FIELD OF GOING BACK TO SCHOOL

Your first problem is *what you want to go back to school for.* Your second problem is *where you want to go, and why?* Your third problem is *how to finance it.*

As for the first: *There are five reasons why most people go back to school:*

1. To learn more about the world in which we are called to do our mission, e.g., *business, astronomy, black culture,* etc.

2. To pick up additional skills for the work we are presently doing full-time, e.g., *Counseling.*

3. To pick up (or sharpen) skills in other fields; i.e., to prepare for "that day." e.g., *business administration.*

4. To broaden the horizons of our mind, *e.g., Many authorities maintain mathematics is a means of making the spirit more elastic and receptive to change.*

5. To postpone decision, and create a never-never land between one's past and any future career. The "eternal student" is becoming a more and more familiar figure in our land.

If you want to go back for the third reason, dear friend, please be very sure you have done the exercises in Chapter Five, in detail, because you can get to taking some courses that are, in retrospect, a waste of time—in terms of your priority goals and skills.

Read the rash of books (e.g., Berg, Ivar, *Education and Jobs: The Great Training Robbery,* New York: Department NM, The Center for Urban Education, 105 Madison Avenue, New York, N.Y. 10016, $7.50) and articles (e.g. "Let's Break the Go-to-College Lockstep" in *Fortune,* November 1970) that have appeared in recent years *if your only reason for going back is to get a degree. ("That ol' black magic.")*

Confirmation of the futility of degrees is found in a study done by Richardson of 367 Air Force officers who got full-time secular jobs. They agreed that *"higher" education credentials were asked of them in order to get hired, than were necessary for the actual performance of the job.* (p. 173, 199—see Appendix B). You can get around this, if you faithfully follow Chapters Six and Seven. If you want to know what colleges are available, see the College Blue Book (three volumes) or The Blue Book of Occupational Information (MacMillan) at your local library. For overseas opportunities (if that interests you), there is: *International Education: A Directory of Resource Materials on Comparative Education and Study in Another Country* by Lily von Klemperer. (Garrett Park, Maryland 20766: Garrett Park Press. $5.95 if payment is enclosed with order.)

If you have done private study, and feel you could pass equivalency examinations without taking (at least some) courses, write The College Entrance Examination Board, Box

592, Princeton, New Jersey 08540 or Box 1025, Berkeley, CA 94701 and ask for details of their College-Level Examination Program.

If it's *a doctorate* you want, viable ones are in business administration (even a Masters in same is highly regarded from one of the *great* schools), economics, and computer-related sciences (but beware of *useless* computer schools—see *The Wall Street Journal,* June 10, 1970 at your local library).

If you don't care about a degree, but *just want knowledge,* there are several ways you can get it:

1. *Seminars, workshops,* etc. Get your hands on *National Directory of Adult and Continuing Education*-by Steven Goodman. Approximate price $15.00. Education and Training Associates, P.O. Box 304-BK, Dunellen, New Jersey 08812.

2. *Independent study at home: guided by others.* Get your hands on *Guide to Correspondence Study in Colleges and Universities,* from National University Extension Association, One Dupont Circle, Washington, D.C. 20036. ($.50). Or: *Directory of Accredited Private Home Study Schools,* from National Home Study Council, 1601 18th St., N.W., Washington, D.C 20009.

Or: if you *really* want to try new methods of study, under guidance, try education by Cassettes. This is going to be very popular in the future. Companies already in the field: Automated Learning, Inc., 1275 Bloomfield Ave., Fairfield, N.J. 07006; The Parish of the Air, 15 Sixteenth St., N.E., Atlanta, Georgia 30309; Thesis, P.O. Box 11724, Pittsburgh, Pa. 15228; The Executive Voice, *Fortune,* Time & Life Bldg., Rockefeller Center, N.Y., N.Y. 10029; Instructional Dynamics Incorporated, 166 East Superior St., Chicago, Ill. 60611; Norelco Training and Education Systems, 100 East 42nd St., N.Y., N.Y. 10017; Charles E. Merrill Publishing Co., 1300 Alum Creek Drive, Columbus, Ohio 43216; Cassettes Unlimited, P.O. Box 13119, Pittsburgh, Pa. 15243; Xerox Learning Systems, Dept. 109, 600 Madison Ave., N.Y., N.Y. 10022; Creative Resources, Box 1790, Waco, Texas 76703. Write to any of these, requesting a list of the cassettes they have, their cost, etc.

If you want *self-guided, independent study* and you know what subject you want to dabble in, write ERIC Clearing-house, on Adult Education, 107 Roney Lane, Syracuse, New York 13210 asking them what Clearinghouse in the country could give you a print-out of recent resources in the subject that interests you.

3. *Study at community college, college extension division, university, etc.* In case you don't know, *The Education Directory, Part 3 (Higher Education)* will tell you which schools of this nature are near you (or near the area where you would like to go and live). Consult the directory at your local library.

For non-school type learning, you know "in places that will let you get your hands dirty and places that will leave you alone to work out the struggle between you and whatever hunk of the world you're grappling with", there are 400 such places listed in the Center for Curriculum Design's *SOMEWHERE ELSE: a living-learning catalog* (The Swallow Press Inc., 1139 South Wabash Avenue, Chicago, Illinois 60605. Published 1973. $3.00).

As for your *finances,* there are three possible ways to get finances: a) Consult your university or college office to see what resources they have for aiding people in financial binds (like you); b) Consult your local service clubs (in town) to see if they have, or know of, similar kinds of aid: scholarship or whatever; c) Get your hands on: *Catalog of Federal Domestic Assistance,* Supt. of Documents, U.S. Government Printing Office, Washington, D.C. 20402. $7.

You can also get financed, by various ingenious methods, on your own. One cleric, for example, wrote to all the clergy whom he knew in large parishes, and asked for gifts from their *discretionary funds or other special funds.* He secured enough money to cover his whole study program.

The government, incidentally, has "guaranteed loans" in a program which enables banks to lend you money at lower rates. But this program has run into real difficulty this past year, and many students were left high and dry. Consult your local college for details about the viability of this program, and any others that may exist.

AND FINALLY, SOME RESEARCH NOTES ABOUT WORKING OVERSEAS

Mandatory reading for anyone contemplating overseas living is Hopkins, Robert. *I've Had It: A Practical Guide to Moving Abroad.* New York: Holt, Rinehart & Winston, 1972. $7.95.

We still advise following the techniques of Chapters Five-Seven, in the end.

If you want to know the kinds of places you might target in on, overseas, there is the *Dictionary of American Firms Operating in Foreign Countries*, by Juvenal L. Angel (World Trade Academy Press, 1971; look it up, in your local library, and ask your librarian for similar directories.)

---

1 "The Management of Human Resources: A Symposium" (See Bibliography), p. 24. Haire is the source of the statistic (p. 19) that human resources comprise about two-thirds of the value of a typical company.

2 In *Dun's Review*, February, 1969.

3 Uris, *Action Guide*, p. 196.

4 Saxenian (see Bibliography), p. 57. He suggests this as a helpful criterion for interviewers to use, in the process of hiring. It should be equally a criterion for job-hunters to use, in order to measure how much they ought to speak about themselves during an interview.

Those entering the job-market for the
first time, and desiring a simpler skill-list
than we have provided here, are referred
to *The Three Boxes of Life*, in which
the Beginning Version of the Quick Job-
Hunting Map may be found. Or that
version may be ordered separately, by
writing directly to Ten Speed Press,
Box 7123, Berkeley, California 94707.
$1.25.

Appendix A:

The Quick Job-Hunting Map

A fast way to help

*For the undecided college student
or the housewife going back to work,
or the mid-career changer, or the man or
woman whose job has been terminated,
or anyone else facing obstacles in the job hunt*

ADVANCED VERSION

Introduction: What You Need Before You Go Job-Hunting

You need to know that the traditional way of going about looking for a job—using want-ads in the newspapers, private employment agencies, the Federal/State employment agency, job listings, and the mailing out of resumes by the hundreds,—is not very effective, for *most* of the people who follow it.

For example, in a recent study of a major U.S. city, it was discovered that only 15% of the firms in that city had hired *anyone* during the entire year, as the result of a want-ad.*

For this, and other reasons, experts say that 80% of all the vacancies which occur in the work force (above entry level, at least) are never advertised through any of the avenues that job-hunters traditionally turn to. And resumes are notoriously unsuccessful in turning up vacancies, for many if not most people.

We need a better way of changing jobs, or of finding work for the first time. Especially because the average person has to go looking for a job up to fifteen times in his or her life.

What do you need to know, in order to be the most successful in your job-hunt, and to accomplish a successful conclusion to your job-hunt as quickly as possible? You need to know three things—which we have symbolized by the figure of

        a) a cart;
        b) a horse; and
        c) a road.

---

* *A Study to Test the Feasibility of Determining Whether Classified Ads in Daily Newspapers Are An Accurate Reflection of Local Labor Markets and of Significance to Employers and Job Seekers.* 1973. Olympus Research Corporation, 1290 24th Avenue, San Francisco, California 94122.

a. THE CART. You need to know that the most important thing about you to an employer (or to clients or customers directly) is not a recital of your past Experience, nor what field you were Trained in, [but *what* skills you have.] This is the common denominator that you always take with you, no matter how many different organizations you may (or may not) have worked for, or how often you change careers. You *must* know, for now and all the future, not only what Skills you *have*, but more importantly, what Skills you have *and enjoy*, if you are to find a job, or change jobs, quickly and effectively.

b. THE HORSE. The Skills you have and enjoy are like a cart without a horse, unless you know *where* you want to use those Skills—i.e., what you want to hook them up to. Other people can help you here, by telling you what the Possibilities are, but—in the end—this must be a self-directed search, on your part. Only you can define and decide where you want to use your Skills.

c. THE ROAD. The third thing you then need to know is *How* to identify the places where you would like to work, and How to get hired in one of those places. This step is the hardest step of all, *if* you have not spent any time on the preceding two questions. It is the easiest step of all, however, if you have done your homework on the WHAT (skills do I enjoy?) and the WHERE (do I want to use those skills?).

This Quick-Job-Hunting Map, then, is devoted to helping you work through these three steps, to put together the information you need in order to go about your job-hunt quickly and effectively. How long will your job-hunt take? No one can say. It can be as short as a week or as long as nine months. A lot depends upon how hard you work at it, full-time, and on various other factors, principally Luck. What you are doing here is organizing your Luck. One thing is sure: the time you invest in this Map will *greatly* shorten the time it takes for your job-hunt.

The Party

Below is an aerial view of a room in which a party is taking place.
At this party, people with the same or similar interests have
(for some reason) all gathered in the same corner of
the room—as described below:

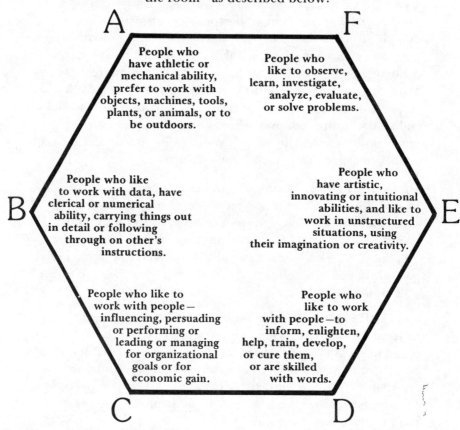

A

People who
have athletic or
mechanical ability,
prefer to work with
objects, machines, tools,
plants, or animals, or to
be outdoors.

F

People who
like to observe,
learn, investigate,
analyze, evaluate,
or solve problems.

B

People who like
to work with data, have
clerical or numerical
ability, carrying things out
in detail or following
through on other's
instructions.

E

People who
have artistic,
innovating or intuitional
abilities, and like to
work in unstructured
situations, using
their imagination or creativity.

People who like to
work with people—
influencing, persuading
or performing or
leading or managing
for organizational
goals or for
economic gain.

People who
like to work
with people—to
inform, enlighten,
help, train, develop,
or cure them,
or are skilled
with words.

C

D

(1) Which corner of the
room would you instinctively
be drawn to, as the group
of people you would most
enjoy being with for the
longest time? (leave aside
any question of shyness,
or whether you would
have to talk with them.)
Write the *letter* for that
corner in this box:

(2) After fifteen minutes,
everyone in the corner you
have chosen, leaves for
another party crosstown,
exept you. Of the groups
that still remain now, which
corner or group would
you be drawn to the most,
as the people you would
most enjoy being with for
the longest time? Write
the letter for that corner
in this box:

(3) After fifteen minutes.
this group too leaves for another
party, except you.
Of the corners, and groups,
which remain now, which
one would you most
enjoy being with for the
longest time?
Write the letter for that
corner in this box:

Your Seven Most Enjoyed or Satisfying Accomplishments

I. THE MAGNIFICENT SEVEN

"The Party" exercise, which you have just completed, is based on a simple truth discovered by Dr. John L. Holland: that we all tend to be attracted to the people who have the same (interests and) SKILLS as we do. Or at least the same Skills that we MOST ENJOY (or would most enjoy) using. So, what you have done in the party exercise, actually, is to define (at least in a general fashion) the Skills you most enjoy using: just read back, in the diagram, the description of the people in each of the three corners you preferred: that is actually a description of YOU, and your Skills.

But now you MUST HAVE more detailed information about your most enjoyable natural talents and developed skills. The first step toward this is for you to take

SEVEN SHEETS OF PAPER
(lined paper, if you are not going to type it)

What you want to put on these seven separate pieces of paper is a description of some *experiences* in your life which you can then examine, to see what skills you were using when you were most enjoying yourself.

You have a choice as to what you write on the seven sheets of paper. Here are three possibilities:

Possibility A: You can describe the seven *most satisfying accomplishments or achievements* you have ever done. e.g., "I learned how to sew my own dress" or "I learned how to fix a car". The best way to get at this is to make a much longer list to begin with, of accomplishments from all different portions of your life—e.g., two or three for each five year period of your life, thus far. Then, from that longer list, choose the seven which are most meaningful TO YOU. If you find it impossible to make such a list, then consider this alternate way of getting at the task:

Possibility B: You can describe seven *jobs* you have held in your life (the seven most meaningful TO YOU, if you have had more than seven so far). These jobs can be paid or unpaid, full or part-time. The key is: describe jobs you most *enjoyed* doing. If this doesn't work either, then try this:

Possibility C: You can describe seven *roles* you have (or have had) in life. e.g., wife, mother, cook, housekeeper, volunteer worker, student, and friend. If you have more than seven to choose from, then choose the seven which you have *enjoyed* the most.

II. THE FLESHING OUT

Whichever you choose, "A", "B", or "C", once you have put a separate item on each of the seven sheets, then go back and DESCRIBE IN DETAIL what you did under each of these items— in as much detail as if you were describing it to a five year old child (whom you could count on to know Nothing about the activity you are describing, say).

You may fill each sheet, and write on the back of it if necessary. You must *not* cut corners here, or you will simply not be able to do the next part of this Map.

Here is an example of how detailed you will need to be:

SAMPLE 66 My Halloween experience when I was seven years old. Details: When I was seven, I decided I wanted to go out on Halloween dressed as a horse. I wanted to be the front end of the horse, and I talked a friend of mine into being the back end of the horse. But, at the last moment he backed out, and I was faced with the prospect of not being able to go out on Halloween. At this point I decided to figure out some say of getting dressed up as the whole horse, myself. I took a fruit basket, and tied some string to both sides of the basket's rim, so that I could tie the basket around my rear end. This filled me out enough so that the costume fit me, by myself. I then fixed some strong thread to the tail so that I could make it wag by moving my hands. When Halloween came I not only went out and had a ball, but I won a prize as well. 99

When you have fleshed the seven out, *thoroughly*, turn to page 206 and in the seven columns at the top of the chart, put some words which will recall each sheet to your mind. For a sample, we have called the story above "The Halloween Experience".

III. THE EXAMINING FOR SKILLS

Rather than use all the pages of the chart, to examine each experience, we suggest you begin with the 'skill families' corresponding to your answers to The Party exercise (page 202) earlier. If your first answer to The Party exercise was "A", then use the A^1 and A^2 sections of the chart. If "B", then use the B^1 and B^2 sections. If "C", then use the C^1, C^2, C^3, and C^4 sections of the chart (the fact that some letters have "more" skill families, or a longer list of skills is not of any significance; sometimes a longer list just means the skills are harder to describe). If "D", then use the D^1, D^2, and D^3 sections of the chart. If "E", then use the E^1, and E^2 sections. And if your answer to the first question in The Party exercise was "F", then use only the F^1, and F^2 sections of the chart—to begin with.

If you have the patience (and the time) you can later go on to the parts of the chart corresponding to your SECOND answer in The Party exercise. And still later, to the parts of the chart corresponding to your THIRD answer.

For the most complete analysis, it is of course most helpful to go on to the remaining sections; but this is optional— depending on the degree of thoroughness you wish.

Color me "intuitive"

Your Functional/Transferable Skills

Directions

- Go down the parts or sections of the checklist you have chosen, to begin with (see previous page).
  Take Experience #1, first. In doing it, did you use *any* of the skills in the first paragraph (or 'box')? If so:
  a) Color the box under #1, opposite it; AND
  b) Underline the exact skill (or skills) you used.

- Don't be bothered by the fact that some lists sound repetitive. That's deliberate. We've often said the same thing in two different ways. Just underline the way you like best. Or feel free to change the wording, fill in the blanks, or do what ever you wish, in order to make this YOUR list—not ours.

- If the answer was "No", then skip a) and b).

- Repeat with each succeeding paragraph, or 'box', until you have completed that section for Experience #1. Then repeat the whole procedure for Experience #2. Then for #3. And so forth. Run through the sample, to get the idea.

- *Italics* below belong to the Halloween story we have used as the 'sample'. We have used italics instead of underlining.

- Two different ways of coloring (or using two different color pens) may be helpful. One if you *used* the skill; and the other if you *used and enjoyed it.*

Sample: The Halloween Experience

1 2 3 4 5 6 7

Additional thoughts that occur to me about other times when I used these skills

A¹

Machine or Manual Skills

I can do because I did do:

	sample	1	2	3	4	5	6	7	Additional experiences
Designing ___ ; Molding ___ ; Shaping; Developing ___ ; Composing ___ (e.g., type)									
Preparing ___ ; Clearing ___ ; Building ___ : Constructing ___ ; Assembling ___ ; Setting Up ___ ; Installing ___ ; Installation of ___ ; Laying ___									
Lifting/Pushing/Pulling/Balancing ___ ; Carrying ___ ; Unloading/Moving/Shipping ___ ; Delivering ___ ; Collecting ___									
Handling/fingering/feeling ___ ; Keen sense of touch; Keen sensations; Finger dexterity (as in typing, etc.); *Manual*/hand *dexterity*; Handling ___ ; *Manipulating* ___ ; Weaving/Knitting; Handicrafting/craft skills; Making models									
Precision-working; Punching ___ ; Drilling ___ ; Tweezer dexterity; Showing dexterity or speed									
Washing; Cooking/culinary skills									
Feeding ___ ; Tending ___									
Controlling/Operating ___ ; Blasting ___ ; Grinding ___ ; Forging ___ ; Cutting ___ ; Filling ___ ; Applying ___ ; Pressing ___ ; Binding ___ ; Projecting ___									
Operating tools; operating machinery (e.g. radios); operating vehicles/equipment; Driving ___ ; Switching ___									
Fitting ___ ; Adjusting ___ ; Tuning ___ ; Maintaining ___ ; Fixing/Repairing ___ ; Masters machinery against its will; Trouble-shooting ___									
Producing ___									
Other skills which you think belong in this family but are not listed above:									

Machine or Manual Skills continued

and I used the above skills with:

	sample	1	2	3	4	5	6	7	Additional experiences
Tools (specify kinds):									
Work aids (what kinds?):									
Trees/stones/metals/other:									
Machines/equipment/vehicles:									
Processed materials (kinds?):	▨								
Products being made (kinds?):									
Other:									

A2

Athletic/ Outdoor/ Traveling Skills

I can do because I have proven:

	sample	1	2	3	4	5	6	7	Additional experiences
Motor/Physical coordination & agility; *Eye-Hand-Foot coordination*; Walking/Climbing/Running	▨								
Skilled at general sports: Skilled in small competitive games; Skilled at ___ (a particular game)									
Swimming: Skiing/ Recreation; Playing. Hiking/ Backpacking/Camping/Mountaineering; Outdoor survival skills; Creating, planning, organizing outdoor activities; Traveling									
Drawing samples from the earth; Keen oceanic interests; Navigating									
Horticultural skills; Cultivating growing things; Skillful at planting/nurturing plants; Landscaping and groundskeeping									
Farming; Ranching; Working with animals									
Other skills which you think belong in this family, but are not listed above:									

B¹

Detail/Follow-through Skills.

I can do because I did do:

	sample	1	2	3	4	5	6	7	Additional experiences
Following-through; Executing ____ ; Ability to follow detailed instructions; *Expert at getting things done*; Implementing decisions; Enforcing regulations; Rendering support services; Applying what others have developed; Directing production of ____ (kind of thing)	▨								
Precise attainment of set limits, tolerances or standards; Brings projects in on time, and within budget; Skilled at making arrangements for events, processes; Responsible; Delivering on promises, on time.									
Expediting ____ ; Dispatching ____ ; Consistently tackles tasks ahead of time; Adept at finding ways to speed up a job; Able to handle a great variety of tasks and responsibilities simultaneously and efficiently; *Able to work well under stress, and still improvise*; Good at responding to emergencies	▨								
Resource expert; Resource broker; Making and using contacts effectively; Good at getting materials; Collecting things; Purchasing ____ ; Compiling ____									
Approving ____ ; Validation of information; Keeping confidences or confidential information.									
A detail man or woman; Keen and accurate memory for detail; Showing careful attention to, and keeping track of, details; Focusing on minutiae; High tolerance of repetition and/or monotony; Retentive memory for rules and procedures (e.g. protocol); *Persevering* ____	▨								
Checking ____									
Explicit, ordered, systematic manipulation of data; Good at the processing of information; Collates data accurately, comparing with previous data; Tabulation of data; Keeping records (time, etc.); Recording ____ (kinds of data)									
Facilitating/Simplifying other people's finding things; Orderly organizing of data or records									

	sample	1	2	3	4	5	6	7	Additional experiences
Organizing written and numerical data according to a prescribed plan; Classification skills; Classifying materials expertly; Filing; Filing materials; Retrieving data									
Clerical ability: Typing; Operating business machines and data processing machines to attain organizational and economic goals; Copying; Reproducing materials									
Other skills which you think belong in this family, but are not listed above:									
Numerical ability; Expert at learning and remembering numbers; number memory; Remembering statistics accurately, for a long period of time									
Counting; Taking inventory; Calculating; Computing; Arithmetical skills; High accuracy in computing /counting; Rapid manipulation of numbers; Rapid computations performed in head or on paper									
Managing money; Financial planning and management; Keeping financial records; Accountability									
Appraising ____; Economic research and analysis; Doing cost analysis; Effective Cost Analyses, Estimates, Projections, and Comparisons; Financial/Fiscal Analysis and Planning/Programming									
Developing a budget; Budget Planning, Preparation, Justification, Administration, Analysis and Review									
Extremely economical; Skilled at Allocating Scarce Financial Resources									
Preparing financial reports; Bookkeeping; Doing accounting; Fiscal Cost Audits, Controls, and Reductions									
Using numbers as a reasoning tool; Very sophisticated mathematical abilities; Effective at solving statistical problems									
Others which you think belong in this family of skills, but are not listed above:									

B²

Numerical/ Financial/ Accounting/ Financial (Money) Management Skills

I can do because I did do:

C¹

Influencing/Persuading Skills

I can because I did:

	sample	1	2	3	4	5	6	7	Additional experiences
Develop rapport/trust; Inspiring trust in the minds and hearts of others; Encouraging people									
Helping people identify their own intelligent self-interest									
Persuading____; Expert in reasoning persuasively/developing a thought; Debating; Influencing the attitudes or ideas of others									
Promoting____; (Face to face) Selling of tangibles/intangibles; Selling ideas or products without tearing down competing ideas or products; Selling an idea, program or course of action to decision-makers; Developing targets/building markets for ideas or products; Fund-raising/money-raising									
Recruiting talent or leadership; Attracts skilled, competent creative people; Enlisting; Motivating others; Mobilizing____; Stimulating people to effective action									
Getting diverse groups to work together; Wins friends easily from among diverse or even opposing groups or factions; Adept at conflict management									
Arbitrating/mediating between contending parties or groups; Negotiating to come jointly to decisions; Bargaining; Crisis intervention; reconciling____									
Renegotiating____; Obtaining agreement on policies, after the fact									
Charting mergers; Manipulating____ to achieve____; Arranging financing									
Other skills which you think belong in this family, but are not listed above:									

and I used the above skills with:

Opinions									
Attitudes									
Judgments, Decisions									
Products									
Money									
Other:									

C2
Performing Skills

I can do because I did do:

	sample	1	2	3	4	5	6	7	Additional experiences
Getting up before a group; Very responsive to audiences' moods or ideas; Diverting; Contributes to others pleasure consciously; Performing									
Demonstrating____ (products, etc.); Modelling____; Artistic (visual) presentations	▓								
Showmanship; A strong theatrical sense; Poise in public appearances	▓								
Addressing large or small groups; (Exceptional) speaking ability/articulateness; Public address / public speaking/oral presentations; Lecturing; Stimulating people/stimulating enthusiasm; Poetry reading									
Playing music; Making musical presentations; Singing; Dancing									
Making people laugh; Understands the value of the ridiculous in illuminating reality									
Acting; Making radio and TV presentations/films									
Public sports									
Conducting and directing public affairs and ceremonies; Conducting musical groups									
Other skills which you think belong in this family, but are not listed above:									

C3
Leadership Skills

I can do because I did do:

	sample	1	2	3	4	5	6	7	Additional experiences
Initiating____; Able to move into totally new situations on one's own; Able to take the initiative or first move in developing relationships; Skilled at striking up conversations with strangers									
Driving initiative; Continually searches for more responsibility; Persevering in acquiring things (like____)									
Excellent at organizing one's time; Unusual ability to work self-directedly, without supervision;									

Additional experience

	Sample												Additional experience

Unwillingness to automatically accept the status quo; Keen perceptions of things as they could be, rather than passively accepting them as they are; Promoting and bringing about major changes, as change agent; Planning for/and effecting/initiating change; *Sees and seizes opportunities*

Sees a problem and acts immediately to solve it; Deals well with the unexpected or critical; Very decisive in emergencies; Adept at confronting others with touchy or difficult personal matters

Showing courage; No fear of taking manageable risks; Able to make hard decisions; Adept at policy making; Able to terminate projects/people/processes when necessary

Leading others; guiding ____; Inspiring, motivating and leading organized groups; Impresses others with enthusiasm and charisma; Repeatedly elected to senior posts; Skilled at chairing meetings

Deft in directing creative talent; Skilled leadership in perceptive human relations techniques

Other skills which you think belong in this family, but are not listed above:

C4

Developing/
Planning/
Organizing/
Executing/
Supervising/
Management
Skills

Planning ____; Planning and development ____; Planning on basis of lessons from past experience; A systematic approach to goal-setting

Prioritizing tasks; Establishing effective priorities among competing requirements; Setting criteria or standards; Policy-making; Policy formulation or interpretation

Designing projects; Program development/Programming; Skilled at planning and carrying out well-run meetings, seminars or workshops

Organizing ____; Organizational development; Organizational analysis, planning and building; adept at organizing, bringing order out of chaos with masses of (physical) things

Developing / Planning / Organizing / Executing / Supervising / Management Skills, *continued*	sample	1	2	3	4	5	6	7	Additional experiences
I can do because I did do:									
Organizing others, bringing people together in cooperative efforts; Selecting resources; Hiring; Able to call in other experts/helpers as needed; Team-building; Recognizing and utilizing the skills of others; Contracting/Delegating____									
Scheduling____; Assigning____; Setting up and maintaining on-time work-schedules; Coordinating operations/details; Arranging/Installing____									
Directing others; Making decisions about others; Supervising others in their work; Supervising and administering____									
Managing/Being responsible for others' output; Management____; Humanly-oriented technical management; Real property, plant and facility, management; R&D Program and Project Management; Controlling____									
Producing____; Achieving____; Attaining____									
Maintaining____; Trouble-shooting____; Recommending____									
Reviewing____; Makes good use of feed-back; Evaluating____; Recognizes intergroup communication gaps; Judging people's effectiveness									
Other skills which you think belong in this family, but are not included above:									
and I used those skills with:									
Individuals									
Personnel									
Groups									
Organizations									
Management systems									
Office procedures									
Meetings									
Projects / Programs									
Educational events									

D1

Language/ Reading/ Writing/ Speaking/ Communications Skills

I can do because I did do:

	sample	1	2	3	4	5	6	7	Additional experiences
Reading; Love of reading voraciously or rapidly; Love of printed things; Relentlessly curious									
Comparing ____ ; Proofreading ____ ; Editing effectively ____ ; Publishing imaginatively ____									
Composing ____ (kinds of words)									
Communicating effectively; Expresses self very well; Communicates with clarity; Making a point and cogently expressing a position; Thinking quickly on one's feet; Talking/Speaking; Encouraging communication									
Defining ____ ; Explaining concepts; Interpreting ____ ; Ability to explain difficult or complex concepts, ideas and problems									
Translating ____ ; Verbal/linguistic skills in foreign languages; Linguistics; Teaching of languages; Adept at translating jargon into relevant and meaningful terms, to diverse audiences or readers									
Summarizing ____ ; Reporting accurately; Very explicit and concise writing; Keeping superior minutes of meetings									
Outstanding writing skills; Ability to vividly describe people or scenes so that others can visualize; Writes with humor, fun and flair (related to *Diverting*, below); Employs humor in describing experiences, to give people courage to embrace them									
Uncommonly warm letter composition; Flair for writing reports; Skilled speech-writing									
Promotional writing; Highly successful proposal writing for funding purposes; Imaginative advertising and publicity programs									
Other skills which you think belong in this family, but are not listed above:									

Language / Reading / Writing / Speaking Communications Skills continued

	sample	1	2	3	4	5	6	7	Additional experiences
Ideas									
Feelings									
Facts									
Articles									
Reports/Newsletters									
Brochures/catalogs/journals									
Books									
Other:									

and I used those skills with:

D2

Instructing/ Interpreting/ Guiding/ Educational Skills

I can because I have:

Proven myself to be very knowledgeable; Having a commitment to learning as a life-long process

Briefing ___ ; Informing ___ ; Enlightening ___ ; Explaining ___ ; Instructing ___ ; Teaching ___ ; In-Service training

(Unusually) skillful teaching; Fosters a stimulating learning environment; Creating an atmosphere of acceptance; Patient teaching; Adept at inventing illustrations for principles or ideas; Down to earth; Adept at using visual communications (charts, slides, chalkboards, etc.); Instills love of the subject; Conveys tremendous enthusiasm

Coaching about ___ (finances, etc.); Advising/aiding people in making decisions; Giving advice about ___ ; Giving insight concerning ___

Encouraging ___ ; (cf. Influencing/Persuading Family of Skills, above)

Adept at two-way dialogue; Communicates effectively; Ability to hear and answer questions perceptively; Acceptance of differing opinions; (Keen) ability to help others express their views; Consulting

	sample	1	2	3	4	5	6	7	Additional experiences
Enabling/Facilitating personal growth and development; Helping people make their own discoveries in knowledge; Helping people to develop their own ideas or insights; Clarifying goals and values of others; Counseling; Putting things in perspective; Brings out creativity in others; Shows others how to take advantage of a resource									
Group-facilitating; Discussion group leadership; Group dynamics; Behavioral modification									
Empowering____; Training and Development____; Training someone in something; Designing educational events; Organization and administration of inhouse training programs									
Other skills which you think belong in this family, but are not listed above:									
Information									
Ideas / Generalizations									
Values / standards									
Goals / decisions									
Other									

and I used those skills with:

D3
Serving/ Helping/ Human Relations Skills

	sample	1	2	3	4	5	6	7	Additional experiences
Relates well in dealing with the public/public relations									
Servicing____; Customer relations and services; Attending____; Adjusting____ (e.g. bills); Referring (people)____									
Rendering services to____; Being of service; Helping and serving____									
Sensitivity to others; Interested in/manifesting keen ability to relate to people; Intense curiosity about other people—who they are, what they do; Remembers people and their preferences; Adept at treating									

Serving/Helping
Human Relations Skills *continued*

I can because I did:

Human Relations Skills *continued*	sample	1	2	3	4	5	6	7	Additional experiences
people fairly; Listening intently and accurately; A good trained effective listener; Good at listening and conveying awareness; Consistently communicates warmth to people; Conveying understanding, patience and fairness; Readily establishes warm, mutual rapport with ____; Able to develop warmth over the telephone									
Interpersonal competencies; (Unusual) perception in human relations; Expertise in interpersonal contact; Keen ability to put self in someone else's shoes; Empathy: instinctively understanding how someone else feels; Understanding; Tact, Diplomacy and Discretion; Effective in dealing with many different kinds of people / Talks easily with all kinds of people									
Caring for / Nursing children or the handicapped; Watching over ____; Love of children; Guiding ____									
Administering a household; Hostessing; Shaping and influencing the atmosphere of a particular place; Providing comfortable, natural and pleasant surroundings; Warmly sensitive and responsive to people's feelings and needs in social or other situations; Anticipating people's needs									
Works well on a teamwork basis; Has fun while working, and makes it fun for others; Collaborates with colleagues skillfully; Treats others as equals, without regard to education, authority, or position; Refuses to put people into slots or categories; Ability to relate to people with different value systems; Motivates fellow workers; Expresses appreciation faithfully; Ready willingness to share credit with others									
Takes human failings/limitations into account; Able to ignore undesirable qualities in others; Deals patiently and sympathetically with difficult people; Handles super-difficult people in situations, without stress; Handles prima donnas tactfully and effectively; Works well in a hostile environment									

Serving/Helping
Human Relations Skills continued

	sample	1	2	3	4	5	6	7	Additional experiences
Nursing _____ ; Skillful therapeutic abilities; Curing _____ ; Gifted at helping people with their personal problems; Raises people's self-esteem; (Thorough) understanding of human motivations; Understands family relationships and problems; Aware of people's need for supportive community; Adept at aiding people with their total life adjustment/Mentoring									
Unusual ability to represent others; Expert in liaison roles; Ombudsmanship									
Other skills which you think belong in this family, but are not included above:									

and I used those skills with:

	sample	1	2	3	4	5	6	7	Additional experiences
Children									
The young									
Adolescents									
Adults or *Peers*	▨								
The aging									
All age groups									
Other:									

E¹ Intuitional and Innovating Skills

	sample	1	2	3	4	5	6	7	Additional experiences
Imagining _____ ; Highly imaginative; *Possessed of great imagination, and the courage to use it*	▨								
Ideaphoria/Continually conceiving, developing and generating ideas; Conceptual ability of the highest order; Being an idea man or woman; Inventing; *Inventive; Ability to improvise on the spur of the moment*	▨								
Innovating; Having many innovative and creative ideas; Creative, perceptive effective innovator; *Willing to experiment with new approaches;* Experimental with ideas, procedures, and programs; Strongly committed to experimental approaches; Demonstrating continual originality; Love of exercising the mind-muscle	▨								

Intuitional and Innovating Skills continued

	sample	1	2	3	4	5	6	7	Additional experiences
Synthesizing perceptions, etc.; Seeing relationships between apparently unrelated factors; Integrating diverse elements into a clear coherent whole; Effective dissolution of barriers between ideas or fields; Ability to relate abstract ideas; Balancing factors/Judging/Showing good judgement									
Deriving things from others' ideas; Improving ____; Updating ____; *Adapting* ____; Reflection upon ____; Sees the theoretical base in a practical situation; Significant theoretical modeling; *Model developing;* Developing ____; Formulating ____; Developing innovative program ideas									
Generating ideas with commercial possibilities; Able to see the commercial possibilities of abstract ideas or concepts; Applying ____; Applying theory; Applied research; Creating products; Entreprenurial									
Form perception; Perception of patterns and structures; *Visualizing shapes;* Graphing and reading graphs; Visualizing in the third-dimension; Able to read blueprints									
Spatial memory; Memory for design; Able to notice quickly (and/or remember later) most of the contents of a room; Remembering ____; Memory for faces									
Showing foresight; Recognizing obsolescence before compelling data is yet at hand; Instinctively gathering resources even before the need for them becomes clear; Forecasting									
Perceiving intuitively; Color-discrimination (of a very high order)									
Other skills which you think belong in this family, but are not listed above:									

I can do because I did do:

E2

Artistic Skills

I can because I did:

	sample	1	2	3	4	5	6	7	Additional experiences
Shows strong sensitivity to, and need for, beauty in the environment; Adept at coloring things; instinctively excellent taste									
Expressive; Exceptionally good at facial expressions used to express or convey thoughts, without (or, in addition to) words; Ability to use the body to express feelings eloquently; Uses voice tone and rhythm as unusually effective tool of communication; Skilled in telephone-voice; Can accurately reproduce sounds (e.g., foreign languages spoken without accent); Mastery of all forms of communication									
Good sense of humor/playfulness	▨								
Creative imagining/Creating original _____; Operates well in a free, unstructured, unsupervised environment; Bringing new life to traditional (art) forms; Translating _____; Restoring _____	▨								
Aware of the value of symbolism, and deft in its use; Skilled at symbol formation (words, pictures, and concepts); Visualizing concepts; Creating poetry, or poetic images; Designing and/or using audio-visual aids; Photographing									
Visual & spatial designing; Artistic talent (drawing, etc.); Illustrating; Mapping; Drafting/Mechanical drawing	▨								
Fashioning/Shaping things; *Making* _____; Designing in wood or other media; Redesigning structures; Styling _____; Decorating _____									
Writing; Playwriting; Assisting in/directing the planning, organizing and staging of theatrical productions									
Musical knowledge and taste; Tonal memory; Uncommon sense of rhythm, Exceedingly accurate melody recognition; Composing									
Other skills which you think belong in this family, but are not listed above:									

Artistic Skills continued	sample	1	2	3	4	5	6	7	Additional experiences
Colors									
Spaces									
Shapes, faces									
Handicrafts									
Arts, drawing, paints									
Fashion, jewelry, clothing, furs, furniture									
Music									
Other:									

and I used those skills with:

F¹

Observa-tional/Learning Skills

I can do because I did do:

	sample	1	2	3	4	5	6	7	Additional experiences
Observing____; (Highly) observant of people/data/things; (Keen) awareness of surroundings									
Reading____ (e.g., dials); Adept at scanning radar or other sophisticated observational systems; Estimating____ (e.g., speed)									
Listening skillfully; Hearing accurately; Keen sense of smell; (Tremendously) sensitive sense of tasting									
Perceptive: Perceiving____; Detecting____; Discovering____; A person of perpetual curiosity/discovery, delighting in new knowledge; Continually seeking to expose oneself to new experiences; Highly committed to continual personal growth and learning; Learns from the example of others; Learns quickly									
Alert in observing human behavior; Studying other people's behavior perceptively; Perceptive in identifying and assessing the potential of others; Recognizes and appreciates the skills of others									
Appraising____; Assessing____; Screening applicants; Realistically assessing people's needs; Accurately assessing public moods; *Quickly sizes up situations and instinctively understands political realities*									

	sample	1	2	3	4	5	6	7	Additional experiences
Exceptional intelligence, tempered by common sense									
Other skills which you think belong in this family, but are not listed above:									
Data (what kinds?)									
People (any special kinds?)									
Ideas									
Behavior									
Procedures									
Operations									
Phenomena									
Instruments									
Other									

and I used those skills with:

F2
Research/ Investigating/ Analyzing/ Systematizing/ Evaluating Skills

	sample	1	2	3	4	5	6	7	Additional experiences
Anticipates problems before they become problems; Recognizing need for more information before a decision can be made intelligently; Skilled at clarifying problems or situations									
Surveying _____; Interviewing _____; Adept at gathering information from people by talking to them; Researching resources, ways and means; Researching personally, through investigation and interviewing; Inquiring									
Inspecting _____; Examining _____; Surveying organizational needs; Researching exhaustively; Collecting information/Information gathering; Academic research and writing									
Analyzing _____; Dissecting _____; *Breaking down principles into parts;* Adept at atomizing/breaking down into parts; Analyzing community needs, values, and resources; Analyzes communication situations; Analyzing manpower requirements; Analyzing performance specifications									

Research / Investigating / Analyzing / Systematizing / Evaluating Skills continued	sample	1	2	3	4	5	6	7	Additional experiences
I can because I did: Diagnosing ___; Organizing/Classifying ___; Identifies elements, relationships, structures, and organizing principles of organizations to be analyzed; Isolating elements; *Able to separate 'wheat from chaff'*; Reviewing large amounts of material and extracting essence; Perceiving and Defining Cause & Effect relationships; Ability to trace problems, ideas, etc. to their source									
Grouping ___; Perceiving common denominators; Systematizing/Organizing material/information in a systematic way									
Testing ___ (e.g. an idea, or hypothesis)									
Determining/Figuring out ___; Solving ___; Problem-solving; Trouble-shooting									
Reviewing/Evaluating ___; Screening ___ (e.g., fund proposals); Critiquing ___; Evaluating by measurable or subjective criteria; Accurately evaluating ___ (e.g., programs administered by others; experiments; loan applications; papers; quizzes; work; records; staff; program bids; evidence; options; qualifications; etc.)									
Decision-making skills; Re-evaiuating									
Other skills which you think belong in this family, but are not listed above:									
and I used those skills with: People (what kinds?)									
Data (what kinds?)									
Things (what kinds?)									
Ideas (theoretical, abstract, symbolic, systematic?)									
Articles, artifacts, or processes									
Matter (inert or moving) or Energy									
Phenomena (physical, biological, scientific, mathematical, or cultural?)									
Other:									

NOW THAT YOU'RE DONE WITH THE CHART

When you've finished the chart (sure you can go ahead and fill it all out, if you want to) you have some decisions to make. WHICH OF THE SKILL 'FAMILIES' (like A^1, etc.) that you colored in, do you ENJOY ABSOLUTELY THE MOST? Enter its name *plus* the skills that you've underlined, on page 228. Then decide which 'family' came in second, and enter it next, on page 228. And so on, through the fifth family.

And now it is time to consider:

Where You Would Most Enjoy Using These Skills

It's nice to 'stay loose' and be willing to use your skills any place that there is a vacancy, but—as we said—vacancies are hard to discover. You are going to have to go out and canvass, or research, or interview, a particular area. The more you can cut this area down to manageable size, before you go out, by using some principles of *elimination* or *exclusion*, and the clearer a picture you can have in your own mind of what kind of place you want to use your skills in, the faster and more effective will be your search—to discover a vacancy, or even create your own job.

There are six principles of exclusion or narrowing down the area you need to focus on:

The six principles of exclusion or narrowing down the area you need to focus on:

1

Where would you most like to uncover a job, geography-wise?

(What city, rural area, county, or whatever, in this country or the world?)

2

Where, in terms of the kinds of people you would like to be surrounded by?

(Here copy the answers you gave to The Party Exercise on page 4, for those answers were a description of People-environments that you prefer, as well as of skills. Add any other inportant descriptions—thinking of the kinds of people who have turned you off, in the past; and then describing their exact opposites here.)

3

Where in terms of What goals, purposes, or values do you want your skills to serve?

(Two exercises will help here. Write out your answer (on a separate sheet of paper) to the question: What do I hope others will solve or change about this world, while I am still alive to see it; Brainstorm this with some friends of yours, if possible. Then, from this list select the five most important items (to you) and write a paragraph about each one of those five, as to why you would or would not like to be involved yourself, and in what fashion.

(Don't disqualify yourself on the grounds your talents are too peculiar to fit this particular 'cause'. Remember, Pete Seeger was concerned about the pollution of the Hudson River, and his talent was not engineering but singing. Still he used his voice to sing about pollution there, and alert people to the need to do something about it.)

Another exercise to get at this is: if you had $10 million and didn't have to ever work, what would you do with your spare time for the rest of your life? If it turns out to be simply gardening, or making kites and flying them, then think about places which might pay you to do this (like horticultural stores, or kite factories).

Another version of the same exercise: if you had another $10 million and had to give it away, to what or to whom would you give it? To which causes, needs of our society, or unmet needs?

4

Where in terms of Special Knowledges you have picked up, that you still want to be able to use because you enjoy them?

(Consider the school subjects you especially loved, languages you know and enjoy, or other special knowledges related to particular fields or professions that are still important to you, to be able to use in the future.)

5

Where in terms of the particular Working Conditions you would prefer?

(Do you need a lot or very little of such things as: Authority/Supervision; Change; Consistency; Dress Codes; Opportunity for Initiative; Self-Management, at your work? If you have had experience already in the world of work, list the Distasteful Living/Working Conditions you have experienced, in the past, and then state these in a positive form for the Future.)

6

Where in terms of level, amount of responsibility, and (to put it another way) at what salary level?

The Quick Job-Hunting Map

(PUTTING IT ALL TOGETHER)

⬤ I am looking for a job where I could
use the following skills:

....

1. First Family of Skills Most Enjoyed: _____
   [Individual skills in this family used and enjoyed:]   *(title)*

....

2. Second Family of Skills: _____
   [Individual skills:]   *(title)*

....

3. Third Family _____
   [Individual skills]:   *(title)*

....

4. Fourth Family _____
          (title)

....

5. Fifth Family _____

          (title)

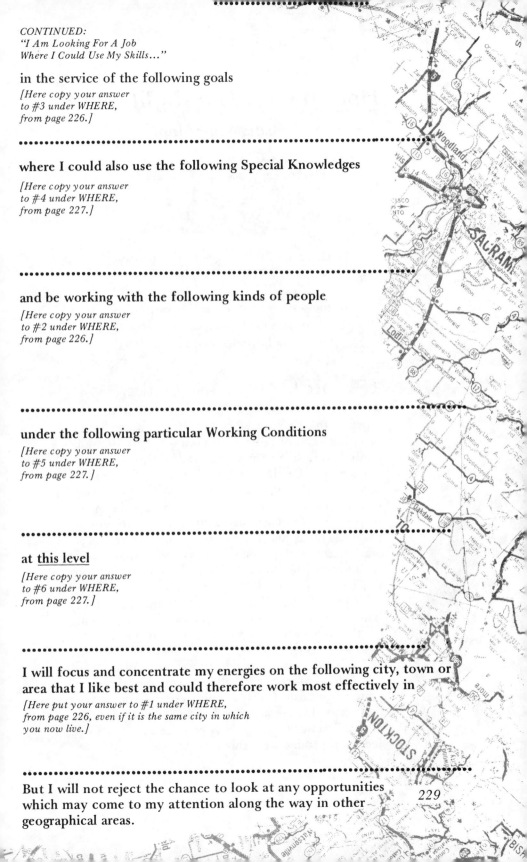

CONTINUED:
*"I Am Looking For A Job
Where I Could Use My Skills..."*

in the service of the following goals

*[Here copy your answer
to #3 under WHERE,
from page 226.]*

where I could also use the following Special Knowledges

*[Here copy your answer
to #4 under WHERE,
from page 227.]*

and be working with the following kinds of people

*[Here copy your answer
to #2 under WHERE,
from page 226.]*

under the following particular Working Conditions

*[Here copy your answer
to #5 under WHERE,
from page 227.]*

at <u>this level</u>

*[Here copy your answer
to #6 under WHERE,
from page 227.]*

I will focus and concentrate my energies on the following city, town or area that I like best and could therefore work most effectively in

*[Here put your answer to #1 under WHERE,
from page 226, even if it is the same city in which
you now live.]*

But I will not reject the chance to look at any opportunities which may come to my attention along the way in other geographical areas.

229

How to Find The Right Place
(Using Your Map)

There are three stages to this process
of finding the place
where you can use your skills,
in the service of those values or purposes
or needs of our society that
you have decided upon:

1st Stage   JUST FOR PRACTICE

At home on vacation, or in the city where you live
most of the year, or wherever, choose some hobby
or enthusiasm or interest of yours—totally non-job-
related, at best. Say, painting, skiing, music, garden-
ing, stamp collecting, affirmative action for women,
or whatever. Go visit someone—anyone—picked out
of the yellow pages or from what somebody suggests
to you, *and if you are shy take a friend with you, of
course.* This is just for information. Just for information. ● Ask the person you visit, who shares your
enthusiasm (one hopes): (1) How did you get into
this work? (2) What do you like the most about it?
(3) What do you like the least about it? and (4)
Where else could I find people making their living
off this, or sharing this enthusiasm, in places I would
not have thought of? ● Then, go visit those people,
and ask the same four questions. And so on, until
you feel comfortable in talking to people who share
your enthusiasm (most shyness comes from having
to talk with people who don't share our enthusiasms). Practice this as long as you need to, until you
feel comfortable with this stage.

2nd Stage JUST FOR INFORMATION

In the city or geographical area *of your choice*, now armed with the clues from your completed map (on previous page), you need to go out as INFORMATION GATHERER, to discover all the places that fit the description on your map.

You start with the Chamber of Commerce, or the Yellow Pages in the phone book, or your friends (contacts) — anyone you know who can tell you. What you want to discover is just one place that is even *remotely* like the place you have described on your map. That's all you need. That place will lead you to others.

Example: One woman felt her most enjoyable (and effective) skills were with people, counseling them, in one to one situations face to face, in a place (she hoped) that was a private organization (as opposed to government or college), but was concerned enough about its employees to want to help them with their career development. So much for her "map".

The way she used this map was, in the city of her choice, to discover from her contacts (e.g. the alumni list from her college) where in that city was even *one* private organization that had a program of career development for its employees. (It turned out to be a bank.) Then to visit the officer in charge of that program to ask: a) how they got started in the program; b) what they were trying to accomplish with the program; c) how it worked; and d) what its strengths and limitations had—so far—turned out to be. Then: where else in that city were similar programs, and who was in charge of them?

Her task then as INFORMATION GATHERER only, to visit each one in turn, and ask the same sorts of questions, until she had surveyed them all. Then to return to the two or three organizations whose program she liked best, and tell them so—together with *why*, and the skills she wanted to use with them.

3rd Stage FOR HIRING, AT LAST

> One thing must be very clear about the two stages above: *you* are the Screener, and the employers or organizations you look at are the *Screenees* all during the first two stages.

If you forget this, you will lapse into the mentality of a Screenee early on, and every employer or organization will know it. Thereby you will lose whatever advantage you had, in this job-hunt process.

But now, when you get to this third stage, when you are going back to the two or three places you already have visited in your Second Stage, and which you decided fitted your description on The Map better than any other, now you are the Screenee. You are now, but only now, coming to visit them as Job-hunter. Whether they have a vacancy or not, is immaterial. You are going to seek out in each organization among your top three or so, the person who has the power to hire (not the personnel department); and you are going to tell him or her

● what impressed you about their organization, during your information survey (stage 2),

● what sorts of challenges, needs or "problems" (go slow in using this latter word with sensitive employers) your survey suggested exist in this field in general, and with this place in particular—that intrigue you.

● what skills seem to you to be needed, in order to meet those challenges or needs in his or her organization.

● the fact that you have these skills (here use the information summarized on the Map, pp. 228–229).

● For more detailed information about this third, or final, stage, see Crystal's book (below), or Haldane's, or Djeddah's.

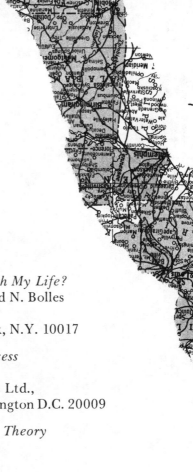

Bibliography
(if you want additional help)

Where Do I Go From Here With My Life?
by John C. Crystal and Richard N. Bolles
$7.95, from: Seabury Press,
815 Second Avenue, New York, N.Y. 10017

How To Make A Habit of Success
by Bernard Haldane
$3.50, from: Acropolis Books Ltd.,
2400 17th Street, N.W., Washington D.C. 20009

*Making Vocational Choices: A Theory
of Careers*
by John L. Holland
$4.95, from: Prentice-Hall, Inc.,
Englewood Cliffs, New Jersey 07632

Moving Up
by Eli Djeddah
$4.95 from: Ten Speed Press,
900 Modoc, Berkeley, CA 94707

Those entering the job-market for the
first time, and desiring a simpler skill-list
are referred to *The Three Boxes of Life*,
in which the Beginning Version of the
Quick Job-Hunting Map may be found.
Or that version may be ordered
separately, by writing directly to
Ten Speed Press, Box 7123, Berkeley,
California 94707. $1.25

My son, be admonished:
of making many books there is no end;
and much study is a weariness of the flesh.

Ecclesiastes

Appendix B: Bibliography

Books

Books are an inexpensive way of getting information, advice, coaching, and supervision.

Books are an inexpensive way of transporting *Someone Knowledgeable* into your library or living room, for an hour's conversation or two, with you.

On the other hand:

Books are also large blocks of black print, often boring, sometimes filled with mis-information delivered with a pontifical ring—which may, however unwittingly, lead the reader down some primrose path.

So, you will have to read with caution and care—except for the first two books we list here, which are recommended absolutely without reservation of any kind:

HIGHLY RECOMMENDED

Crystal, John, and Bolles, Richard N., *Where Do I Go From Here With My Life? The Crystal Life Planning Manual.* A more detailed step-by-step explanation of the process described in Chapters 5-7 of this book you are now reading. From: Seabury Press, 815 Second Avenue, New York, N.Y. 10017. $7.95.

Lathrop, Richard, *Who's Hiring Who.* 1977, Ten Speed Press, Box 7123, Berkeley, CA 94707. Simply excellent resource. Now back in print, revised and improved. $5.95 paper, $8.95 cloth.

Holland, John L., *Making Vocational Choices: a theory of careers.* Englewood Cliffs, New Jersey: Prentice-Hall, Inc. 1973. $4.95 paper. This book is simply excellent, including as it does John Holland's instrument (The Self-Directed Search) for determining the people-environments that you prefer. (We recommend, however, that after you have arrived at your final 'people-environment code,' you do not at that point turn back to the sample Occupations Finder, since this is a very limited classification. Instead, we recommend you use the translation of the Holland 'code' into the 'codes' of the Dictionary of Occupational Titles (p. 136f in Holland's book) in order to find out *clues;* and then we urgently recommend you go on your own information-gathering expeditions around town, as we suggested on page 109, asking people who are in the D.O.T. occupations that go with your Holland 'people-environment': "What other occupations are there, that surround you with the same kind of people?" You will begin to discover some very unbelievable ways in which people make their living while at the same time being surrounded by the kinds of people that appeal to *you*. Thus, when you begin to focus down on the kinds of occupations that interest you, you will be doing so from a multitude of possibilities. Confucius say: when you choose a card, be sure it is from a full deck.)

Bolles, Richard N., "The Quick Job-Hunting Map: a fast way to help." For the undecided college student or the housewife going back to work, or the mid-career changer, or the man or woman whose job has been terminated, or anyone else facing obstacles in the job-hunt. 1975. Ten Speed Press, Box 7123, Berkeley, CA 94707. $1.25. Specify Beginning Version or Advanced Version. See Advanced Version p. 198ff of this book.

BETTER THAN SOME

Djeddah, Eli, *Moving Up: How to get high-salaried jobs,* Berkeley: Ten Speed Press. 1977. $4.95.

Haldane, Bernard, *How to Make a Habit of Success.* Warner Books, Box 690, New York, N.Y. 10019. 1975. $1.95 plus 35¢ postage and handling.

Irish, Richard K., *Go Hire Yourself An Employer.* New York: Anchor Press (Doubleday & Co., Inc.). 1973. $2.95 paper.

Miller, Arthur F., and Mattson, Ralph T., *The Truth About You: Discover what you should be doing with your life.* Old Tappan, New Jersey. Fleming H. Revell Company. $6.95.

FOR SPECIAL REFERENCE
OR BROWSING

Libraries are just filled with books related to the world of work, choosing careers, and the job-hunt process. The worse the economy becomes, at any time, the more publishers dust off old titles, or run to find new ones. Now: every book, to be sure, has something valuable in it. But in some books (no names) it's like panning for gold. You may strike an ore-vein the first five minutes. In other cases, hours, even days may go by, without your getting much.

We have listed these books under several categories.

1. The World of Work in America Today
2. General Books on Job-Hunting
3. On Vocational Counseling in High School or College
4. Shedding Light on Special Problems
5. For Analysis of Skills
6. Interviewing and Employeeship
7. Concerning Being Fired
8. For High School and College Students
9. On Your Own
10. For Women
11. For Minorities
12. For Executives and Those Interested in the Business World
13. For Mid-Life or Second Careers

In general, within each category, the first books listed are the most useful, in our judgment. The rest are for browsing —the kind of stuff you find in most bibliographies. We list them for the sake of completeness.

Not that we have any great confidence many of our readers will read them. As almost everyone knows, the only people who usually read bibliographies are:

people who want to know what some other good books are in the general field that they have been trained in; or

people who are knowledgeable in the subject, and want to see what new books have appeared that they may not be aware of; or

people who question seriously the scholarship and/or orthodoxy of the author, and want to scrutinize the bibliography as a test of his credentials; or

speed-reading graduates who have run through three libraries already, and are desperate for some new fodder for a long winter's night.

I will offer no comment on any of these prospective users of *this* bibliography, except to say that yours truly is a speed reading dropout.

1. THE WORLD OF WORK
IN AMERICA TODAY

Work in America. Special Task Force to the Secretary of Health, Education, and Welfare, administered by the W. E. Upjohn Institute for Employment Research. Cambridge, Massachusetts: MIT Press, 1973. Or: Available from National Technical Information Service, U.S. Department of Commerce, Springfield, VA 22151. December 1972. PB– 214 779. $6.75.

Terkel, Studs, *Working.* New York: Avon Paperback, 1974. $2.25.

Bartlett, Laile E., *New Work/New Life.* 1976. Harper & Row, 10 E. 53rd Street, New York, N.Y. 10022. $8.95 hardcover.

O'Toole, James. "The Reserve Army of the Underemployed. I. The World of Work. II. The Role of Education," a series of articles appearing in CHANGE Magazine, May and June, 1975.

Scoville, James G., *The Job Content of the U.S. Economy 1940-1970.* New York: McGraw-Hill Book Company, 1969. $7.95.

Clark, Ann, *New Ways to Work: a gestalt perspective.* Vitalia, Box 27253, San Francisco, CA 94127. 1975. $1.50.

Babson, Steve, and Brigham, Nancy, *What's Happening to Our Jobs?* 1976. Popular Economics Press, Box 221, Somerville, MA 02143. $1.45 paper.

Changing Schedules of Work: patterns and implications. American Institutes for Research, prepared for the Manpower Administration. 1973. Available from: NTIS, U.S. Department of Commerce, Springfield, VA 22151. PB 219 117.

Poor, Riva, ed., *4 Days, 40 Hours: Reporting a Revolution in Work and Leisure.* Foreword by Paul A. Samuelson. Cambridge, Massachusetts: Bursk and Poor Publishing (66 Martin Street, Cambridge, MA), 1970. $5.00.

Marconi, Katherine, *Survey of Research on Job Satisfaction.* Washington, D.C.: The George Washington University Graduate School of Arts & Sciences. Available from: NTIS, U.S. Department of Commerce, Springfield, VA 22151. June 1973. TR 1117.

"The New Markets and the New Entrepreneurs" in Drucker, Peter F., *Men, Ideas & Politics.* New York: Harper and Row. 1971.

Sheppard, Harold L., and Herrick, Neal Q., *Where Have All the Robots Gone? Worker Dissatisfaction in the 70s.* New York: The Free Press, A Division of The Macmillan Company. 1972. $7.95.

Lasson, Kenneth. *The Workers: Portraits of Nine American Jobholders.* Afterword by Ralph Nader. New York: Bantam Books. 1971. $1.50.

2. GENERAL BOOKS ON JOB-HUNTING

The number of books coming out on job-hunting, to (hopefully) aid the job-hunter, increases each year. We are listing here and in the following sections as many of them as we have heard of, purchased, and read. Many—if not most of them—simply tell you all about "the numbers game." Why are we listing them here? Well, first of all, we know of no such extensive list anywhere else. For sure, someone somewhere out there is looking for a list like this, for some purpose or other (to cure insomnia?) and now at last, his or her search is over.

Secondly, since we digested most of these books either before writing *Parachute* or since (in which case any exceptionally worthwhile ideas they had were incorporated into subsequent revisions of this book), you will now be reassured that we digested *a lot. Parachute* is partly a compendium, you see, of all that has come out to date, in addition to its own hopefully original ideas.

Well, all of this is but a preamble to the $64,000 question: should you buy and/or read any of these books, to supplement what you have learned from this book you presently hold in your hands? Well, sure, under either of two conditions: (1) You have some spare time for further reading on the job-hunt, and you see a title, an author, or a glimmer, below that intrigues you. Go buy. Go read. You will find something helpful in any of these books, to supplement what you have already read. *Parachute* is not after all, a compendium of *all* wisdom about the job-hunt. It would have to have been 2000 pages long, and cost you $45 if it were to be that. In other words, for most of you, this sort of supplementary reading is Optional

—depending on how much time and curiosity you have.
(2) If however, after reading all of *Parachute,* you thought the most fascinating chapter—and the only one you want to follow —was Chapter Two, then reading some of the following books is absolutely Obligatory. You'll need all the help you can get.

Sheppard, Harold L., and Belitsky, A. Harvey, *Promoting Job Finding Success for the Unemployed.* (Summarizing part of the authors' book: *The Job Hunt: Job-Seeking Behavior of Unemployed Workers in a Local Economy.* Baltimore: The John Hopkins Press, 1966.) Kalamazoo, Michigan: The W. E. Upjohn Institute, 1968. An excellent pioneer research study.

Noer, David, *How to Beat the Employment Game*, 1975. Ten Speed Press, Box 7123, Berkeley, CA 94707. Highly recommended.

Turmail, Richard L., "Job Hunters, be prepared to scramble!," *Electronic Design 16,* August 2, 1970. pp. 60ff.

Wein, Ess. *The Complete Job Hunting Guide.* New York: Cornerstone Library. 1966. $1.00.

Payne, Richard A., *How to Get a Better Job Quicker.* New York: Taplinger Publishing Company. 1972. $5.95.

Butler, E. A., *Move In and Move Up.* New York: The Macmillan Company. 1970. $5.95.

Law, Bill, *Decide for Yourself.* Cambridge, England: Hobsons Press (Cambridge) Ltd., Bateman Street, Cambridge CBZ ILZ, England. $2.00 softback. "A new approach to assessing individual abilities and values," put out by The Careers Research and Advisory Centre, in Britain.

Kirn, Arthur, and Kirn, Marie. *Lifework Planning.* New York: McGraw-Hill Book Company. Participant's Workbook $10.00, Trainer's Manual $15.00.

Walter, Verne, and Wallace, Melvin, *"Self-Motivated Personal Career Planning Program."* Published by Walter and Kinzer, Consultants to Management, Box 3330, Santa Monica, CA 90403. 1974.

Schwartz, Eileene, "Game Plan: A Workbook for Group Consulting Participants." Mission Employment Development Department Center, 2948 - 16th Street, San Francisco, CA 94103. 1975.

McKee, Bill, *How to Get a Higher Paying Job Now.* Consumers Digest, Book Dept. CG-11, 6416 N. Lincoln Avenue, Chicago, Illinois 60659. 1974. $1.95.

"A Job-Hunter's Handbook" by Elliott Bernstein, MONEY Magazine, June 1975. Deals with the financial problems of the job-hunt period in one's life.

Moore, Charles G., *The Career Game.* New York: The National Institute of Career Planning (Box 938, Ansonia Station, New York, N.Y. 10023). 1975. $10.95. Written by an economist, from an economist's point of view.

Bryant, John Talbot, *You Can Get a Better Job . . . and this book tells you how! The Complete Handbook for Job Seekers and Those Who Hire Them.* Buffalo: TMC Publishing, Division of Trenton Moncton Corp. (1275 Delaware Ave., B-1, Buffalo, N.Y. 14209, or 345 Lakeshore Road East, Oakville, Ontario, Canada). 1974. $10.00.

Taylor, Phoebe, *How to Succeed in the Business of Finding a Job.* Chicago: Nelson-Hall Company (325 West Jackson Blvd., Chicago, Illinois 60606). 1975. $7.95.

File, Norman & Howroyd, Bernard, *How to Beat the Establishment and Get That Job!* Los Angeles, Apple/One Publishing Company. 1971. $2.95.

Uris, Auren, *Turn Your Job Into a Successful Career.* New York: An Essandess Special Edition, Simon and Schuster, Inc. 1967. $1.00.

Snelling, Robert, *The Opportunity Explosion.* New York: The Macmillan Company. 1969. $6.95.

Biegeleisen, J. I., *How to Go About Getting a Job with a Future.* New York: Grosset & Dunlap, 1967.

_____. *Job Resumes.* New York: Grosset & Dunlap, 1969.

Johansen, I. Norman, *Write Your Ticket to Success: A Do-It-Yourself Guide to Effective Resume Writing & Job Hunting.* Annapolis, MD 21403: Job Hunter's Forum 1976. $7.95.

Jackson, Tom, *28 Days to a Better Job.* "A day-by-day action approach that has helped thousands to find jobs they want." New York. Hawthorn Books, Inc. $6.95

Buus, Virginia, *A Time to Be Born: A practical guide to vocational planning.* Minneapolis: Augsburg Publishing House. 1977.

————, *A Time to Be Born: A practical guide to vocational planning.* Leader's Guide. Minneapolis: Augsburg Publishing House, 1977.

Inter-Cristo. The International Christian Organization. A New Service on Christian Work Opportunities. Box 9323, Seattle, WA 98109.

Anderson, Jack, *The Plum Book.* The Official United States Guide to Leading Positions in the Government, Presidential and Executive Appointments, Salaries, Requirements and Other Vital Statistics for Job Seekers. New York. Bolder Books. $5.95.

3. ON VOCATIONAL COUNSELING IN HIGH SCHOOL OR COLLEGE

McClure, Larry, *Career Education SURVIVAL MANUAL: A Guidebook for Career Educators and Their Friends.* Olympus Publishing Company, 1670 East Thirteenth South, Salt Lake City, Utah 84105. 1975. An absolutely superb little handbook for everyone who wants to understand more about how to relate education to the world of work (and vice versa). Imaginatively laid out, and written by one of the experts in this field.

Career Education: What It Is and How to Do It. Kenneth Hoyt and others. Second Edition, 1974. Olympus Publishing Company, 937 East Ninth South, Salt Lake City, Utah 84105. $6.95.

Career Education Wall Charts, ed. by Carl McDaniels. From: Garrett Park Press, Garrett Park, MD 20766. $14.95 per set of 15. Charts on "Earnings by Occupation," etc.

Crites, John O., *Vocational Psychology.* New York: McGraw Hill Book Company, 1969.

Dunnette, Marvin D., *Handbook of Industrial and Organizational Psychology.* New York: Rand McNally College Publishing Company. 1975. 1500 pages. $45.00. Is likely to be the most comprehensive publication covering the whole field of vocational, organizational and industrial psychology ever put together.

Flanagan, John C., et al, *The Career Data Book: Results from Project TALENT's Five-Year Follow-Up Study.* Palo

Alto, California: American Institutes for Research (Box 1113, Palo Alto 94302). 1973. $5.50. Student's booklet $3.00 for 25 copies, $10.00 for 100 copies.

Stephens, Everett W., *Career Counseling and Placement in Higher Education: A Student Personnel Function.* Bethlehem, Pennsylvania: The College Placement Council, Inc., 65 East Elizabeth Avenue, 1970.

Isaacson, Lee E., *Career Information in Counseling and Teaching.* Boston: Allyn and Bacon, Inc. (Rockleigh, New Jersey 07647). 1971. $11.95.

Windle, J. L.; Van Mondrans, Adrian P.; and Kay, Richard S., *Review of Research: Career Planning and Development, Placement, and Recruitment of College-Trained Personnel.* Published by the College Placement Council, Inc., 65 East Elizabeth Avenue, Bethlehem, PA 18018. 1972. $10.00.

Hoppock, Robert, *Occupational Information: Where to Get It and How to Use It in Counseling and in Teaching.* 3rd Edition. New York: McGraw Hill. 1967.

Kirk, Barbara A., and Michels, Marjorie E., *Occupational Information in Counseling: Use and Classification.* Palo Alto, California: Consulting Psychologists Press, Inc. 1964.

Ghiselli, Edwin E., *The Validity of Occupational Aptitude Tests.* New York: John Wiley and Sons, Inc.

Fine, Sidney A., *Use of the Dictionary of Occupational Titles to Estimate Educational Investment.* Kalamazoo, Michigan: The W. E. Upjohn Institute for Employment Research, Inc. 1968.

Hoffmann, Banesh, *The Tyranny of Testing.* New York: Collier Books. 1964. 95¢.

Atherton, J. C., and Mumphrey, Anthony, *Essential Aspects of Career Planning and Development.* Danville, Illinois: The Interstate Printers and Publishers, 1969.

Vocational Biographies Career Subscriptions Service. Box 146, Sauk Centre, MN 56378. For grades 7-14.

4. SHEDDING LIGHT ON
SPECIAL PROBLEMS

Our whole vocational system is oriented toward people with verbal skills, rather than intuitive; and toward achievement, rather than relationship goals. Those who wish to delve further into this realm will find the following books very helpful:

Ornstein, Robert E., *The Psychology of Consciousness.* New York: Viking Press. 1972. $8.95. Fascinating book about the two sides of the brain; raises acute questions about how much we have oriented our whole culture toward one side of the brain rather than the other.

McClelland, David C., and Steele, Robert S., *Human Motivation, A Book of Readings.* Morristown, New Jersey: General Learning Press (250 James Street, Morristown 07960). 1973. $7.80. Superb.

Knowles, Malcolm S., *Self-Directed Learning: A Guide for Learners and Teachers.* New York: Association Press (291 Broadway, New York, N.Y. 10007). 1975. Fascinating.

5. FOR ANALYSIS OF SKILLS

First of all, there are books or pamphlets dealing with the theory of (and behind) skills analysis. Most of these are from the brilliant brain of Sidney Fine:

The W. E. Upjohn Institute for Employment Research's Studies on Functional Job Analysis and Career Design

—*Guidelines for the Design of New Careers.* Sidney A. Fine. September 1967.

—*A Systems Approach to New Careers: Two Papers.* Methods for Manpower analysis, No. 3. Wretha W. Wiley and Sidney A. Fine. November 1969.

—*An Introduction to Functional Job Analysis: A Scaling of Selected Tasks from the Social Welfare Field.* Methods for Manpower Analysis, No. 4. Sidney A. Fine and Wretha W. Wiley. September 1971.

—*Functional Job Analysis Scales: A Desk Aid.* Methods for Manpower Analysis, No. 5. Sidney A. Fine. April 1973.

We particularly recommend the last two publications, above. They are all available from The W. E. Upjohn Institute for Employment Research, 300 South Westnedge Avenue, Kalamazoo, Michigan 49007.

U.S. Department of Labor, Manpower Administration.
A Handbook for Job Restructuring. Superintendent of Documents, U.S. Government Printing Office, Washington, D.C.
20402. 1970. 55¢.

"Nature of Skill: Implications for Education and Training"
by Sidney A. Fine, W. E. Upjohn Institute for Employment
Research, 1101 - 17th Street N.W., Washington, D.C. 20036.
A superb summary of the latest thinking from the father of
skills analysis in the Dictionary of Occupational Titles.

*Task Analysis Inventories: A Method for Collecting Job
Information.* U.S. Department of Labor Manpower Administration. 1973. Stock No. 2900 00163 US SUP DOC $2.60.

U.S. Department of Labor (Bureau of Labor Statistics,
Middle Atlantic Regional Office), *"Resources for Manpower
Planning.* From: Mr. Herbert Biestock, Assistant Regional
Director for Bureau of Labor Statistics, 1515 Broadway, New
York, New York 10036.

An Occupational Clustering System and Curriculum Implications for the Comprehensive Career Education Model Human
Resources Research Organization, Alexandria, Virginia,
January 1973. Center for Vocational and Technical Education. The Ohio State University.

Handbook for Analyzing Jobs. U.S. Department of Labor.
J. D. Hodgson, Secretary. Manpower Administration 1972S.
Stock No. 2900 0131. Superintendent of Documents. $2.50.

6. INTERVIEWING AND
   EMPLOYEESHIP

"Making the Most of Your Job Interview." New York Life
Insurance Company. Available from any New York Life Insurance Company office.

"Interviewing Techniques for the Non-Personnel Executive"
(for those who have to sit on the other side of the desk), by
Robert M. Hecht, Joel E. Aron, and Morton D. Siegel. Personnel
Data Systems, Inc., 274 Madison Avenue, New York, N.Y.
10017.

Addeo, Edmund G., and Burger, Robert E., *EgoSpeak: Why
No One Listens to You.* Radnor, Pennsylvania: Chilton Book
Company, 1973. $6.95. An excellent tongue-in-cheek, and

very helpful book on how to be sure your conversation conveys what you want it to, about your concern for others instead of just yourself.

Saxenian, Hrand, "To Select a Leader," *Technology Review,* Vol. 72, No. 7, May 1970, pp. 54f. Written to guide both interviewer and interviewee. *Very* helpful. (Ask your local public library for it.)

Drucker, Peter F., "How to Be an Employee," in *Psychology Today,* March 1968 (an issue on "The Great Job Dilemma"). Excellent, as anything from Peter Drucker's pen is.

7. CONCERNING BEING FIRED

Catt, Ivor, *How to Hang Onto Your Job While Everyone Else Is Losing His: THE CATT CONCEPT, the New Industrial Darwinism.* New York: G. P. Putnam's Sons, 1972. $2.95.

Howell, Barbara, *Don't Bother to Come in on Monday: What to Do When You Lose Your Job.* New York: St. Martin's Press. 1973. $6.50.

Irish, Richard K., *If Things Don't Improve Soon I May Ask You to Fire Me: The Management Book for Everyone Who Works.* Garden City, New York: Anchor Press/Doubleday. 1975. $7.95 hardcover.

Reid, Clyde H., *Help! I've Been Fired.* Philadelphia, Pa.: United Church Press. 1971. $1.95.

Bielski, Robin, *The Out-of-Work Book: How to Predict It; What to Do When It Happens.* Allen Advertising Company, Inc., New York, N.Y. 10028. 1974. Paper.

8. FOR HIGH SCHOOL AND COLLEGE STUDENTS

Working Loose, New Vocations Project, San Francisco: American Friends Service Committee, 1972. $1.95. Order from American Friends Service Committee, 2160 Lake St., San Francisco, CA 94121.

College Graduates and Jobs: Adjusting to a New Labor Market Situation. A Report and Recommendations by The Carnegie Commission on Higher Education. Highstown, New Jersey: McGraw Hill Book Company, 1973. $4.50.

The Graduates: A Report on the Characteristics and Plans of College Seniors. Leonard L. Baird, Principal Investigator, with chapters by Mary Jo Clark and Rodney T. Hartnett. Princeton, New Jersey: Educational Testing Service. 1973.

Cartter, Allan M., *Ph.D.s and the Academic Labor Market.* New York: McGraw-Hill, 1976. $12.50. Actual and projected data relating to the employment outlook for Ph.D.s. (Read before enrolling in graduate school.)

Gottlieb, David, *Youth and the Meaning of Work.* The Pennsylvania State University, University Park, PA 16802. Washington, D.C.: Department of Labor, Manpower Administration, Contract No. 81 11 72 04.

Sandman, Peter, and Goldenson, Daniel R., *How to Succeed in Business Before Graduating: 307 Tested Money-Making Ideas for the Undergraduate Entrepreneur.* New York: Collier Books. 1968. $1.95.

Harvard Student Agencies, Inc., *Making It: A Guide to Student Finances.* New York: E. P. Dutton & Co., Inc. 1973. $4.95.

Berg, Ivar, *Education and Jobs: The Great Training Robbery.* Foreword by Eli Ginzberg. Boston: Beacon Press. 1971. $2.95.

Williams, Gerald D., *Student Perceptions of Occupational Congruency.* Baltimore, Maryland: The Johns Hopkins University Center for Social Organization of Schools (Dr. John L. Holland, Director).

Buskirk, Richard H., *Your Career: How to Plan It, Manage It, Change It.* 1976. Cahners Books Inc., 221 Columbus Avenue, Boston, Mass. 02116.

Chapman, Elwood N., *Career Search: A Personal Pursuit,* 1976. Science Research Associates, Inc. A subsidiary of IBM, Chicago, Illinois.

Job Guide for Young Workers, Manpower Administration, U.S. Department of Labor, 0 415 741. Washington, D.C.: U.S. Government Printing Office. $1.50.

Herzog, Doug, and Anderson, Bill. "Cluster Interest Inventory," Watertown, South Dakota: Career Education Systems (Box 391, Watertown, SD 57201).

"Career Interest Guide for Students," available from John P. Knievel, Supervisor, Educational Services, Northern States Power Company, 414 Nicollet Mall, Minneapolis, Minn. 55401. Groups a multitude of jobs into fifteen 'career clusters.'

Carkhuff, Robert, *The Art of Developing a Career.* Amherst, Massachusetts: Human Resource Development Press (Box 863, Dept. M-18, Amherst, Massachusetts 01002). 1974. For grades 10-16. $6.95 for students' guide; $9.95 for helper's guide.

"The Strength Deployment Inventory," Personal Strengths Assessment Service, 571 Muskingum Avenue, Pacific Palisades, CA 90272. $2.50. An inventory to help the individual decide how he or she usually uses their strengths in relating to others under two conditions: when everything is going well, vs. when you are faced with conflict.

Ostrom, Dr. Stan, *Self-Appraisal and Assessment Structure.* 1972. From: Dr. Stan Ostrom, Box 1423, San Jose, CA 95109. $5.00. Includes a rating scale, a student handbook (for groups or individuals), and a covering manual.

Campbell, David P. *If you don't know where you're going, you'll probably end up somewhere else.* Niles, Illinois, Argus Communications, 1974. $1.95 paper.

"Career World—The Continuing Guide to Careers" (a periodical), Joyce Lain Kennedy, Executive Editor. From $3.25 up, per subscription. Curriculum Innovations, Inc., 501 Lake Forest Avenue, Highwood, Illinois 60040.

Haight, Tim, *Careers After High School: 251 Selected Jobs for High School Graduates.* New York: Collier Books. 1970. $1.25.

Endicott, Frank S., *How to Get the Right Job and Keep It: A Guide to Jobs for High School Students.* Miami, Florida 33145: Education Division, Management Information Center, Inc., 1450 Coral Way, Box 357. 1970.

Malnig, Lawrence R., and Morrow, Sandra L., *What Can I Do with a Major in . . . ?* Jersey City: Saint Peter's College Press (2641 Kennedy Blvd., Jersey City, N.J. 07306). 1975. Describes how 10,000 alumni (based on a 76 per cent sample) actually used their college training and what fields various majors went into. The answer to 'what can I do with a major in . . . ?' ultimately proves to be the same as the answer to 'what does a 2000 pound gorilla do on his birthday?—namely, Anything he wants to.

Ferguson, Jeff, ed., *The Career Guidance Class.* Camarillo, California: Walter T. Metcalf and Associates (2034 Ciprian Avenue, Camarillo, CA 93010). 1974.

The College Placement Council, *Four Year Liberal Arts Graduates: Their utilization in business, industry, and government—the problem and some solutions.* From: College Placement Council, Inc., Box 2263, Bethlehem, PA 18001.

The College Placement Council, *Directory of College Recruiting Personnel.* From: CPC (Box 2263, Bethlehem, PA 18001). $5.00 each for CPC members, $8.00 for non-members.

Calvert, Robert, Jr., and Steele, John E., *Planning Your Career.* New York: McGraw-Hill Book Company, Inc., 1963. $1.95.

Cosgrave, Gerald, *Career Planning: Search for a Future.* Guidance Centre/Faculty of Education/University of Toronto. 1973. Unusual, in that it relates its explorations to John L. Holland's six people-environments.

Figler, Howard E., *PATH: A Career Workbook for Liberal Arts Students.* Cranston, Rhode Island: Carroll Press (43 Squantum Street, Cranston, Rhode Island 02920) 1974. Quite helpful.

Muraski, Ed. J., *Corner Your Career: Choose, Change or Confirm Your Career.* D & E Publishing Company, 22042 Rockport Lane, Huntington Beach, CA 92646. $2.75 plus 25¢ postage and handling. 1973.

Hutchinson, Marilyn A., and Spooner, Sue E., "Job Search Barometer." Published by The College Placement Council, Inc., Box 2263, Bethlehem, PA 18001. $3.00 to CPC members, $5.00 to non-members.

Pell, Arthur R., *The College Graduate Guide to Job Finding.* New York: Simon and Schuster. 1973. (1 West 39th Street, New York, N.Y. 10018) $2.45.

Longhary, John W., and Ripley, Theresa M., *This Isn't Quite What I Had in Mind: A Career Planning Program for College Students.* United Learning Corporation, 3255 Olive Street, Eugene, Oregon 97405. 1974. Very entertaining.

Brown, Newell, *After College—Junior College—Military Service—What?* New York: Grosset and Dunlap, 1971. $3.95.

Lembeck, Ruth, *Teenage Jobs.* New York: David McKay Co., Inc. 1971. $6.95.

Rubin, David M., *The Independent Teen-Ager: 350 Summer Jobs for High School Students.* New York: Collier Books. 1971. $1.25.

Barron's Teen-age Summer Guide. 4th rev. ed. 1972. $2.25.

Goldenthal, Allan B., *The Teenage Employment Guide.* New York: Simon & Schuster, 1969. $2.95.

Mitchell, Joyce Slayton, *I Can Be Anything: Careers and Colleges for Young Women.* College Entrance Examination Board, Publications Orders, Box 2815, Princeton, New Jersey 08540. Item No. 219850. 1976. $4.50 paper.

Leith, Myrena A., *Summer Employment Director of the United States.* 23rd ed. National Directive Service, 1974. $5.95.

World-Wide Summer Placement Directory. Includes permanent career and part-time opportunities. Annual. Advancement and Placement Institute, 169 N. 9th Street, Brooklyn, New York. $10.00.

9. ON YOUR OWN

Weaver, Peter, *YOU, INC. A detailed escape route to being your own boss.* Garden City, New York: Doubleday & Company, Inc. 1973. $7.95.

Wood, Jane, *Selling What You Make.* Baltimore, Maryland: Penguin Books, Inc. 1973. $2.25.

Dible, Donald M., *Up Your OWN Organization: A Handbook for the Employed, the Unemployed, and the Self-Employed on How to Start and Finance a New Business.* Santa Clara, California 95051: Entrepreneur Press, Mission Station, Drawer 2759. 1972. $14.95.

Kalins, Dorothy, *Cutting Loose: A Civilized Guide for Getting Out of the System.* New York: Saturday Review Press. 1973. $6.95.

Handel, Lawrence, *The Job Handbook for Postcollege Cop-Outs.* New York: Pocket Books (1 West 39th Street, New York, New York 10018). 1973. $1.25.

Ellis, John. *A financial guide for the self-employed: taxes, employees, accountants, insurance, bill collecting, loans, time*

management, retirement, paperwork. Chicago, Illinois: Henry
Regnery Company. 1972. $7.50.

Nicholas, Ted, *How to Form Your Own Corporation With-
out a Lawyer for Under $50.00. Complete with tear-out Forms,
Certificate of Incorporation, Minutes, By-Laws.* Wilmington,
Delaware: Enterprise Publishing Co., Inc. (1000 Oakfield Lane,
Wilmington, Delaware 19810). 1973. $7.95 plus 45¢ for
postage and handling.

Henderson, Bill, *The Publish It Yourself Handbook: Literary
tradition and how to.* Yonkers, New York: Pushcart Book
Press (Box 845, Yonkers 10701).

Goodman, Joseph, *How to Publish, Promote and Sell Your
Book.* Chicago, Illinois: Adams Press. 1970. $2.00.

Logsdon, Gene, *The Organic Homesteader.* Rodale Press.
$7.95. Advice for those going back to the land.

Woodstock Craftsman Manual I, II. New York: Prager.
1972, 1973. $4.95 each. A paperback encyclopedia for would-
be artisand, written by the crafts people of Woodstock, with
instruction on all kinds of crafts: needlework, candlemaking,
pottery, book publishing, song writing, videotaping, etc.

Young, Jean and Jim, *Garage Sale Manual.* New York:
Praeger. 1973. $3.95. Alternative economics for the people:
hints on garage sales, running restaurants, buying real estate,
running flea markets, antique shops, etc.

Henry, Leon, Jr., *The Home Office Guide: How to Work
at Home and Like It.* New York: Arco Publishing Co. 1968.
$1.45. Available from: Home Office Report, 17 Scarsdale
Farm, Scarsdale, New York 10583. Prepaid orders only. For
those interested in working out of an office at home, on their
own. Henry also publishes a monthly Report ($15 a year)
and other helps. Ask for his catalog.

10. FOR WOMEN

Now, just a (perhaps unnecessary) word of common sense
—uncommon common sense, sad to say—about this whole
business of job-hunting publications for women. There is a
difference between *form* and *content.* In these days of liberated consciousness (or conscious liberation?) there is a great
preoccupation with *form:* i.e., does this book use non-sexist

language? But let us not forget *content,* please. A book that does little more than outline the old numbers game (see Chapter Two) is not going to do you much good, no matter how superb (i.e., non-sexist) its form may be. On the other hand, a book with helpful *content* (i.e., the creative minority's prescription) is going to help you, no matter how chauvinistic its language might be (just shut your eyes, and grit your teeth). The best of all possible worlds, of course, is to have both: a book whose form *and* content are both superb: that's the ideal woman's book. But don't get hypnotized just by *form,* please.

Catalyst, *Planning for Work.* Self-Guidance Series G1, 1973. Catalyst, 14 East 60th Street, New York, N.Y. 10022. $1.75.

Catalyst, *Your Job Campaign.* Self-Guidance Series G2. 1975. Catalyst, 14 East 60th Street, New York, N.Y. 10022. $1.75.

Pogrebin, Letty Cottin, *Getting Yours: How to Make the System Work for the Working Woman.* 1975. Avon Books, 959 Eighth Avenue, New York, N.Y. 10019. $1.75 paper.

Friedman, Sande, and Schwartz, Lois C., *No Experience Necessary: A Guide to Employment for the Female Liberal Arts Graduate.* Dell Publishing Co., Inc., 750 Third Avenue, New York, N.Y. 10017. 1971. $1.25.

"Work and Money: Jobs—Feminist Enterprises—Alternatives," Chapter Six in *The New Woman's Survival Catalog.* New York: Coward, McCann & Geoghegan, Inc./Berkley Publishing Corporation, 206 Madison Avenue, New York, N.Y. 10016. 1973. $5.00. Lists facts, figures, books, resources, centers, and what your rights are.

Schwartz, Felice N.; Schifter, Margaret H.; and Gillotti, Susan S., *How to go to work when your husband is against it, your children aren't old enough, and there's nothing you can do anyhow.* New York: Simon and Schuster, 630 Fifth Avenue, New York, N.Y. 10020. 1973. $8.95 hardback.

Bird, Carolyn, *Everything a Woman Needs to Know to Get Paid What She's Worth.* Edited by Helene Mandelbaum. New York: David McKay Company, Inc. 1973. $8.95.

Lembeck, Ruth, *Job Ideas for Today's Woman for Profit, for Pleasure, for Personal Growth, for Self-Esteem. Ways to Work Part-Time, Full-Time Free-Lance at Home and in the Office, and as an Entrepreneur.* Englewood Cliffs, New Jersey: Prentice-Hall. 1974. $6.95.

Wetherby, Terry, *Conversations: Working women talk about doing a "man's Job."* Millbrae, California: Les Femmes Publishing. $4.95.

Epstein, Cynthia Fuchs, *WOMAN'S PLACE. Options and Limits in Professional Careers.* 1971. Berkeley, Los Angeles, and London. University of California Press. $2.45.

Roesch, Roberta, *There's Always a Right Job for Every Woman.* New York: Berkley Publishing Corporation. 1976. $2.95.

Ross, Susan C., *The Rights of Women: An American Civil Liberties Union Handbook.* New York: Avon Books. $1.75.

Pettman, Barrie O., *Equal Pay for Women: Progress and Problems in Seven Countries.* Washington–London: Hemisphere Publishing Corporation. McGraw-Hill Book Company.

Farmer, Helen S., and Backer, Thomas E., *New Career Options: A Woman's Guide.* New York: Human Sciences Press, 72 Fifth Avenue, New York 10011. 1976.

Abarbanel and Siegel, *Woman's Work Book: How to Get Your First Job. How to Re-Enter the Job Market. How to Fight for Your Rights in the Work World, and More.* New York: Praeger Publishers. 1976 Second Printing.

Careers for Women in the 70's. Washington, D.C.: U.S. Government Printing Office (Superintendent of Documents, U.S. Govt. Printing Office, Washington, D.C. 20402). 1973. 50¢.

Women: A Selected Bibliography. Woman and the Human Revolution, Wittenberg University, Patricia O'Connor, Coordinator. August 1973. Available from: The Wittenberg Bulletin (Vol. 70, No. 6), Wittenberg University, Springfield, Ohio 45501. Section on books related to Women and Work.

It is frequently argued that a 21-year-old woman is perfectly free to choose a career if she cares to do so. This argument conveniently overlooks the fact that our society has spent twenty long years carefully marking the woman's ballot for her. Society has controlled not her alternatives but her motivation to choose.

—Sandra L. and Daryl J. Bem, 1973

Women: A Bibliography. Lucinda Cisler. Available from Ms. Cisler, Box 240, New York, N.Y. 10024. 50¢. Section on more books related to Women and Work.

"The Myth and the Reality," Washington, D.C.: U.S. Department of Labor Employment Standards Administration, Women's Bureau. 1971. Available from: Superintendent of Documents, U.S. Government Printing Office, Washington, D.C. 20402. 10¢. Stock No. 2902-0041.

"Fact Sheet on the Earnings Gap." Washington, D.C.: U.S. Department of Labor Wage and Labor Standards Administration Women's Bureau. 1971. Available from: Superintendent of Documents, U.S. Government Printing Office, Washington, D.C. 20402. WB 71-86.

"Underutilization of Women Workers," Washington, D.C.: U.S. Department of Labor Workplace Standards Administration Women's Bureau. 1971. Available from: Superintendent of Documents, U.S. Government Printing Office, Washington, D.C. 20402. 35¢. 0-413-102.

"Publications of the Women's Bureau." Washington, D.C.: U.S. Department of Labor Workplace Standards Administration Women's Bureau. 1971. Available from: Superintendent of Documents, U.S. Government Printing Office, Washington, D.C. 20402. 0-415-816.

Jobfinding Techniques for Mature Women. Washington, D.C.: U.S. Department of Labor, Wage and Labor Standards Administration, Women's Bureau. 1970. Lists women's associations in various fields and professions, among other things, which may be of interest to women of *any* age. Plays the numbers game in its job-hunting techniques, however. Available from: Superintendent of Documents, U.S. Government Printing Office, Washington, D.C. 20402. 30¢.

"Who Are the Working Mothers?" Washington, D.C.: U.S. Department of Labor, Employment Standards Administration, Women's Bureau. 1972. Available from: Superintendent of Documents, U.S. Government Printing Office. 10¢. Stock No. 1916-0007.

A Guide for Affirmative Action. Equal Employment Opportunity in State and Local Governments. Washington, D.C.: U.S. Civil Service Commission. 1972. They also publish a wealth of other material on Equal Opportunity for those who want to pursue the legal route, *while at the same time* using the principles in this book as their alternative route. (Court cases in some places are alleged to have a backlog equivalent to a two-year waiting period, and you don't want to wait *that* long for a job, do you?) Materials available from: U.S. Civil Service Commission, Bureau of Intergovernmental Personnel Programs, Washington, D.C. 20415.

Loring, Rosalind, and Wells, Theodora, *Breakthrough: Women into Management*. New York: Van Nostrand Reinhold Company (450 West 33rd Street, New York, N.Y. 10001). 1972. $3.95 paper.

Hennig, Margaret, and Jardim, Anne, *The Managerial Woman*. New York: Anchor Press/Doubleday. 1976. $7.95.

Epstein, Cynthia Fuchs, *Woman's Place: Options and Limits in Professional Careers*. Berkeley, California: University of California Press. 1970. $2.45.

"Womanpower," A Monthly Report on Fair Employment Practices for Women. Tells what's happening in the whole field with fair employment for women, and what's going to happen next. Primarily for organizations rather than individuals. One-year subscription: $37.00. Available from: *Womanpower*, Betsy Hogan Associates, 222 Rawson Road, Brookline, Massachusetts 02146.

Cowan, Susan, *From College Girl to Working Woman: 201 Big-City Jobs for Girl Graduates*. New York: Collier Books Career Guide, Macmillan Company, 866 Third Avenue, New York, N.Y. 10022. 1970. $1.50.

Prentice, Barbara, *The Back to Work Handbook for Housewives: 500 Job and Career Ideas*. New York: Collier Books. 1971. $1.50.

Scobey, Joan, and McGrath, Lee Parr, *Creative Careers for Women: A Handbook of Sources and Ideas for Part-Time Jobs*. New York: Essandess Special Editions, Simon & Schuster, 630 Fifth Avenue, New York, N.Y. 10020. 1968. $1.00.

11. FOR MINORITIES

Johnson, Willis L., ed., *Directory of Special Programs for Minority Group Members: Career Information Services, Employment Skills Banks, Financial Aid Sources—Second Edition.* Garrett Park, Maryland: Garrett Park Press (Garrett Park, Maryland 20877). $8.50 if payment is enclosed with order.

A Study of Successful Persons from Seriously Disadvantaged Backgrounds. Human Interaction Research Institute, Los Angeles, CA. March 31, 1970. PB 199 438 NTIS.

12. FOR EXECUTIVES AND THOSE INTERESTED IN THE BUSINESS WORLD

Drucker, Peter, *Management: Tasks, Responsibilities, Practices.* New York: Harper & Row, Publishers (10 East 53rd Street, New York, N.Y. 10022). 1973. $15.00. Should be absolutely required reading for anyone contemplating entering, changing to, or becoming a professional within, the business world, or any organization.

Louis, Arthur M., "The Year of the Executive Axing," *Fortune,* September 1970, pp. 142ff.

Performance Dynamics, Inc., *The Professional Job Changing System: The world's fastest way to get a better job!* Verona, New Jersey: McCormack Services. 1974. $10.50. (Performance Dynamics, Inc., 17 Grove Avenue, Verona, New Jersey 07044)

Boll, Carl R., *Executive Jobs Unlimited.* New York: The Macmillan Company. 1965. $4.95.

Schoonmaker, Alan N., *Executive Career Strategy.* New York: American Management Association, Inc. (135 West 50th Street, New York, N.Y. 10020). 1971. $14.00.

German, Donald R. and Joan W., *Successful Job Hunting for Executives.* Henry Regnery Company, 180 North Michigan Avenue, Chicago, Illinois 60601. 1974. $4.95.

Adams, Edward L., Jr., *Career Advancement Guide.* New York: McGraw-Hill, Inc. 1975.

Kent, Malcolm, *Successful Executive Job-Hunting.* New York: Laddin Press. 1967. $5.95.

Uris, Auren, *Action Guide for Executive Job Seekers and Employers.* (Original title: The Executive Job Market) New York: Arco Publishing Company. 1968. $2.95.

Miner, Charles S., *How to Get an Executive Job After Forty*. New York: Collier Books. 1963. $1.50.

Drucker, Peter F., *Technology, Management and Society*. New York: Harper and Row, 1970.

Vicino, Franco L., and Miller, John A., PROSPECTS: A Program in Self-Planning and Evaluation of Career and Training Needs. Scottsville, New York: Transnational Programs Corporation. 1971. For managers, looking ahead.

Townsend, Robert, *Up the Organization: How to Stop the Corporation from Stifling People and Strangling Profits*. New York: Alfred A. Knopf, 1970.

Burton, Anthony, *A Programmed Guide to Office Warfare*. New York: Ballantine Books. 1972. 95¢.

Rodman, Irwin L., *The Executive Jungle*. New York: Warner Paperback Library (Warner Books, Inc., 315 Park Avenue South, New York, N.Y. 10010). 1973. $1.25.

Kaufman, H. B., *Obsolescence and Professional Career Development*. New York, N.Y.: Amacom (a division of American Management Associations, 135 West 50th Street, New York, N.Y. 10020). 1974. $11.95.

Peter Laurence F., and Hull, Raymond, *The Peter Principle: Why Things Always Go Wrong*. New York: William Morrow & Company, Inc. 1969. $4.95 hardback.

Uris, Auren, and Tarrant, John J., *How to Win Your Boss's Love, Approval... and Job*. Van Nostrand-Reinhold Co. 1974. $7.95.

Crosby, Philip, *The Art of Getting Your Own Sweet Way*. New York: McGraw-Hill, Inc. 1974. A description of how to be a situation manager, from the point of view of a vice president of a large corporation.

13. MID-LIFE OR
SECOND CAREERS

LeShan, Eda J., *The Wonderful Crisis of Middle Age: Some Personal Reflections*. New York: David McKay Company, Inc. 1973. $7.95.

Hills, L. Rust, *How to Retire at Forty-One: Or, Dropping Out of the Rat Race Without Going Down the Drain*. Garden City, New York: Doubleday & Company, Inc. 1973. $6.95.

Sheppard, Harold L., "The Emerging Pattern of Second Careers" in *Vocational Guidance Quarterly,* December 1971 issue: Second Careers as a Way of Life: A Symposium. (Read at your local public library.)

"Studies on Problems of Work and Age: Second Careers." A special issue of *Industrial Gerontology,* Spring 1973. Published by the National Council on the Aging. (At your public library)

Albee, Lou, *Job Hunting After Forty.* New York: Arco Publishing Company, Inc. 1971. (Former title: Over Forty— Out of Work? 1970) $1.45.

Secrets of Successful Job Hunting. Chemical Engineering, McGraw-Hill, Inc. Engineer's Career Development Series. 1972. Lists resources in its appendix, which engineers can turn to for special help. Many of these resources have already gone out of existence, unfortunately.

AIAA Employment Workshops. Volume II. An Analytic Report on Some Effects of Twenty-Two Workshops. Leonard Smith, American Institute of Aeronautics and Astronautics. January 1972. PB: 209 367. NTIS.

Harper, Maxwell J., and Pell, Arthur R., *How to Get the Job You Want After Forty.* New York: Pilot Books, 1967.

McNeil, John S., and Giffen, Martin B. "Military Retirement: The Retirement Syndrome," *American Journal of Psychiatry,* 123:7 January 1967. (See your local public library.)

Target: tomorrow. Second Career Planning for Military Retirees. Office of the Assistant Secretary of Defense, Manpower and Reserve Affairs. March 1972. Available from: Superintendent of Documents, U.S. Government Printing Office, Washington, D.C. 20402. 55¢.

"Problems after Forty," Publication No. 328 of the American Institute of Family Relations, 5287 Sunset Boulevard, Los Angeles, California 90027.

Richardson, Robert Brooks, *An Examination of the Transferability of Certain Military Skills and Experience to Civilian Occupations. No. PB 177 372.* Distributed by Clearinghouse for Federal Scientific and Technical Information, Springfield, Virginia 22151. September 1967.

Bartlett, Laile E., *The Vanishing Parson*. Boston: Beacon Press, 1971.

Strategic Research Services Group, *The Problems of the Priest: Have his concerns become the church's crisis?* Report on a comprehensive survey conducted among the Episcopal parish clergy. New York: The Executive Council of the Episcopal Church, 1970.

Jud, Gerald J., and Mills, Edwar W., Jr., and Burch, Genevieve Walters, *Ex-Pastors. Why Men Leave the Parish Ministry.*

Harris, John C., *The Minister Looks for a Job, Finding Work As a Parish Minister.* 1974. From: The Alban Institute, Inc., Mount St. Alban, Washington, D.C. 20016. $1.50.

Two are better than one;
    for if they fall,
the one will lift up his fellow;

but woe to him that is alone when he falleth,
and hath not another to lift him up.

Ecclesiastes

Appendix C:
Professionals

HELP

A WORD (OR THREE) ABOUT THIS DIRECTORY

The listing of an organization, agency, or person in this directory of professional help for the job-hunter does *not necessarily* constitute an endorsement of their program or services. There are some here that we think very highly of. However, you are urged, indeed exhorted, to do comparison shopping, according to the principles in Chapter Four, and make up *your* own mind about which places are best. If you don't comparison shop, you will deserve what you get.

While information concerning the groups listed here is believed to be accurate and reliable, it is not possible to guarantee the accuracy of all information given. We apologize in advance to anyone who is thereby offended. Moreover, be wary. Phone numbers change, staffs change, and places fold up, almost weekly, in this field.

Needless to say, this is not a complete directory in any sense of the word. It is only intended to indicate *kinds* of places that exist. If you want help badly, you will need to supplement this directory with your own research in your own city.

Cost for professional help will range from $75 or less (for aptitude testing only) to $3000 or more (for complete guidance throughout the whole job-hunting process). Read Chapter Four again, please. The wallet you save may be your own.

In this job-hunting and career counseling field, some counselors have all the right training and credentials, but have a miserable record as 'enabler' of those looking for a job or career. Others with or without credentials have a fabulous rate of success as 'enabler' of men and women in the job-hunt process. The only thing that counts are the results. The credentialing is, so far as a prospective client is concerned, irrelevant. Someday, to be sure, we may see a credentialing process which sets as its principal test the *counselor's* ability to go out and get the job he or she wants, where he or she wants it, and at the proper level—*before* he or she presumes to counsel others in the job hunt ... even as a psychoanalyst must undergo analysis before he or she presumes to analyze others. Until then, you're going to have to be wary.

A. HELP FOR ANYONE

I. Irrespective of where you live (correspondence courses by mail or services by mail)

CRYSTAL MANAGEMENT SERVICES, INC. Our good friend John C. Crystal has dissolved his Crystal Management Services, Inc., and is now Principal Consultant to a new firm recently incorporated by Hal and Marilyn Shook. John's new address is John C. Crystal, Principal Consultant, Life Management Services, Inc., 6825 Redmond Drive, McLean, Virginia 22101, phone (703) 356-2630. LMS conducts courses and seminars not only in McLean and nearby areas, but also in the Shenandoahs (Bryce Mountain), Maryland (Columbia and College Park), and the New York Metropolitan Area; for information about the latter, contact Bob Marshall at (516) 671-5477 (day) or (516) 627-3631 (night).

• There are a number of places which offer help by mail on an hourly basis to anyone who wants to pay their fee. Among such professionals are:

MANFRED F. ETTINGER. 2020 Ventura Avenue, Springfield, Missouri 65804. $36 per hour for advisory services.

II. Somewhat dependent on where you live: workshops or seminars

JOB FORUMS. These are run in various cities by the Chamber of Commerce, service organizations, sales executives clubs, advertising clubs. These are usually run on a weekly or bi-weekly basis, at some central location, and afford an opportunity for some expert to speak on some phase of marketing, plus an opportunity for questions from those attending on any phase of the marketing process. (Some cities call them *man marketing clinics,* or such like—instead of *job forums.*) Usually there is no charge for these forums, or only a nominal one. Consult your Chamber for information as to what exists in *your* city.

DIRECTORY OF APPROVED COUNSELING AGENCIES. Is prepared by the International Association of Counseling Services, Inc., a board created by the American Personnel and Guidance Association, and lists reputable counseling agencies which maintain high professional standards, and have been approved by the board, after requesting evaluation previously. (Whether they know anything about the techniques in this book is something else again.) Your local library may have this, or it can be procured (for $4.00) from International Association of Counseling Services, Inc., 1607 New Hampshire Avenue N.W., Washington, D.C. 20009. Anywhere from one to fourteen agencies are listed for most states.

FLORIDA CAREER AND LIFE-PLANNING INSTITUTE, Box 12919 University Station, Gainesville, Florida 32604. Offers one-day workshops primarily in the State of Florida. Fee.

CENTER FOR CREATIVE LIVING AND SPIRITUAL GROWTH. Fred McKirachan, Th.M., Associate in Career Assessment. 2580 W. Broad Street, Athens, Georgia 30601. A two-day process in residence, with testing. Fee.

CAREER WORKSHOPS, INC., Executive Office Building, 1801 East Franklin Street, Chapel Hill, North Carolina 27514, (919) 929-8338. Patricia Grandstaff and Daniel Grandstaff, Directors. Workshops, seminars, and individual counseling on Creative Job Hunting. Fees vary.

ALEX METHVEN, Suite 400, 1730 North Lynn St., Arlington, VA 22209, (703) 938-8945. Offers seminars in Creative Job Hunting and Career Development, on weekends. Minimum number of participants, ten; maximum, sixteen.

THE MID-ATLANTIC CAREER CENTER. Formerly of Washington, D.C., was discontinued as of the end of 1977. Bart Lloyd, its excellent director, is now with the New England Career Development Center (see page 285).

FJN CAREER DEVELOPMENT PROGRAM. Francis J. Nead, Professional Career Consultant, 14 Eggert Avenue, Metuchen, New Jersey 08840; (201) 494-6280. Formerly Senior Career Consultant at Mainstream Associates and at Bernard Haldane Associates, both in Manhattan. Individual counseling. Fees vary.

CAREER MANAGEMENT ASSOCIATES, 14 East 60th Street, New York, N.Y. 10022. James J. Gallagher, President. For those in the New York–New Jersey area, offers a group program for men and women seeking new careers and new jobs, or organizations seeking help with 'outplacement' (termination) of their employees. One set fee. (212) 752-8715.

THE COUNSELING SERVICE OF THE METROPOLITAN HARTFORD YMCA, INC., 160 Jewel Street, 3rd Floor, Hartford, CT 06103. (203) 522-4183. Offers personal vocational counseling to all ages, both sexes. Fees vary; scholarship aid available for those unable to afford the full counseling fee.

PEOPLE MANAGEMENT INCORPORATED, 10 Station Street, King's Head Row, Simsbury, CT 06070. (203) 658-1800. Arthur F. Miller, Jr., President. Works with individuals, groups and organizations, assisting them in identifying their strengths, translating their gifts into viable career/job objectives, and teaching them how to identify and land a job suitable for their gifts. Experienced in motivational patterns, and in use of the technique Miller calls SIMA (System for Identifying Motivated Abilities). Fees vary.

CAREER DEVELOPMENT DIVISION. Nathan Barry Associates, Inc., 29 Commonwealth Avenue, Boston, Mass. 02116. Christopher Ruggeri, Manager. Fee.

COMMUNICATION RESOURCES, 75 Parker Road, Wellesley, MA 02181. John C. Zacharis, Counselor. (617) 237-3599. Program of career counseling. Fees vary.

EUGENE B. SHEA & ASSOCIATES. Eugene B. Shea, President, Suite 209, 800 Enterprise Drive, Oak Brook, Illinois 60521. (312) 654-4266. Offers two executive Development Programs—with cost depending on earnings of candidate; plus fee if placed, from either the employer (sponsored program) or from the candidate (non-sponsored program). Uses a job-seeker's manual entitled "How to Step Into the Executive Position of Your Choice," written by Mr. Shea.

LIFE/CAREER COUNSELORS. Donald R. Wageck and Samuel M. Kirk, Counselors. Ed-Venture Associates, Inc., 1418 S. Race Street, Denver, Colorado 80210. (303) 722-3629. Offers individual counseling, workshops and small-group participation. Fees vary.

AWARE ADVISORY CENTER, YWCA South Lounge, Second Floor, 2019 - 14th Street (near Pico Blvd.), Santa Monica, CA 90405. (213) 392-1303. Aware support groups, career planning classes, and individual counseling. Mondays and Wednesdays, 10:00 a.m. to 5:00 p.m.; and 7:00 p.m. to 9:00 p.m. No appointment necessary. Donation: $3.00 per visit (may be waived).

VIKI ZENOFF, Career Alternatives Specialist, c/o National Career Development Project, Box 379, Walnut Creek, CA 94596. (415) 935-1865. Individual counseling, plus weekend seminars and group workshops. Fees vary.

CAREER INFORMATION SERVICE, 4036 Everett Avenue, Oakland, California 94602. Janice A. Kay, Vocational Consultant. After extensive research in career fields, Mrs. Kay has created her own system of vocational assessment, dealing with analysis of vocational potential, an exploration of the world of work, identifying the occupational step-ladder, and the projected trends in your chosen field. Fee.

THE BERKELEY CENTER FOR HUMAN INTERACTION, Ann MacKinlay, Director, 1820 Scenic Avenue, Berkeley, CA 94709. This center is developing a whole series of Professional and Career Workshops, including Career Clinics, and workshops on "Careers in Transition," "Career Options for Women," etc. These range from 10 to 18 hours in length, and sometimes are run on weekends, or may be spread over six weeks. Fees vary.

SYLAN PSYCHOLOGICAL & COUNSELING SERVICES, 215 Skyline Building, 2041 SW 58th Avenue, Portland, Oregon 97221, (503) 292-9867. Joseph A. Dubay, Life/Work Counselor. Offers workshops helping the individual find an enriched life-style and fulfillment in the world of work and of leisure.

PASTORAL INSTITUTE OF WASHINGTON, 527 Lowman Building, 107 Cherry St., Seattle, Washington 98104. A full career evaluation, of a full-scale intensive nature. Fee.

COOPER/HAMILTON ASSOCIATES, 77 Shallmar Blvd., Toronto, Ontario m6c. (2K2) 789-1717. Elaine Cooper and John Hamilton, Principals. Consultants in Career and Life/ Work Planning. Work with individuals and groups.

In addition to the above resources, the National Career Development Project has trained some 300 people—in the U.S. and Canada—in the particular techniques described in chapters five, six and seven of this book. Each of these people has had over 120 hours of training with Ye Olde Author. Should you desire a list of the people in your state, or in adjoining areas, who have been so trained, you may secure that list by sending a check for $1.00, payable to The National Career Development Project, together with a stamped, self-addressed envelope, to: National Career Development Project, Attn: Erica Chambre-Hubartt, Box 379, Walnut Creek, CA 94596. This request must be made by mail, not by phone, as we are not equipped to handle phone requests.

B. HELP FOR THOSE WHO
ARE UNEMPLOYED

FORTY-PLUS CLUBS. Not a national organization, but a voluntary group of autonomous non-profit clubs, manned by members, paying no salaries, supported by initiation fees and monthly dues of members. Clubs now operating in New York City (Manhattan), Philadelphia, Washington, D.C., Cincinnati, Chicago, Denver, Seattle, Los Angeles and the Bay Area (Oakland) of California. (See phone book for exact addresses.) *Only open normally to those who are forty years or older, unemployed, seeking employment, making an average of at least $12,000-15,000 (varies from one club to another) for the preceding five years, and able to pass a screening process.* Club's name may vary; e.g., the club in Seattle is called Sea-VEST (Seattle Volunteer Service Team for Professionals), located at 515 Thomas Street, Seattle, WA 98109. (206) 464-5344. Screening procedures of all these 'Forty-Plus' type groups may also vary, but usually they involve personal interview, checking out of business references, and informal meeting with representative active members. Process may take two to three weeks, in normal course. Insiders say a club (like New York) may have one hundred active members, and placements at the rate of two to five a week. Insiders say it takes the average member about three months to find placement, and one (at least) alleges that about one-third leave without finding placement—or hang around for indefinite periods. Members must agree to give (typically) sixteen hours a week or two and one-half days to the club. Fees and dues vary from club to club.

EXPERIENCE UNLIMITED. An organization for unemployed professionals, based in California. Contact: Mr. Herman L. Leopold, Experience Unlimited Coordinator, Department of Human Resources Development, 1111 Jackson Street, Room 1009, Oakland, CA 94607. (415) 464-1337.

ASSOCIATION FOR THE FULL EMPLOYMENT OF DOCTORATES. The first of perhaps other chapters across the nation; designed to help unemployed Ph.D.s. 448 - 14th Street, Santa Monica, CA 90402. (213) 394-2529; (213) 838-9462.

C. HELP FOR COLLEGE STUDENTS OR GRADUATES

As we stated earlier (page 26), most of the colleges in this country—two-year or four-year—have some kind of Career Planning or Placement Office. Usually the office on a particular campus can be found under the above title, although sometimes it is "buried" in the Counseling Department, or in the Dean of Student Services Office. How helpful the Career Planning office is, on the particular campus you are attending, depends on the staffing, philosophy, and funding of that office —and this may vary from year to year (and even from season to season). So, go explore for yourself.

A Directory of these offices is published, and is available for perusal in most Placement Offices. It is called the *Directory of Career Planning and Placement Offices,* and is published by the College Placement Council, Inc., Box 2263, Bethlehem, PA 18001. It costs, incidentally, $8.00 to non–CPC members, $5.00 to members. This Directory is not a complete listing of all such offices in the country. For example, the Career Planning and Placement Office (c/o Office of Counseling and Testing) at Western Nevada Community College is not included. (7000 Sullivan Lane, Reno, Nevada 89505, (702) 673-4666.)

Now, if you are not only a college graduate but also a hopeless romantic, you will have a vision of blissful cooperation existing between all of these placement offices across the country. So that if you are a graduate of an east coast college, let us say, and subsequently you move to California, and want help with career planning, you should in theory be able to walk into the placement office on any California campus, and be helped by that office (a non-altruistic service based on the likelihood that a graduate of that California campus is, at the same moment, walking into the placement office of your east coast college—and thus, to coin a phrase, "one hand is washing another.") Alas and lack, dear graduate, in most cases it doesn't work like that. You will be told, sometimes with genuine regret, that *by official policy,* this particular placement office on this particular campus is only allowed to aid its own students and alumni. One Slight Ray of Hope: on a number of campuses, there are career counselors who think this policy is absolutely asinine, so if you walk into the Career Planning office on that campus, *are lucky enough to get one of Those Counselors,* and you don't mention whether or not you went to that college—the counselor will never ask, and will proceed to help you just as though you were a real person.

This restriction (to their own students and graduates) is less likely to be found at Community Colleges than it is at four-year institutions. So, if you run into a dead end, try a Community College near you.

D. HELP FOR WOMEN

Resource centers for women are springing up all over the country, faster than we can record them. We are listing here only a sampling of same, sent in to us by our readers or courtesy of Catalyst. If you have a favorite, let us know, and we'll list it in our next edition. Any of these centers, incidentally, will know (in all probability) what other centers or recourses there are in your geographical area. Also, try your yellow pages.

In all of this you will remember won't you, our earlier description (page 51) of all career counseling professionals, as falling into one of three groups: (1) Sincere and skilled; (2) Sincere but inept; and (3) Insincere and inept? Well, dear friend, groups or organizations or centers which have been organized specifically to help women job-hunters or career-changers are not—by that act—made immune to the above distinctions. Think about it. Then read Chapter Four again, before you agree to put your (vocational) life into somebody else's hands. Remember: the numbers game (Chapter Two), even if it is expressed in non-sexist language, is still the numbers game.

RESOURCES FOR WOMEN

ALABAMA
UNIVERSITY OF ALABAMA
Counseling Service
Box 60, NBSB
University Station—UAB
Birmingham, Ala. 35294
(205) 934-4173
Monday-Friday, 8:30 a.m. to 5:00 p.m.
Official college office.
Educational and career counseling;
personal and emotional counseling.
No fees.

ARIZONA
UNIVERSITY OF ARIZONA
Student Counseling Service
200 W. Old Psychology Building
Tucson, Ariz. 85721
(602) 884-2575
Monday-Friday, 8:00 a.m. to 12:00 p.m.
1:00 p.m. to 5:00 p.m.; Tues., Wed.,
6:30 p.m. to 9:00 p.m. at Continuing
Education Office
Official college office.
Restricted to students.
Educational and career counseling,
and personal and marital counseling,
continuing education courses.
No fees.

CALIFORNIA
ADVOCATES FOR WOMEN, INC.
256 Sutter Street, 6th Floor
San Francisco, Cal. 94105
(415) 495-6750
Monday-Friday, 8:30 a.m. to 4:30 p.m.
Independent non-profit agency.
Career counseling, job referral, placement.
No fees.
Offices also in Berkeley & Hayward.

CALIFORNIA STATE UNIVERSITY,
SACRAMENTO
Career Development & Placement Center
6000 J Street
Sacramento, Cal. 95819
(916) 454-6231
Monday-Friday, 8:00 a.m. to 5:00 p.m.
Official college office. Restricted
to students and alumnae.
Educational and career counseling, job
referral, placement. Continuing
education courses.
No fees.

CAREER DESIGN
An affiliate of Ranny Riley & Assoc.
2398 Broadway, San Francisco, Cal. 94115
(415) 929-8161
      929-8150
Offers a variety of intensive seminars and
comprehensive workshops. Fees vary.

CAREER PLANNING CENTER
1623 South La Cienega Blvd.
Los Angeles, Cal. 90035
(213) 273-6633
Monday-Friday, 10:00 a.m. to 4:00 p.m.
Thursday, 7:00 p.m. to 9:00 p.m.
Independent nonprofit office.
Labor market/career information and
counseling, job referral, placement,
resume preparation. Continuing
education programs.
No registration fee. Other fees vary.

CAREERWISE
Ann Morton, Career Development
Specialist
3174 Turk St., No. 3
San Francisco, Cal. 94118
(415) 387-9045
Offers variety of evening and Saturday
workshops.
Fees vary.

CENTER FOR NEW DIRECTIONS
5800 Fulton Ave.
Van Nuys, Cal. 91401
(213) 785-3955, 785-9171
Monday-Friday, 8:30 a.m. to 4:00 p.m.
Non-profit community service agency,
co-sponsored by Los Angeles Valley
College and the San Fernando Branch
of the American Association of
University Women.
Career and educational counseling;
referral placement.
Workshops and seminars designed to
promote personal and career development.
Reasonable fees; scholarships available.

THE CLAREMONT COLLEGES
Special Academic Programs and
Office for Continuing Education
Harper Hall 160
Claremont, Cal. 91711
(714) 626-8511
Monday-Friday, 9:00 a.m. to 5:00 p.m.
College-sponsored office
Educational and career counseling,
job referral, continuing education
courses.
Registration fee.

272

CYPRESS COLLEGE
Career Planning Center
9200 Valley View Street
Cypress, Cal. 90630
(714) 826-2220, Ext. 221
Monday-Friday, 8:00 a.m. to 4:00 p.m.
Monday-Thursday, 6:00 p.m. to 9:00 p.m.
Official college office.
Educational and career counseling.
No fees.

DISPLACED HOMEMAKERS CENTER, INC.
Mills College, Box 9996
Oakland, Cal. 94613
(415) 632-4600
Designed for the person over 35, who
has worked without pay as a homemaker
for one's family, and is not gainfully
employed at present.

FOOTHILL COLLEGE
Continuing Education for Women
12345 El Monte
Los Altos Hills, Cal. 94002
(415) 948-8590, Ext. 363
Monday-Friday, 10:00 a.m. to 3:00 p.m.
Official college office
Educational and career counseling,
job referral, continuing
education courses.
No fees.

ANITA J. GOLDFARB
18340 Ventura Blvd., M218
Tarzana, Cal. 91356
(213) 881-6760
Monday-Friday, 9:30 a.m. to 4:00 p.m.
Independent, private office.
Educational and career counseling,
class in Transitional Woman.
Fees vary.

SUSAN W. MILLER
1710 S. Durango Avenue
Los Angeles, Cal. 90035
(213) 837-7768
Job and career development for women,
using a structured task-oriented approach.
Life planning workshops for small groups.

NEW WAYS TO WORK
457 Kingsley Avenue
Palo Alto, Cal. 94301
(415) 321-WORK
Monday-Friday, 10:00 a.m. to 2:30 p.m.
Independent non-profit agency.
Career counseling, job referral, placement.
No fees.

**INFORMATION ADVISORY SERVICE,
UCLA EXTENSION**
10995 Le Conte Avenue, Room 114
Los Angeles, Cal. 90024
(213) 825-2401, Ext. 250 or 261
Monday-Friday, 9:00 a.m. to 5:00 p.m.
College-sponsored office.
Educational and career counseling,
job referral information, continuing
education courses.
No fees.

**INFORMATION ADVISORY SERVICE,
UCLA EXTENSION**
1100 S. Grand Ave., Room 115
Los Angeles, Cal. 90015
(213) 747-2433, 748-7079
Monday-Friday, 9:00 a.m. to 4:00 p.m.
Educational and career counseling,
job referral information, continuing
education courses.

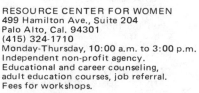

RESOURCE CENTER FOR WOMEN
499 Hamilton Ave., Suite 204
Palo Alto, Cal. 94301
(415) 324-1710
Monday-Thursday, 10:00 a.m. to 3:00 p.m.
Independent non-profit agency.
Educational and career counseling,
adult education courses, job referral.
Fees for workshops.

SAN JOSE STATE UNIVERSITY
Re-Entry Advisory Program
Old Cafeteria Building
San Jose, Cal. 95192
(408) 277-2189
Monday-Thursday, 8:00 a.m. to 8:00 p.m.
Friday, 8:00 a.m. to 5:00 p.m.
Official college program.
Educational and career counseling,
continuing education courses, referral
to other services.
No fees.

**UNIVERSITY OF CALIFORNIA,
BERKELEY**
Women's Center for Continuing
Education of Women
T-9 Building
Berkeley, Cal. 94704
(415) 642-4786
Monday-Friday, 9:00 a.m. to 5:00 p.m.
College sponsored office.
Educational and career counseling,
research library.
No fees.

**UCSD EXTENSION COUNSELING
PROGRAMS**
University of California, San Diego
Box 109, La Jolla, Cal. 92037
(714) 453-2000, Ext. 2096
Monday-Friday, 8:00 a.m. to 5:00 p.m.
Official college office.
Educational and career counseling,
continuing education courses, job
referral. Counseling available in relation
to courses.
Fees range from $10 up.

THE WOMEN'S OPPORTUNITIES
CENTER
Univ. of California Extension, Irvine
Irvine, Cal. 92664
(714) 833-7128
Monday-Friday, 10:00 a.m. to 4:00 p.m.
College sponsored office.
Educational and career counseling,
continuing education courses.
No fees.

WOMAN'S PLACE, INC.
1901 Avenue of the Stars
Los Angeles, Cal. 90067
(213) 553-0870
Monday-Friday, 9:30 a.m. to 2:30 p.m.
Independent private agency.
Career counseling, workshops, job
referral, 5-hour day.
Fees vary.

VIKI ZENOFF
Career Alternatives Specialist
c/o National Career Development Project
Box 379, Walnut Creek, Cal. 94596
(415) 935-1865
Conducts monthly weekend workshops,
as well as offering individual counseling.
Fees vary.

COLORADO
DENVER–WOMEN'S RESOURCE
CENTER
1545 Tremont Place
Denver, Colo. 80202
(303) 222-0870
Monday-Friday, 9:00 a.m. to 5:00 p.m.
Monday & Wednesday, 6:00 p.m. to 9:00 p.m.
Tuesday, 5:00 p.m. to 8:00 p.m.
Independent non-profit agency.
Educational and career counseling,
job referral.
No fees.

CARROL DENMARK
Magnolia Star Route
Nederland, Colo. 80466
(303) 443-2017 or 258-7289
Independent, private office.
Conducts workshops, courses.
Fees vary.

WOMEN ENTERPRISES, INC.
158 Fillmore Street, No. 307
Denver, Colo. 80206
(303) 388-5623
Gloria Golbert, Director
Women are assisted on an individual
basis, or may attend group seminars
and workshops. Designed to assist
professionals in all areas of job
preparation.
Fees vary.

CONNECTICUT
INFORMATION & COUNSELING
SERVICE FOR WOMAN
215 Park Street, Box 5557
New Haven, Conn. 06520
(203) 436-8242
Five days a week—by appointment only.
Independent nonprofit agency.
Career counseling, education and
employment information, job referral.
Registration fees, fees for career events.

NEW CONCEPT
111 Saugatuck Avenue
Westport, Conn. 06880
(203) 226-5841
Monday-Friday, 9:30 a.m. to 3:30 p.m.
Independent private agency.
Job referral, resume preparation,
career counseling.
No registration fee. Other fees vary.

TODAY'S WOMAN
Placement Service
21 Charles Street
Westport, Conn 06880
A division of Bolles Associates, Inc.
(No relation to the author of
this book.)
A nation wide placement service,
where all fees are paid by the
employer. Gave some 5000 clients
access to over 200 employers, (or
200 employers access to 5000 clients,
depending on your point of view),
so far. For experienced women in the
$10-30,000.00 range.

UNIVERSITY OF CONNECTICUT
Continuing Education for Women, U-56W
Storrs, Conn. 06268
(203) 486-3441
Monday-Friday, 8:30 a.m. to 4:30 p.m.
Official college office.
Educational and career counseling,
continuing education courses.
Fees vary.

YOUNG WOMEN'S CHRISTIAN
ASSOCIATION
422 Summer Street
Stamford, Conn. 06901
(203) 348-7727
Monday-Friday, 9:00 a.m. to 5:00 p.m.
and by appointment.
National organization.
Educational and career counseling,
adult education courses.
Registration fee.

DELAWARE
UNIVERSITY OF DELAWARE
Division of Continuing Education
Clayton Hall
Newark, Del. 19711
(302) 738-8432
Monday-Thursday, 8:30 a.m. to 9:00 p.m.
Friday, 8:30-5:00. Saturday, 9:00-noon.
Official college office.
Educational and career counseling,
continuing education courses.
No registration fee. Other fees vary.

DISTRICT OF COLUMBIA
GEORGE WASHINGTON UNIVERSITY
Continuing Education for Women
2130 H Street, N.W.
Washington, D.C. 20006
(202) 676-7036
Monday-Friday, 9:00 a.m. to 5:00 p.m.
College sponsored.
Educational and career counseling,
continuing education courses,
job referral.
Fees vary.

JOB MARKET, INC.
1816 Jefferson Place, N.W.
Washington, D.C. 20036
(202) 785-4155
Monday-Friday, 9:00 a.m. to 5:00 p.m.
Independent private agency.
Job placement.
No registration fee.
Employer pays placement fee.

WIDER OPPORTUNITIES FOR WOMEN
1649 K Street N.W.
Washington, D.C. 20006
(202) 638-4868

FLORIDA
COUNCIL FOR CONTINUING
EDUCATION FOR WOMEN OF
CENTRAL FLORIDA, INC.
Valencia Community College,
Downtown
1 West Church Street, Third Floor
Orlando, Fla. 32801
(305) 423-4813
Monday-Friday, 9:00 a.m. to 5:00 p.m.
Independent non-profit agency.
Educational and career counseling,
adult education courses, testing.
No fees.

THE GREATER MIAMI COUNCIL
FOR THE CONTINUING EDUCATION
OF WOMEN
Miami-Dade Community College
300 N.E. Second Avenue
Miami, Fla. 33132
(305) 577-6840
Monday-Friday, 8:30 a.m. to 5:00 p.m.
College sponsored office.
Educational and career counseling,
limited job referral, continuing
education courses.
No registration fee. Other fees vary.

GEORGIA
KENNESAW JUNIOR COLLEGE
Office of Counseling & Placement
P.O. Box 444
Marietta, Ga. 30061
(404) 422-8770, Ext. 203
Monday-Friday, 8:00 a.m. to 5:00 p.m.
Tuesday-Thursday, 8:00 a.m. to 8:30 p.m.
Official college office. Restricted to
students. Educational and career
counseling, job referral and placement,
continuing education courses.
No registration fee. Other fees vary.

ILLINOIS
APPLIED POTENTIAL
Box 19
Highland Park, Ill. 60035
(312) 432-0620
Monday-Friday, 9:00 a.m. to 5:00 p.m.
Non-profit educational corporation.
Professional counselors.
Educational, career and personal
counseling.
No registration fee. Other fees vary.

FLEXIBLE CAREERS
Loop Center YWCA
37 South Wabash Avenue
Chicago, Ill. 60603
(312) 263-2488 or 2514
Monday-Wednesday 10:30 a.m. to 2:30 p.m.
Thursday, 3:30 p.m. to 7:30 p.m.
Independent nonprofit organization.
Career Information Center.
Job Development Project.
Registration fee.

HARPER COLLEGE COMMUNITY
COUNSELING CENTER
Palatine, Ill. 60067
(312) 359-4200
Monday-Thursday, 8:30 a.m. to 4:30 p.m.
Monday-Thursday, 6:00 p.m. to 10:00 p.m.
Friday, 8:30 a.m. to 4:30 p.m.
College sponsored office.
Educational and career counseling.
No registration fee. Other fees.

MORAINE VALLEY COMMUNITY
COLLEGE
Adult Career Resources Center
10900 South 88th Avenue
Palos Hills, Ill. 60465
(312) 974-4300
Monday-Friday, 9:00 a.m. to 5:00 p.m.
Tuesday, Wednesday, Thursday,
9:00 a.m. to 9:00 p.m.
Official college office.
Educational, career and personal
counseling.
No registration fee.

OAKTON COMMUNITY COLLEGE
Women's Outreach Resource Center
7900 N. Nagle
Morton Grove, Ill.
(312) 967-5120, Ext. 350
Rotating center located in six
community facilities. Call for
location.
Monday-Friday, 9:00 a.m. to 3:00 p.m.
Thursday, 7:00 p.m. to 9:30 p.m.
College sponsored.
Educational and career counseling,
continuing education courses.
No registration fee. Other fees vary.

SOUTHERN ILLINOIS UNIVERSITY
General Studies Division
Office of Continuing Education
Edwardsville, Ill. 62025
(618) 692-2242
Monday-Friday, 8:00 a.m. to 5:00 p.m.
Official college office.
Educational and career counseling,
continuing education courses.
No fees.

SOUTHERN ILLINOIS UNIVERSITY
Women's Programs Office
Woody Hall, B-244/245
Carbondale, Illinois 62901
(618) 453-3655
Monday-Friday, 8:00 a.m. to 5:00 p.m.
Individual advising, group discussions.
No appointment needed.

UNIVERSITY OF ILLINOIS
URBANA-CHAMPAIGN
Student Services Office for Married
Students and Continuing Education
for Women
610 East John Street
Champaign, Ill. 61820
(217) 333-3137
Monday-Friday, 8:00 a.m. to 5:00 p.m.
Official college office.
Educational and career counseling.
No fees.

WOMEN'S EMPLOYMENT
COUNSELING CENTER
Y.W.C.A.
1001 South Wright
Champaign, Ill. 61820
(217) 344-0721
Monday-Friday, 9:00 a.m. to 5:00 p.m.
Independent, nonprofit office.
Educational and career counseling,
job referral and placement.
No fees.

WOMEN'S INC.
15 Spinning Wheel Rd., Suite 14
Hinsdale, Ill. 60521
(312) 325-9770
Monday-Saturday, 9:00 a.m. to 9:00 p.m.
Independent private agency.
Educational and career counseling,
job referral and placement.
No registration fee. Other fees vary.

INDIANA
CONTINUING EDUCATION SERVICES
Indiana University/Purdue University
1201 East 38th Street
Indianapolis, Ind. 46205
(317) 264-4501
Monday-Friday, 8:00 a.m. to 5:00 p.m.
Official college office.
Educational and career counseling,
continuing education courses.
Fees vary.

INDIANA UNIVERSITY
Continuing Education for Women
Owen Hall
Bloomington, Ind. 47401
(812) 337-1684
Monday-Friday, 8:00 a.m. to 5:00 p.m.
Official college office.
Educational and career counseling,
continuing education courses.
Fees vary.

ST. MARY'S COLLEGE
Career Development Center
Notre Dame, Indiana 46556
(219) 284-4431
Monday-Friday, 9:00 a.m. to 5:00 p.m.
Official college office.
Restricted to students and alumnae.
Educational and career counseling.
No fees.

UNIVERSITY CENTER FOR WOMEN
Purdue University
2101 Coliseum Blvd. East
Fort Wayne, Ind. 46805
(219) 482-5527
Monday-Friday, 8:00 a.m. to 12:00 noon.
College sponsored office.
Educational and career counseling,
continuing education courses,
job referral.
Fees vary.

IOWA
DRAKE UNIVERSITY
Women's Programs
College for Continuing Education
Des Moines, Iowa 50311
(515) 271-2183
Monday-Friday, 8:00 a.m. to 5:00 p.m.
Official college office.
Educational and career counseling,
continuing education courses.
No fee for individual counseling.
Fee for group sessions.

UNIVERSITY COUNSELING SERVICE
Iowa Memorial Union
University of Iowa
Iowa City, Iowa 52242
(319) 353-4484
Monday-Friday, 8:00 a.m. to 5:00 p.m.
College sponsored office.
Educational, vocational and personal
counseling.
Fees vary for non-students.

UNIVERSITY OF IOWA
Office of Career Planning and Placement
Iowa City, Iowa 52242
(319) 353-3147
Monday-Friday, 8:00 a.m. to 5:00 p.m.
Wednesday, 5:30 p.m. to 7:30 p.m.
Official college office.
Educational and career counseling,
job referral, placement.
Fee for job placement only.

WOMEN'S WORK
820 First National Building
Davenport, Iowa 52801
(319) 326-6249
Monday-Friday, 9:00 a.m. to 4:00 p.m.
Independent, private agency.
Job referral and placement.
Fees vary.

KANSAS
UNIVERSITY OF KANSAS
Student Services
Extramural Independent Study Center
Division of Continuing Education
Lawrence, Kan. 66044
(913) 864-4792
Monday-Friday, 8:00 a.m. to 12:00 noon
Monday-Friday, 1:00 p.m. to 5:00 p.m.
College sponsored.
Educational and career counseling,
continuing education (independent
study, classes).
No registration fee. Other fees vary.

MARYLAND

BALTIMORE NEW DIRECTIONS
FOR WOMEN
1100 N. Eutaw Street, Room 205
Baltimore, Md. 21201
(301) 383-5579
Monday-Thursday, 10:00 a.m. to 2:00 p.m.
Government agency.
Educational and career counseling,
continuing education courses, job
referral, placement. Information center.
No fees.

COLLEGE OF NOTRE DAME
OF MARYLAND
Continuing Education Center
4701 N. Charles Street
Baltimore, Md. 21210
(301) 435-0100
Monday-Friday, 9:00 a.m. to 4:30 p.m.
College sponsored.
Educational and career counseling,
continuing education courses,
job referral.
Fees vary.

WOMANSCOPE
Suite 240
Wilde Lake Village Green
Columbia, Md. 21044
(301) 997-2916
A volunteer, non-profit career and
vocational counseling service.
Services provided at no cost to the
client or the employer.

MASSACHUSETTS

CIVIC CENTER AND CLEARING
HOUSE, INC.
14 Beacon Street
Boston, Mass. 02108
(617) 227-1762
Monday-Friday, 10:00 a.m. to 4:00 p.m.
Independent non-profit agency.
Educational and career counseling,
job information.
$15.00 for consultation of the Career
and Vocational Advisory Service.

NEW ENVIRONMENTS FOR WOMEN
ASSOCIATES
44 Bertwell Road
Lexington, Mass. 02173
(617) 862-0663
Monday-Friday, 9:00 a.m. to 5:00 p.m.
Independent private agency.
Educational and resource counseling,
career and life planning; personal
growth workshops; limited job referral.
Fees vary.

SMITH COLLEGE
Vocational Office
Pierce Hall
Northampton, Mass. 01060
(413) 584-2700
Monday-Friday, 8:30 a.m. to 4:30 p.m.
Official college office.
Educational and career counseling.
No fees.

WOMEN's EDUCATIONAL
& INDUSTRIAL UNION
Career Services
264 Boylston Street
Boston, Mass. 02116
(617) 536-5651
Monday-Friday, 9:00 a.m. to 5:00 p.m.
Independent non-profit agency.
Career counseling, job referral and
placement.
No registration fee. Placement fees vary.

WOMEN'S OPPORTUNITY RESEARCH
CENTER
Middlesex Community College
Division of Continuing Education
Spring Road
Bedford, Mass. 01730
(617) 275-1590
Monday-Friday, 9:00 a.m. to 2:00 p.m.
College sponsored office.
Educational and career counseling,
continuing education courses.
Fees vary.

YWCA WOMEN'S RESOURCE CENTER
66 Irving Street
Framingham, MA 01701
(617) 873-9781
Monday-Friday, 9:00 a.m. to 5:00 p.m.
Individual career counseling.
Free.

MICHIGAN

MICHIGAN TECHNOLOGICAL
UNIVERSITY
Center for Continuing Education
for Women
Houghton, Mich. 49931
(906) 487-2270
Monday-Friday, 8:00 a.m. to 5:00 p.m.
Official college office.
Educational and career counseling,
continuing education courses.
No registration fee. Other fees vary.

MONTCALM COMMUNITY COLLEGE
Area Guidance Center
Career Guidance Model
Sidney, Mich. 48885
(517) 328-2111
Monday-Friday, 8:00 a.m. to 5:00 p.m.
Evenings by appointment
College sponsored office.
Education and career counseling.
No fees.

NORTHERN MICHIGAN UNIVERSITY
Women's Center for Continuing Education
Marquette, Mich. 49855
(906) 227-2219
Monday-Friday, 8:30 a.m. to 4:30 p.m.
Official college office.
Educational and career counseling,
job referral, continuing education
courses.
Fees vary.

OAKLAND UNIVERSITY
Continuum Center for Adult Counseling
and Leadership Training
Rochester, Mich. 48063
(313) 337-3033
Monday-Friday, 8:00 a.m. to 5:00 p.m.
College affiliated.
Personal, educational and career
counseling, continuing education
courses.
Fees vary.

UNIVERSITY OF MICHIGAN
Center for Continuing Education of
Women
330 Thompson Street
Ann Arbor, Michigan 48108
(313) 764-6555

WESTERN MICHIGAN UNIVERSITY
Continuing Education for Women
Kalamazoo, Mich. 49001
(616) 383-1860
Monday-Friday, 8:00 a.m. to 3:00 p.m.
Official college office.
Educational and career counseling,
continuing education courses.
Fees vary.

WOMEN'S RESOURCE CENTER
226 Bostwick N.E.
Grand Rapids, Mich. 49503
(616) 456-8571
Monday, 9:00 a.m. to 8:00 p.m.
Tuesday-Friday, 9:00 a.m. to 5:00 p.m.
Independent non-profit agency.
Educational and career counseling,
job referral.
Fees vary.

MINNESOTA
MINNESOTA WOMEN'S CENTER
University of Minnesota
306 Walter Library
Minneapolis, Minnesota 55455
(612) 373-3850
Monday-Friday, 7:45 a.m. to 4:30 p.m.
Official college office.
Educational and career counseling.
No fees.

SOUTHWEST MINNESOTA STATE
COLLEGE
Personal Development Center
Marshall, Minnesota 56258
(507) 537-7150
Monday-Friday, 8:00 a.m. to 4:30 p.m.
Evening schedule varies.
Official college office.
Educational and career counseling,
job referral and placement,
continuing education courses.
Placement fee only

MISSOURI
UNIVERSITY OF MISSOURI,
ST. LOUIS
Extension Division—Women's Programs
8001 Natural Bridge Road
St. Louis, Missouri 63121
(314) 453-5961
Monday-Friday, 8:00 a.m. to 5:00 p.m.
Official college office.
Educational and career counseling,
adult education courses, limited
job referral.
No registration fee. Other fees vary.

WASHINGTON UNIVERSITY
Continuing Education for Women
Box 1099
St. Louis, Missouri 63130
(314) 863-0100, ext. 4261
Monday-Friday, 8:30 a.m. to 5:00 p.m.
Official college office.
Educational and career counseling,
continuing education courses.
Fees Vary.

THE WOMEN'S RESOURCE SERVICE
University of Missouri, Kansas City
5325 Rockhill Road
Kansas City, Missouri 64110
(816) 276-1442
Monday-Friday, 10:00 a.m. to 2:00 p.m.
Official college office.
Educational and career counseling,
job referral, continuing education
courses.
No fees.

NEW JERSEY
BERGEN COMMUNITY COLLEGE
Community Counseling Service
295 Main Street
Hackensack, N.J. 07601
(201) 489-1556
Monday-Friday, 9:00 a.m. to 5:00 p.m.
College sponsored office.
Educational and career counseling,
adult education courses.
No fees.

CALDWELL COLLEGE
Career Planning and Placement
Caldwell, N.J. 07006
(201) 228-4424, Ext. 60
Monday-Friday, 9:00 a.m. to 4:30 p.m.
College-sponsored office.
Educational and career counseling,
limited job referral.
No fees.

DOUGLASS COLLEGE
Women's Center
Gate House
New Brunswick, N.J. 08903
(201) 932-9603
Monday-Friday, 9:00 a.m. to 12 noon,
1:00 p.m. to 4:00 p.m.
Educational and career counseling.
No fees.

DREW UNIVERSITY
Career Planning and Placement Center
Madison, N.J. 07940
(201) 377-3000
Monday-Friday, 9:00 a.m. to 5:00 p.m.
Official college office.
Educational and career counseling,
continuing education courses,
job referral and placement.
No fees

EVE—Women's Center
Kean College of New Jersey
Kean Building
Union, N.J. 07083
(201) 527-2210
Monday-Friday, 8:30 a.m. to 4:30 p.m.
College sponsored.
Educational and career counseling,
job referral.
No registration fee. Other fees vary.

JERSEY CITY STATE COLLEGE
The Women's Center—1-407
Jersey City, N.J. 07305
(201) 547-3189
Monday-Friday, 9:00 a.m. to 5:00 p.m.
Official college office.
Educational and career counseling,
continuing education courses.
No fees.

JEWISH VOCATIONAL SERVICE
454 William Street
East Orange, N.J. 07017
(201) 674-6330
Five days, thirty-seven hours.
Independent, non-profit office.
Educational and career counseling,
job referral and placement.
Fees vary.

MONTCLAIR STATE COLLEGE
Women's Center
Upper Montclair, N.J. 07405
(201) 893-5106
Monday-Friday, 8:30 a.m. to 4:30 p.m.
Evenings by appointment.
College-sponsored office.
Educational and career counseling.
No fees.

REACH, INC.
O'Connor Hall
College of St. Elizabeth
Convent Station, N.J. 07961
(201) 267-2530
Monday-Friday, 9:00 a.m. to 12:00 noon
Independent nonprofit office.
Educational and career counseling,
job referral.
Fees vary.

THE PROFESSIONAL ROSTER
5 Ivy Lane
Princeton, N.J. 08540
(609) 921-9561
Monday-Friday, 10:00 a.m. to 1:00 p.m.
Independent, non-profit organization.
Educational and career counseling,
job referral.
No fees.

NEW YORK
ADELPHI UNIVERSITY
Women's Center
Linen Hall
Garden City, N.Y. 11530
(516) 294-8700, Ext. 7490
Monday-Friday, 9:30 a.m. to 4:30 p.m.
Official college office.
Educational and career counseling,
legal and health referrals, etc.
No fees.

BARNARD COLLEGE
Placement and Career Planning Office
606 West 120th Street
New York, N.Y. 10027
(212) 280-2033
Monday-Friday, 9:00 a.m. to 5:00 p.m.
Official college office. Restricted
to alumnae. Career counseling, job
referral, placement.
Registration fee.

CAREER COUNSELING FOR WOMEN
Box 372
Huntington, N.Y. 11743
(516) 421-1948
Monday-Friday, 9:00 a.m. to 5:00 p.m.
Some evenings.
Independent, private agency.
Educational and career counseling,
life-planning.
Fees vary.

CAREER SERVICES FOR
WOMEN, INC.
382 Main Street
Port Washington, N.Y. 11050
(516) 883-3005
Tuesday, Wednesday, Thursday
9:30 a.m. to 2:30 p.m.
Independent non-profit agency.
Educational and career counseling,
job referral.
Fees vary.

COUNTY COUNSELING CENTER
2242 Central Park Avenue
Yonkers, N.Y. 10710
(914) WH 6-0333
Hours by appointment.
Independent, private agency.
Educational and career counseling.
Fees vary.

HOFSTRA UNIVERSITY
Counseling Center
Hempstead, N.Y. 11550
(516) 560-3565
Monday-Friday, 9:00 a.m. to 5:00 p.m.
Monday & Thursday, 6:00 p.m. to 10
Official college office.
Educational and vocational counseling,
testing, continuing education courses.
Fees vary.

HUMAN RELATIONS WORK-STUDY
CENTER
New School for Social Research
66 West 12th Street
New York, N.Y. 10011
(212) 675-2700, Ext. 348-9
Monday-Friday, 9:00 a.m. to 5:00 p.m.
Official college office.
Educational counseling, continuing
education courses. Special training
for human services.
Fees vary.

HUNTER COLLEGE
Career Counseling and Placement
Room 1601, 505 Park Avenue
New York, N.Y. 10022
(212) 360-2874
Monday-Friday, 9:00 a.m. to 5:00 p.m.
Official college office. Restricted
to alumnae.
Career counseling, job referral,
placement
No fees.

JANICE LaROUCHE ASSOC.
Career Workshops for Women
333 Central Park West
New York, N.Y. 10025
(212) MO 3-0970
Monday-Saturday, 9:00 a.m. to 6:00 p.m.
Independent private agency.
Career counseling.
No registration fee. Other fees vary.

MARYMOUNT COLLEGE
Career Development Office
Tarrytown, N.Y. 10591
(914) 631-3200
Monday-Friday, 9:00 a.m. to 5:00 p.m.
Official college office.
Career counseling, continuing education
courses. Referral and job placement
for students and alumnae only.
Counseling fee.

MERCY COLLEGE
Career Counseling & Placement Office
555 Broadway
Dobbs Ferry, N.Y. 10522
(914) 693-4500
Monday-Friday, 9:00 a.m. to 5:00 p.m.
Official college office.
Career counseling.
Fees.

MORE FOR WOMEN, INC.
52 Gramercy Park So.
New York, N.Y. 10010
(212) 674-4090
Monday-Friday, 9:00 a.m. to 9:00 p.m.
Saturday, 9:00 a.m. to 4:00 p.m.
Independent private agency.
Educational and career counseling,
workshops.
Fees vary.

NEW DIRECTIONS FOR WOMEN
Pace University
Bedford Rd., Pleasantville, N.Y. 10570
(914) 769-3200, Ext. 211
Pace College Plaza, N.Y.C. 10038
(212) 285-3688

Monday-Friday, 9:00 a.m. to 5:00 p.m.
College sponsored offices.
Educational counseling.
No fees.

ORANGE COUNTY COMMUNITY
COLLEGE
Women's Program
Office of Community Services
115 South Street
Middletown, N.Y. 10940
(914) 343-1614
Monday-Friday, 9:00 a.m. to 5:00 p.m.
Official college office.
Educational counseling, continuing
education courses.
Fees vary.

PERSONNEL SCIENCES CENTER
52 Vanderbilt Avenue
(opp. Pan Am Building)
New York, N.Y. 10017
(212) 684-5300
Monday-Saturday, 9:00 a.m. to 5:00 p.m.
Independent private agency.
Educational and career counseling.
Fees vary.

PROFESSIONAL SKILLS ROSTER
410 College Avenue
Ithaca, N.Y. 14850
(607) 256-3758
Monday-Friday, 9:30 a.m. to 12:30 p.m.
Independent non-profit agency.
Job referral, limited educational
and career counseling.
No fees. Suggested donation.

REGIONAL LEARNING SERVICE
CENTER OF N.Y.
405 Oak Street
Syracuse, N.Y. 13202
(315) 425-5252
Monday-Friday, 9:00 a.m. to 9:00 p.m.
Independent non-profit agency.
Educational and career counseling,
education courses.
Registration fees vary.

SUNY AT BUFFALO
University Placement and
Career Guidance
Hayes Annex "C"
Buffalo, N.Y. 14213
(716) 831-5291
Monday-Friday, 8:30 a.m. to 4:00 p.m.
Official college office.
Educational and career counseling,
job referral and placement.
No fees.

SUNY AT STONY BROOK
Mid-Career Counseling Center
166 Humanities
Stony Brook, N.Y. 11794
(516) 246-3304
Monday-Friday, 9:00 a.m. to 8:00 p.m.
Official college office.
Educational and career counseling,
continuing education courses.
Fees vary.

SYRACUSE UNIVERSITY/
UNIVERSITY COLLEGE
Women's Center for Continuing Education
610 East Fayette Street
Syracuse, N.Y. 13202
(315) 423-3294
Monday-Friday, 9:00 a.m. to 5:00 p.m.
College sponsored office.
Educational and career counseling,
continuing education courses.
No fees.

VASSAR COLLEGE
Office of Career Planning
Poughkeepsie, N.Y. 12601
(914) 452-7000
Monday-Friday, 8:30 a.m. to 5:00 p.m.
Official college office. Restricted
to alumnae. Educational and career
counseling, job referral, placement.
No fees.

NORTH CAROLINA
DUKE UNIVERSITY
Center for Career Development and
Continuing Education
Durham, N.C. 27708
(919) 684-6259
Monday-Friday 8:30 a.m. to 5:00 p.m.
Official college office.
Educational and career counseling,
continuing education courses.
No registration fee. Other fees vary.

SALEM COLLEGE
Lifespan Counseling Center for Women
Lehman Hall, Box 10548, Salem Station
Winston-Salem, N.C. 27108
(919) 723-7961
Monday-Friday, 8:30 a.m. to 4:30 p.m.
College sponsored office.
Lifespan planning, educational
and vocational, personal and social
counseling.
Fees vary.

OHIO
CLEVELAND JEWISH VOCATIONAL
SERVICE
13878 Cedar Road
University Heights, Ohio 44118
(216) 321-1381
Monday-Friday, 9:00 a.m. to 5:30 p.m.
Thursday, 9:00 a.m. to 6:40 p.m.
Independent non-profit agency.
Educational and career counseling,
job referral, placement.
No registration fee. Other fees vary.

OHIO STATE UNIVERSITY
Women's Programs—Division of
Continuing Education
1800 Cannon Drive
Columbus, Ohio 43210
(614) 422-8860
Career Services/Continuing Education
for Mature Women.
Individual counseling (no fee), career

planning courses. Special programs and
workshops.
Fees vary.

RESOURCE
13878 Cedar Road
Cleveland Heights, Ohio 44118
(216) 932-4546
For professional development of
women with one year of college or
more. By appointment only.
No fees.

PROJECT EVE
Cuyahoga Community College
2900 Community College Avenue
Cleveland, Ohio 44115
(216) 241-5966
Monday-Friday, 9:00 a.m. to 5:00 p.m.
Community service. College sponsored
office. Individual educational and
career counseling, no fee. Group
series and programs.
Fees vary.

UNIVERSITY OF AKRON
Office of Student Services
Akron, Ohio 44325
(216) 375-7909
Monday-Friday, 8:00 a.m. to 5:00 p.m.
Educational and career counseling,
adult education courses, job referral,
placement.
No registration fee.

OKLAHOMA
WOMEN'S RESOURCE CENTER, INC.
207½ East Gray
P.O. Box 474
Norman, Okla. 73069
(405) 364-9424
Monday-Friday, 9:00 a.m. to 4:00 p.m.
Independent non-profit agency.
Educational and career counseling,
job referral and placement.
$5.00 registration fee.

OREGON
WOMEN'S PROGRAMS, DIVISION OF
CONTINUING EDUCATION
Oregon State System of Higher Education
1633 S.W. Park Avenue
(mail) Box 1491
Portland, Ore. 97207
(503) 229-4849
Monday-Friday, 8:30 a.m. to 4:30 p.m.
Official college office.
Educational and career counseling,
continuing education courses.
No registration fee. Other fees vary.

PENNSYLVANIA

BRYN MAWR COLLEGE
Office of Career Planning
Bryn Mawr, Pa. 19010
(215) LA 5-1000, Ext. 397
Monday-Friday, 9:00 a.m. to 5:00 p.m.
Official college office.
Educational and career counseling.
Job referral and placement.
No fees.

CEDAR CREST COLLEGE
Career Planning Office
and Women's Center
Allentown, Pa. 18104
(215) 437-4471
Monday-Friday, 8:30 a.m. to 4:30 p.m.
Official college office and
community center.
Educational and career counseling,
continuing education courses, job
referral, alumnae placement.
No fees for alumnae; other fees vary.

INSTITUTE OF AWARENESS
401 South Broad Street
Philadelphia, Pa. 19147
(215) KI 5-4400
Monday-Friday, 9:00 a.m. to 5:00 p.m.
Independent non-profit agency.
Educational and career counseling,
adult education courses, special
workshops, training programs.
Fees vary.

JOB ADVISORY SERVICE
Chatham College
Pittsburgh, Pa. 15232
(412) 441-8200, Ext. 256
Mon. Tues. Thurs. 10:00 a.m. to 2:00 p.m.
Independent non-profit office.
Job counseling and referral; workshops.

LEHIGH COUNTY COMMUNITY
COLLEGE
Alternatives for Women
2370 Main Street
Schnecksville, Pa. 18078
(215) 799-2121 ext. 177
Workshops. Fees Vary.
Sponsored by college
community service office.

OPTIONS FOR WOMEN
8419 Germantown Avenue
Philadelphia, Pa. 19118
(215) CH 2-4955
Monday-Friday, 9:30 a.m. to 3:00 p.m.
Independent non-profit agency.
Educational and career counseling,
job placement. Educational and
business consulting, management
awareness and career development
seminars.
No registration fee. Other fees vary.

SWARTHMORE COLLEGE
Office of Career Counseling & Placement
Swarthmore, Pa. 19081
(215) KI 4-7900
Monday-Thursday, 9:30 a.m. to 3:00 p.m.
Official college office. Restricted

to alumnae. Educational and career
counseling, job referral placement.
No fees.

TEMPLE UNIVERSITY
Career Services/Continuing Education
for Women
Philadelphia, Pa. 19122
Monday-Friday, 8:30 a.m. to 4:30 p.m.
College sponsored offices.
(215) 787-7981 — Career Services
Career counseling.
No counseling fee.
(215) 787-7602 — Continuing Education.
Educational counseling, continuing
education courses.
No registration fee.

UNIVERSITY OF PENNSYLVANIA
Resources for Women
112 Logan Hall
Philadelphia, Pa, 19174
(215) 594-5537
Monday 9:30 a.m. to 3:30 p.m.
Wednesday and Thursday 9:30 a.m.
12:30 p.m.
College sponsored.
Educational and career counseling
center, job referral and placement.
Fees vary.

VILLA MARIA COLLEGE
Career Counseling Center for
Adult Women
2551 West Lake Road
Erie, Pa. 16505
(814) 838-1966
Monday-Friday, 9:00 a.m. to 4:00 p.m.
Official college office.
Educational and career counseling,
job referral, placement, adult
education courses.
No fees.

WILSON COLLEGE
Career Planning Center
Chambersburg, Pa. 17201
(717) 264-4141
Monday-Friday, 9:00 a.m. to 5:00 p.m.
Official college office.
Educational and career counseling,
job referral and placement.
No fees.

TENNESSEE

WOMEN'S SERVICES OF
KNOXVILLE, INC.
4931 Homberg Drive
Knoxville, Tenn. 37919
(615) 584-0092
Monday-Friday, 9:00 a.m. to 2:00 p.m.
Independent, private agency.
Educational and career counseling,
continuing education courses,
psychotherapy, job referral and
placement.
Fees vary.

TEXAS

THE UNIVERSITY OF TEXAS
AT AUSTIN
Continuing Education of Women
and Men
Office of the Dean of Students
Austin, Tex. 78712
(512) 471-1201
Monday-Friday, 8:00 a.m. to 5:00 p.m.
College sponsored office.
Educational and career counseling.
No fees.

VOCATIONAL GUIDANCE
SERVICE, INC.
2529 San Jacinto
Houston, Tex. 77002
(713) 225-0053
Monday-Thursday, 8:30 a.m. to 7:00 p.m.
Friday, 8:30 a.m. to 5:00 p.m.
Non-profit organization.
Educational and career counseling,
job referral and placement.
Fees vary.

WOMEN FOR CHANGE CENTER
3220 Lemmon, Suite 290
Dallas, Tex. 75204
(214) 522-3560
Monday-Thursday, 9:00 a.m. to 3:00 p.m.
Independent non-profit agency.
Educational and career counseling,
adult education courses, job referral.
Fees vary.

VIRGINIA

CAREER PLANNING DIVISION
Psychological Consultants, Inc.
1804 Staples Mill Road
Richmond, Va. 23230
(804) 355-4329
Monday-Saturday, 8:30 a.m. to 5:15 p.m.
Independent private agency.
Educational and career counseling.
No registration fee. Other fees vary.

MARY BALDWIN COLLEGE
Career & Personal Counseling Center
Staunton, Va. 24401
(703) 885-0811, Ext. 294 or 333
Monday-Friday, 9:00 a.m. to 1:00 p.m.
Monday-Friday, 2:00 p.m. to 5:00 p.m.
College affiliated office.
Educational and career counseling.
Fees vary.

UNIVERSITY OF VIRGINIA
Office of Career Planning & Placement
5 Minor Hall
Charlottesville, Va. 22903
(804) 924-3378
Monday-Friday, 8:00 a.m. to 4:00 p.m.
Official college office.
Educational and career counseling,
limited job referral and placement.
No fees.

VIRGINIA COMMONWEALTH
UNIVERSITY EVENING COLLEGE
901 West Franklin Street
Richmond, Va. 23284
(804) 770-6731

Monday-Friday, 8:30 a.m. to 9:30 p.m.
Saturday, 9:00 a.m. to 1:00 p.m.
Official University Office.
Educational counseling, referral to
university career and personal
counseling services, continuing
education courses.

WASHINGTON

INDIVIDUAL DEVELOPMENT
CENTER,INC. (I.D. CENTER)
1020 East John Street
Seattle, Wash. 98102
(206) 329-0600
Monday-Friday, 9:00 a.m. to 4:00 p.m.
Independent private agency.
Career and life decision counseling,
career development workshops for
company and government agency
employees, awareness seminars for
managers and supervisors of women
employees.

UNIVERSITY OF WASHINGTON
Office of Women's Programs
1209 N.E. 41st
Seattle, Wash. 98195
(206) 543-4262
Monday-Friday, 8:00 a.m. to 5:00 p.m.
Official college office.
Educational and career counseling,
testing, job referral, free resume
register. Counseling, testing, course
fees vary.
Scholarships available.

WOMEN'S RESOURCE CENTER
Box 1081
Richland, Wash. 99352
(509) 946-0467
Monday-Saturday, 12:00 p.m. to 4:00 p.m.
Independent, private agency.
Educational and career counseling,
job referral, placement. Resume
preparation.
Fees vary.

WEST VIRGINIA

WEST VIRGINIA UNIVERSITY
Placement Service
MountainLair
Morgantown, West Virginia 26506
(304) 293-2221
Monday-Friday, 8:15 a.m. to 5:00 p.m.
Official college office. Restricted to
alumnae. Educational and career
counseling, job referral.
Registration fee.

WISCONSIN

RESEARCH CENTER ON WOMEN
Alverno College
3401 South 39th Street
Milwaukee, Wisconsin 53215
(414) 671-5400, Ext. 209
Official college office and public
facility. Educational and career
counseling by appointment. Continuing
education courses.
Counseling fee.

WYOMING
UNIVERSITY OF WYOMING
Placement Service
P.O. Box 3915, University Station
Laramie, Wyoming 82071
(307) 766-2398

Monday-Friday, 8:00 a.m. to 5:00 p.m.
Official college office, restricted
to students and alumnae.
Educational and career consulting,
job referral.
No fees.

E. HELP FOR CLERGY & RELIGIOUS

Probably no profession has developed, or had developed for it, so many resources to aid in career assessment as has the clerical profession. Nonetheless, the warning sounded at the introduction to the last section (D. Help for Women) should be read at this point, for it applies with equal force to this section of resources. Where you run into a clerical counselor who is sincere but inept, you will probably discover that his ineptness consists in his failure (thus far) to grasp the distinction between career *assessment*—roughly comparable to taking a snapshot of a person as he, or she, is in one frozen moment of time—vs. career *development*— which is roughly comparable to teaching a person how to take his (or her) own motion pictures of themselves, from there on out.

Having issued this caution, however, we must go on to add that at some of these centers, listed below, are some simply excellent counselors who fully understand this distinction, and are well trained in that empowering of the client which is what career *development* is all about. If you ask the right questions before you sign on the dotted line (see Chapter Four), you will be able readily to identify them.

THE OFFICIAL INTERDENOMINATIONAL CAREER DEVELOPMENT CENTERS

Career Development Center
St. Andrews Presbyterian College
Laurinburg, NC 28352
(919) 276-3162
Alfred E. Thomas, Director

Career Development Center
Eckerd College
St. Petersburg, FL 33733
(813) 867-1166
Frank A. Robinson, Director

American Baptist
Center for the Ministry
7804 Capwell Drive
Oakland, CA 94621
(415) 635-4246
John R. Landgraf, Director-
  Counselor

American Baptist
Center for the Ministry
40 Washington Street
Wellesley Hills, MA 02181
(617) 237-2228
Irene E. Lovett, Director

Church Career Assessment Center
240 Plant Avenue
Tampa, FL 33606
(813) 254-8791
John A. Benton, Jr., Director

Counseling Center
Davis and Elkins College
Elkins, W.V. 26241
(304) 636-1900
C. Joseph Martin, Director

Lancaster Career Development
Center
561 College Avenue,
P.O. Box 1529
Lancaster, PA 17604
(717) 393-7451
Thomas E. Brown, Director

New England Career
Development Center
40 Washington Street
Wellesley Hills, MA 02181
(617) 237-2228
Laurance W. Walton,
Associate Director

North Central Career
Development Center
3000 Fifth Street, N.W.
New Brighton, MN 55112
(612) 636-5120
Warren M. Hoffman, Director

Northeast Career Center
40 Witherspoon Street
Princeton, NJ 08540
(609) 924-4814
Robert G. Foulkes, Director

Midwest Career Development Center
66 East 15th Avenue
Columbus, OH 43201
(614) 294-2587
Frank C. Williams, Director

Midwest Career Development Center
800 West Belden Avenue
Chicago, IL 60614
(312) 935-9340

Southwest Career Development
Center
Suite 712
2723 Avenue E East
Arlington, TX 76011
(817) 265-5541
William M. Gould, Jr., Director-
Counselor

Western Career Development Center
109 Seminary Road
San Anselmo, CA 94960
(415) 453-7000
Don Falkenberg, Director-
Counselor

The above centers are all accredited and coordinated by the Career Development Council, Room 760, 475 Riverside Dr., New York, N.Y 10027. Some of them are accepting directors of Christian Education, ministers of music, and others in their program; some centers are open to all applicants, and not merely church-related professionals.

Also doing work in this field:

THE JUDICATORY CAREER SUPPORT SYSTEM, 3501 Campbell, Kansas City, Missouri 64109. The Rev. Eugene E. Timmons. (816) 931-2516.

THE EPISCOPAL OFFICE OF PASTORAL DEVELOPMENT, 116 Alhambra Circle, Suite 210, Coral Gables, Florida 33134. The Rt. Rev. David E. Richards.

The Career Development Centers are generally Protestant in origin. Within the Roman Catholic fold, a resource is:

SOCIETY OF PRIESTS FOR A FREE MINISTRY, 4231 194th Street, Flushing, New York, 11358. (Mr. Joseph Burns, Secretary). Also: 919 The Alameda, Berkeley, Thomas J. Durkin, Vice President. Works with R.C. priests in transition.

F. HELP FOR THOSE WHO CONCLUDE THEY WANT TO DEAL WITH THEIR INTERIOR FURNITURE

In dealing with people in career transition, three types of problems have surfaced:

1. The problems that the person has carried for a long long time, and which slumbered relatively quietly (maybe), but cry aloud when he or she is considering career transition. These would be hangups such as dependency, feelings of inadequacy, a need for status, a fear of competing, extreme guilt feelings—and the somewhat more exotic problems such as sexual hangups, marital conflict, alcoholism, depression, etc.

2. The problems that appear to come to a person only as the years go on, particularly those that are characteristic of "middle life." Edmund Bergler's classic, *The Revolt of the Middle-Aged Man* (New York: Grosset & Dunlap, 1954,

$1.25) about "those dangerous years when men decide to 'get more out of life' and the erotic games they play with their women" (*that* should sell) is filled with over-generalizations, but it applies to enough middle-aged men to warn us of some false solutions to "the generativity issue," as Erik Erikson calls it. Other middle-age problems: change within the self over the years, in the direction of health, that make the work environment no longer appropriate; or change in the environment over the years (the new introduced, the old taken away) that make it no longer appropriate to that particular Self.

3. The problems that characterize transition from one career system to another. Experts are amassing an impressive amount of data regarding this; for example, let us look at ex-military and ex-clergy: both have been members of a closed social system, somewhat isolated from the mainstream of society, in which roles and status positions were defined, paternalism was encouraged, and security was promised; also, both have worn distinctive uniforms, which they now must shed. In a study reported in *The American Journal of Psychiatry,* McNeil & Giffen found that the transition from military to civilian took (typically) five years, and problems appeared for two years prior to transition, and *could* continue for three years afterward. They included: reduced efficiency, psychosomatic symptoms (chest or intestinal), loss of energy, interest, confidence, and sometimes a singular incident of flagrantly unacceptable behaviour.   Findings of psychiatrists dealing with ex-clerical patients (or clerical contemplating transition) parallel the military findings. The point is, *these* symptoms are often comparatively temporary, for any career transitionist, attending—as they do—the temporary period of role confusion, and role transition. Brawer teaches that temporary symptoms (typical of regression) are ways in which the Ego finds it way around obstacles, regroups energies, and then goes on—*even more rapidly because of the temporary regression.*

Now, the three different kinds of problems outlined above and on the previous page are, to be sure, intertwined. Problems showing up in middle age, for example, are often merely accentuated versions of problems which have long been present. Still, the distinguishing of these three kinds of problems *may afford some clue* as to how earnestly help is needed, and what kinds of help.

The ideal of emotional health to which (presumably) we all aspire has been variously described.

Would you prefer: acceptance of reality; self-acceptance, interest and direction; acceptance of ambiguity and uncertainty; tolerance; flexibility and risk-taking?

Or would you prefer: maleness and femaleness both given acceptance in the self; acceptance of my own weaknesses (not wasting time keeping them hidden); living in the here and now; security, satisfaction and fulfillment found for the self and shared with others?

Or: good reality testing; energy and creativity; providing the ego with opportunities for growth; ability to delay gratification; tolerance of internal and external ambiguity; ability to rebound from challenging experiences; ability to tolerate regression when necessary for ultimately greater development?

Call it emotional health, self-love, or ego strength, or whatever. There is your checklist (or checklists). There are many more around.

Those wishing to feel their psychological pulse (privately) will probably want to grapple with Luscher, Max, *The Luscher Color Test,* New York: Random House, 1969, $6.95. Quite fascinating.

Now, suppose you decide you want help in this area?

This has been called the field of psychological counseling, traditionally. However, this whole field has been undergoing radical changes. The person who decides he needs some professional help with his own personal growth has a decision to make about what kind of help he wants, and accordingly we here categorize the professionals instead by the type of help that they offer and that you may want. Basically, this is

INSTRUCTION,
EXPLORATION, and
PSYCHOTHERAPY.

PROFESSIONAL HELP (FOR A FEE)
BY MEANS OF INSTRUCTION:

1. Local college or university: cf. courses in the psychology department, and adult education.

2. Free universities (informal experimental colleges) have grown to life in a number of communities across the country, and if you know of one, it may be worth investigating to see if they have instructional types of personal growth seminars. Example: Entropy, 1914 Polk Street, Suite 205, San Francisco, CA 94109.

3. Many of the growth centers (see below, under *Exploration*) also have lectures, seminars etc. which offer help by means of instruction.

PROFESSIONAL HELP WITH PERSONAL GROWTH
BY MEANS OF EXPLORATION:

> This covers a wide range of techniques designed to produce new awareness and/or change in the self, in one's relations to others, and in one's relation to God. In general, they are explorations of new experiences which then become (hopefully) challenges to all of the rest of one's experiences, day by day. Techniques include *sensitivity training, encounter groups, gestalt therapy, marathons, sensory awareness, bio-energetics, meditation (including Yoga), auto-analysis (games people play), simulation games, reality-therapy—and even some very exotic stuff like group nudity, "psychological karate," etc. These techniques are, virtually without exception, group techniques, for use by and in groups.*

THE ASSOCIATION FOR HUMANISTIC PSYCHOLOGY, 325 Ninth Street, San Francisco, California 94103. AHP produces a list of Growth Centers with corrections and updatings in its *AHP Newsletter*. Includes other countries' centers, as well as this one's. You can order both the list and the

Newsletter from the Association, at the address above. You can then find the center, or centers, nearest you, and ask them for their catalog and/or schedule of events.

THE ASSOCIATION FOR CREATIVE CHANGE, 107 South 20th Street, Birmingham, Alabama 35233. Composed of persons interested in the use of insights and approaches of applied behavioral science within religious systems, it issued its first annual *Directory* in 1971, listing members and accredited laboratory trainers around the country. By getting this *Directory, you can discover people in your section of the* country who are trained and may be offering various regular events for self-discovery and human growth.

NTL INSTITUTE FOR APPLIED BEHAVIORAL SCIENCE, Rosslyn, Virginia. As of 1967, an independent non-profit corporation associated with the National Educational Association. It certifies competency of leaders; an inquiry to the Institute may secure names of competent leaders in your area of the country, who (likely as not) offer various events.

PROFESSIONAL HELP WITH PERSONAL GROWTH BY MEANS OF PSYCHOTHERAPY:

1. The Directory of Approved Counseling Agencies also lists accredited places which offer psychotherapy.

2. The Psychology Department of your local college or university may be able to suggest plac's or persons which offer psychotherapy.

3. Consult also your local physician for referral suggestions, and/or your local or state psychiatric association, psychologists' association, and psychoanalytic institute (see "Professional Organizations" in your telephone book's yellow pages), for recommendations or lists of accredited personnel.

If you decide to consult a psychologist, psychiatrist, psychotherapist, analyst, or psychoanalyst, here are a few suggestions, or guiding principles for choosing one:

1. Get suggestions of names (see below).

2. We recommend you choose three to go see for a one-hour exploratory visit. You will almost certainly have to pay the going rates for this hour, with each man or woman. It's well worth it.

3. Guidelines in evaluating which one to choose: a) Do you like him/her? (Lack of rapport can kill therapy.) b) How much personal therapy has he/she had? (You have a right to ask. An answer in terms of years doesn't count; hours does. Like, 200-300, or more.) c) Do you feel he is a real person? (If he comes across as pasteboard, maybe that's his ideal for you, too.) d) Does he assiduously avoid giving you advice? Hope so. (You need someone living his life out through you like you need a hole in the head.) Beware of the therapist who gives lots and lots of advice. (Like this!) On the other hand, give him three stars if he comes across as a clarifier.

4. Choose one, after you have weighed your impressions of all three. Give serious consideration to committing yourself to, say, six-eight sessions with him (and telling him so), after which you will each of you evaluate whether or not to continue. That way, if you chose badly, you can terminate it gracefully; if you chose wisely, you have an impetus to begin working immediately.

5. If you have done the exercises in this book, you may have an idea of what goals you have for your own personal therapy: things you want to work on, hangups you want to get rid of, etc. Part of your arrangement with your therapist should be to clarify why you want therapy, so that you will have goals by which to measure progress. With this one proviso: you should feel free to revise these goals, if you want to, as therapy progresses. But therapy without any definition of what you are working toward *can be deadly. Or innocuous*—the way in which lonely people simply *purchase* friendship.

6. A book which summarizes the various options—the different sorts of therapies that are available—is Kovel, Joel, *A Complete Guide to Therapy: From Psychoanalysis to Behavior Modification.* 1976 (Pantheon Books).

7. An excellent manual which summarizes the entire process described above, but in much greater detail, is "Through the Mental Health Maze", for $2.50 (prepaid) from Health Research Group, 2000 P Street N.W., Washington, D.C. 20036.

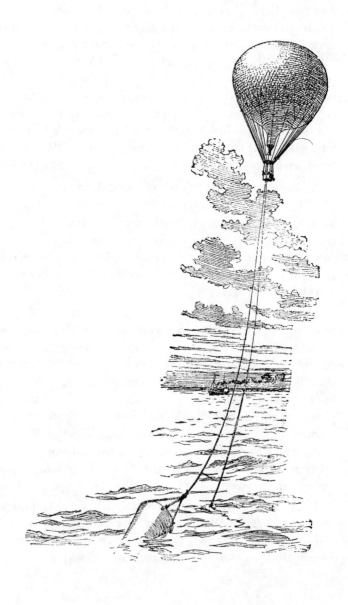

Index

Update

To: PARACHUTE
Box 379
Walnut Creek, California 94596

The information in the '78 edition needs to be changed
regarding

_____

_____

_____

_____

_____

_____

_____

_____

_____

_____

_____

_____

Name _____

Address _____

_____

Hotline

To: PARACHUTE
Post Office Box 379
Walnut Creek, California 94596

I am having trouble with the following part of the career-change/job-hunting process:

_____

_____

_____

_____

_____

_____

_____

_____

_____

_____

_____

If there is a resource in my area, from whom I could get help with this, please let me know.

Name _____

Address _____

_____

OTHER WORKS BY RICHARD N. BOLLES

The three stages of our lives: education, then work then retirement, have tended to become boxes — for learning, achievement, and leisure, argues Richard Bolles. Illustrating and giving substance to the instinctive feeling we all have about this, he proceeds to describe some very effective tools which everyone can use to blend learning, achieving and playing during all the stages of our lives. A long awaited breakthrough in the area of deciding what you want to *do with your life* at any given time. Approximately 320 pages, 6 x 9", $6.95 paper, $9.95 cloth

THE QUICK JOB-HUNTING MAP

is a practical 24-page booklet of exercises designed to give job-hunters detailed help in analyzing their skills, finding the right career field, and knowing how to find job openings and get hired. The **Map** has already sold 50,000 copies in its first year and is becoming an invaluable tool for career-counselors and agencies as well as individuals seeking jobs or changing careers. 8½ x 11", $1.25 paper

THE QUICK JOB-HUNTING MAP —BEGINNING VERSION

Based on the author's original **Quick Job-Hunting Map**, this version for beginners offers special help to new job seekers. For students about to graduate, for housewives going to work for the first time or returning to work, or anyone else entering the world of work and facing obstacles in the job hunt, this workbook gives real and concrete guidance through the maze of the job market. 8½ x 11", 24 pages, $1.25 paper

TEA LEAVES: A New Look At Resumes

Experience shows that in today's market an advertized job opening may well draw more than a thousand applications. This booklet is a new look at effective preparation and use of resumes, the routinely submitted yet only occasionally influential tool of the job seeker. Bolles shows how to create a personal profile that will survive the brutal elimination process, reach the hands of the hiring influence and get you an interview. 6 x 9", 24 pages, $.50 paper

WHO'S HIRING WHO
by Richard Lathrop

"The second-best job-hunting guide on the market"
—Richard N. Bolles, author of **What Color Is Your Parachute?**

Because most people do not know the right steps to take in their job search, most job seekers simply prolong their unemployment in their confusion. Consequently there are more than 600,000 jobs every month that go unclaimed! This book shows the new job seeker how to cope with today's job market by utilizing job hunting techniques which produce satisfying results. Previously published elsewhere, this is an all-new edition. "A fresh and devastatingly accurate analysis of the so-called job market and an invaluable guide... *must* reading for every applicant from entry to executive levels ..."
—John C. Crystal, internationally-known career analyst and consultant. 6 x 9″ $5.95 paper, $8.95 cloth

MOVING UP
by Eli Djeddah

A master in the employment counseling field publishes for the first time in paperback his program for job relocation and advancement which has been available until now only to fee-paying clients. For the man or woman who is between jobs, who is over 45, or just starting out, Djeddah offers an invaluable guide that will lead to the reader's objective: a position for providing maximum compensation and personal effectiveness. 5½ x 8″, 180 pages, $4.95 paper

MOOSEWOOD COOKBOOK
by Mollie Katzen

A delightfully hand-lettered volume which reflects an appreciation for creative uses of fresh and wholesome ingredients and is perfect for people tired of ready-made convenience food who want more nutrition and less hurry-up cooking. The Moosewood Restaurant whose reputation for imaginative and delicious meals has spread across the country by word of mouth, is the source of these 198 recipes emphasizing cheese, eggs, fresh vegetables and grains, using uncommon seasonings and combinations—Mushroom Moussaka, White Bean and Black Olive Soup, Maple Egg Custard, Ukranian Poppyseed Cake—in soups, salads, entrees, breads and desserts. Useful cross-index. Illustrated.
8½ x 11″, 222 pages, $7.95 paper, $9.95 cloth

 Available from
TEN SPEED PRESS • 900 Modoc, Berkeley, California 94707
When ordering please include 50¢ additional for each book for shipping & handling.

To: NEWSLETTER
   Post Office Box 379
   Walnut Creek, California 94596

Yup, we publish a Newsletter (bi-monthly) for job-hunters and professionals in career-counseling. (A professional is someone who is not currently hunting for a job.) The charge for the six issues a year is $10. Check payable to: National Career Development Project.

Subscriptions *must* run from January through December, for a given year. So, if you send us a check in, say, June, we will send you all the issues that have already come out in the period January-June of this year, and then continue your subscription through the end of December, only. Then you have to re-subscribe, if you wish the Newsletter for the next year.

In the Newsletter (its formal name is *Newsletter about life/work planning*) we run articles about special problems that job-hunters are encountering, which are not covered (so far) in *Parachute; plus* descriptions of new research or publications concerning the job-hunt or career-change; *plus* news of the project and where the workshops are, that we periodically hold in different parts of the country; etc.

If you want this Newsletter, tear out this page, fill in your address below, attach your check or money order, and send it on in.

Name _____

Address that you want on the mailing label

_____

_____